Benjamin Franklin,
Genius of Kites, Flights
and Voting Rights

Benjamin Franklin, Genius of Kites, Flights and Voting Rights

by SEYMOUR STANTON BLOCK

McFarland & Company, Inc., Publishers
Jefferson, North Carolina, and London

LIBRARY OF CONGRESS CATALOGUING-IN-PUBLICATION DATA

Block, Seymour Stanton, 1918–
    Benjamin Franklin, genius of kites, flights and voting rights /
by Seymour Stanton Block.
        p.   cm.
    Includes bibliographical references and index.

    ISBN 0-7864-1942-3 (softcover : 50# alkaline paper)

    1. Franklin, Benjamin, 1706–1790.   2. Statesmen — United
States — Biography.   3. Scientists — United States — Biography.
4. Printers — United States — Biography.   5. Inventors — United
States — Biography.   I. Title.
E302.6.F8B624 2004
973.3'092 — dc22

                                            2004012120

British Library cataloguing data are available

On the cover: the Montgolfier balloon of 1783; Benjamin Franklin, 1762,
by Mason Chamberlin, *Burndy Library, Dibner Institute for the History of
Science and Technology, Cambridge, Massachusetts*

Manufactured in the United States of America

McFarland & Company, Inc., Publishers
    Box 611, Jefferson, North Carolina 28640
        www.mcfarlandpub.com

To Peter,
an aspiring young man with great potential.

Acknowledgments

I am happy to acknowledge the invaluable assistance I received from my colleague, Dr. Santiago Tavares, for his help with all my computer problems in writing this book. He not only constructed a computer for me from parts and set it up, but cheerfully answered my urgent calls when things went wrong, which was every day. I am simply amazed that someone can know so much as he does about this esoteric world that I suddenly tumbled into with this book.

Also deserving my appreciation is Debbie Sandoval, who did an expert job converting my handscratch to type before I learned to use voice recognition with the computer. Further, I owe an incalculable debt to my wife, Gertrude Block, who assumed all my chores at home to give me spare time for my research and writing, even though she was working and was herself busy writing a book. I am sure that she would have gladly fed the dog and put out the cat, except we don't have any animals.

I also thank my daughters, Sara Stein and Judith McLaughlin, my son-in-law Dr. Gerald Stein, and my good friend, Dr. Jeffrey Rubin. All did yeoman service in reading the chapters, pointing out the errors, and giving me their suggestions and kind words of encouragement.

Finally, I wish to acknowledge the assistance of the fine, unheralded people at the University of Florida library who have always been generous in their help, whether in the reference department helping me find obscure information, or in the interlibrary loan department obtaining books I needed from distant libraries when so many of our own library's books became unavailable due to new building construction.

Contents

"God grant that not only the love of liberty, but a thorough knowledge of the rights of man, may pervade all the nations of the earth, so that a philosopher may set his foot anywhere on its surface and say: This is my country."

— *Benjamin Franklin, 1789*

Preface

When, in a lecture to the English faculty of my university, the University of Florida, I said that Benjamin Franklin was a renaissance man, they said, "No, Jefferson was a renaissance man." Indeed he was, but Franklin was the first American renaissance man, and Jefferson, more than any of the other founding fathers, appreciated and respected Franklin for his greatness.

This book is not another biography of Franklin; there have been many excellent biographies of that colorful American hero. Instead, this book picks up where the biographies leave off, by exploring several aspects of the life of that many-faceted genius. In his *Poor Richard's Almanac* Franklin wrote, "Men and Melons are Hard to Know." By probing further and deeper, as I have done in this book, we are able to get a better understanding of the man to better appreciate the full flavor of this marvelous melon.

In this book there are ten independent, separate chapters giving examples of Franklin's genius and accomplishments in different fields. There is no necessary order for reading the chapters. In some Franklin is the main actor, while in others he is a minor but important character. Some of the chapters go into depth on his scientific discoveries and inventions, which are then brought up to the present for the reader's interest and to demonstrate the significance of Franklin's original contribution.

Two of the chapters attempt to plow new ground in history. In one, I make the case that Franklin, more than any other American, was responsible for the founding of our new nation. In the other, I present the argument that Franklin was a major cause of the French Revolution. These are both debatable contentions, and the readers can decide for themselves whether or not I have made a convincing case.

Introduction

Benjamin Franklin was an American original. Perhaps it would be better to say that Franklin was "the Original American," for he typifies America in so many ways. He was the first American to be famous on the world scene, and in doing so he exemplified the American expression "he lifted himself by his bootstraps." Born in poverty to a family of 17 children, he achieved recognition and wealth through his remarkable ability and energy. With only two years of elementary education, he educated himself to become admired by the leading people in government, science, philosophy, and literature in America and Europe. Franklin was the oldest of the founding fathers of the United States and his signature appears on all the major documents in the founding of this country. With his *Poor Richard's Almanac* and other writings, he was America's first humorist. He was first in very many ways.

Franklin started many of the American institutions we now take for granted. As our first postmaster general, he traveled all over the country on horseback setting up the postal system. He started the first lending library, the first hospital, the first science society, the first fire insurance company, and the first club for self-improvement and community service like the Rotary and Kiwanis clubs. McDonald's and Burger King also owe him a nod, for Franklin was the first to start the franchising business. He sent his assistants in his printing shop to different cities and set them up in business for a share of the profits. He published the first political cartoon in an American newspaper. It showed a snake in pieces with the name of an American colony on each piece and had the caption "Unite or Die."

Among Franklin's many inventions was the lightning rod, the Franklin stove, bifocal eye glasses, a musical instrument, and swim fins. His wide-ranging interests led him to develop a method of simplified spelling and propose daylight saving time to save energy. Franklin crossed the ocean many times; he studied the Gulf Stream and made the first map of that body of water.

Franklin had more experience in government than any other American of his time. He held positions from village, city, and state to national and international levels of government.

He was America's first diplomat, operating first in England, where he tried to prevent the break with that country, and then in France as America's first ambassador during the Revolutionary War. While he was in France during the war, he created the U.S. Navy, outfitting John Paul Jones, our first admiral, with a ship and armament to attack the coast of England. He was unusually effective in obtaining money and military assistance from the French, without which America could not have won the Revolutionary War. It has been said that George Washington won the battles, but Benjamin Franklin won the war.

Upon his death, Franklin left a sizable amount of money to the two cities—Philadelphia and Boston—to which he felt most indebted. But in his unusual will, he did not leave the money for immediate use but directed that it be used over the years as a fund to assist aspiring young trades people who were unable to get credit for their businesses. They would repay the loan with interest, which would increase the total amount in the fund. After one hundred years the total would increase considerably, and one-third of it was then to be used for the benefit of the cities. The rest of the money was to be lent out for another hundred years, and then the very much-increased total could be used by the designated cities. In this way, due to the power of compound interest, Franklin was able to donate almost one thousand times as much money for good works.

There have been many books written about this unusual American, and more are being written in time for the 300th year celebration of Franklin's birth in 2006. This book is different from the usual biographies. It spotlights different little-known areas of fascinating activity of this many-sided man and is intended to give the reader an entertaining, in-depth insight into the life and times of this amazing American genius.

Chronology of the
Life of Benjamin Franklin

1706 Born in Boston, Massachusetts, the tenth son in a family of 17 children to Josiah Franklin, an English immigrant and candle maker, and Abiah Folger Franklin, Josiah's second wife, who was born and raised on Nantucket Island.

1714–1716 Attends Boston grammar school

1716–1718 Assists father as candle maker and soap boiler

1718–1722 Apprentices to his brother James, printer in Boston

1719 Benjamin Franklin, an avid reader, borrows books by Bunyan, Defoe, and Locke. He enjoys Addison's *Spectator*, a periodical that he attempts to imitate in his writing.

1722 James Franklin publishes newspaper, the *New England Courant*, in which Benjamin anonymously inserts a series of 14 letters supposedly written by a widow, Mrs. Silence Dogood, commenting humorously on life in Boston.

1723 After differences with James, Benjamin leaves Boston and runs away to Philadelphia where he finds work as a printer.

1724 Upon encouragement and promises of financial support by the governor of Pennsylvania, he travels to London to buy equipment to start his own printing business. When the governor's promise fails to materialize, he is stranded in London, where he works for two years in a printing shop.

1726 He returns to Philadelphia and again works for his former employer.

1727   He organizes a club, the Junto, a community service and self-improvement organization, with other, young working men.

1728–1730   He forms a printing partnership with a friend. The partnership dissolves and Franklin buys out the partner. He also buys a failing newspaper, the *Pennsylvania Gazette*, which eventually becomes the largest circulating paper in the American colonies.

1730   A son, William, is born out of wedlock from an unknown mother. Forms common-law marriage with Deborah Read.

1731   Establishes the Library Company of Philadelphia, the first lending library in America. He is named official printer for Pennsylvania. He becomes a Mason. He starts a franchise partnership in Charleston South Carolina.

1732   Publishes the first edition of *Poor Richard's Almanac*. His second son, Francis, is born. Prints first German-language newspaper in America.

1733   He devises and tests his scheme to achieve "moral perfection."

1734   He is elected Grand Master of Masons in Pennsylvania.

1735   Proposes volunteer fire-fighting societies for Philadelphia.

1736   Son Francis dies of smallpox. Franklin is chosen clerk of Pennsylvania assembly. Prints money for New Jersey. Organizes the Union Fire Company, the first fire department in Philadelphia.

1737   Appointed postmaster of Philadelphia.

1739   Befriends famous evangelist, George Whitefield, who preaches in Philadelphia. Publishes Whitefield's sermons.

1740   Becomes official printer for New Jersey.

1741   Announces his new stove and room heater, which he calls the Pennsylvanian fireplace.

1742   Opens a new printing partnership in New York City. Helps fund the botanical expeditions of Philadelphia naturalist John Bartram.

1743   Establishes the American Philosophical Society, the first American scientific society. His daughter, Sarah (Sally), is born.

1744   Publishes the novel *Pamela*, by Samuel Richardson, the first novel printed in America.

1745   Begins his experiments with electricity.

1747   Reports on his research in electricity, which is published by the Royal Society of London. Publishes "Plain Truth," a pamphlet discussing the French expansion and the accompanying Indian military activity on the western frontier of Pennsylvania.

1748   Retires from active business at the age of 42 to devote his life to scientific investigation and public affairs. He is elected alderman of the city council of Philadelphia.

1749   Designs and installs the first lightning rod. He becomes Grand Master of the Mid-Atlantic province of Masons. Writes a booklet on his ideas for the education of youth and Pennsylvania.

1750 Continues his electrical experiments and is severely shocked when he attempts to electrocute a turkey. Proposes the use of lightning rods to protect houses and designs experiment to show that lightning is electricity. He suffers from the first of several attacks of gout.

1751 His book, *Experiments and Observations on Electricity*, is published in London. He is elected to the Pennsylvania assembly. Helps to establish in Philadelphia the first public hospital in America. Starts the first fire insurance company in America.

1752 Conducts kite experiment to prove that lightning is electricity.

1753 Appointed deputy postmaster general of North America. Receives the Copley medal from the Royal Society of London, its most prestigious award, for his electrical work. Negotiates a treaty with Indian tribes at Carlisle, Pennsylvania. Is given honorary degrees from Harvard and Yale.

1754 Publishes his "Join or Die" cartoon in his newspaper, the first political cartoon in America. Represents Pennsylvania and proposes the Albany Plan of Union at the conference with seven other colonies at Albany, New York.

1755 Meets British General Braddock, who is sent to protect Americans from the French. He pledges his personal wealth to obtain wagons and other equipment for the general. Braddock's campaign in the French and Indian War. The Pennsylvania assembly passes Franklin's bill establishing a militia. After Braddock's defeat, Franklin is appointed to oversee construction of forts on the western Pennsylvania frontier and is elected colonel by the regiment recruited in Philadelphia. He travels extensively in western Pennsylvania and New York in this capacity.

1756 An honorary degree is awarded him by William and Mary College in Virginia. He introduces a program of street paving, lighting, and street cleaning in Philadelphia. He conducts military inspections in Pennsylvania and New York.

1757 Appointed agent for Pennsylvania to go to London and attempt to obtain parliament's approval to make taxable the lands in Pennsylvania owned by the family of William Penn. Deborah chooses not to accompany him. He takes his son, William, who will attend law school in London. On the way he writes his famous "The Way to Wealth," a compilation of aphorisms on the subject from his earlier 25 annual editions of *Poor Richard's Almanac*. In London, he finds lodging with Margaret Stevenson, a widow and her daughter Mary (called Polly).

1758 In London, Franklin meets with British officials about the Penn family tax problem. He meets many famous English citizens and is invited to join many scientific and literary organizations. He and his son travel to the family birthplace in England and meets relatives. The Penn family agrees to a compromise on the taxes as proposed by Franklin, but insists that their appointed governor, not the elected legislature of the colony, should decide.

1759   Receives honorary doctor's degree from St. Andrews University in Scotland. In Scotland he meets Lord Kames, Adam Smith, and William Robertson.

1760   He writes a pamphlet on the importance of Canada to Britain and to the colonies. He joins a group called the Associates of Dr. Bray, which raises money for the education of blacks in America, and is elected chair.

1761   In London he attends the coronation of King George III. He and William with friend and member of parliament Richard Jackson travel to Belgium and Holland. As member of a committee of the Society of Arts, he studies agricultural methods and arranges the exchange of plants between England and the American colonies.

1762   Franklin receives an honorary doctorate from Oxford University. He invents a new musical instrument that he calls the "glass armonica," for which Mozart and Beethoven will compose music. To help settle a boundary dispute between Pennsylvania and Maryland, he confers with Charles Mason (astronomer) and Jeremiah Dixon (surveyor). They go to America and survey the famous Mason-Dixon line. Then Franklin goes back to Philadelphia while his son remains in London, is married, and is appointed royal governor of New Jersey.

1763   In America, in his capacity as deputy postmaster general, he travels extensively in the northern colonies conducting post office inspections and establishing postal routes. Upon visiting a school for blacks in Philadelphia, he is impressed with the students' natural capacities for learning.

1764   Elected Speaker of the Pennsylvania assembly. Protests massacre of friendly Indians in Pennsylvania by the "Paxton boys." Defeated in reelection for his seat in the Pennsylvania assembly in a nasty, bitterly fought race. Appointed by the assembly to be their agent again in London to oppose the stamp tax. His wife again chooses not to accompany him. Arrives in London and moves into previous lodgings with Mrs. Stevenson.

1765   Opposes the stamp act, but it is passed nevertheless. In Philadelphia, a mob, believing that Franklin favored the stamp act, attempts to attack his house, but his wife holds them off.

1766   Organizes support in opposition to the stamp act and is successful in having it repealed. Partnership in printing business expires, and partner buys out Franklin's share. He travels to Holland and Germany with Dr. John Pringle, a fellow member of the Royal Society. He is elected to the German Academy of Sciences.

1767   Visits Paris with Dr. Pringle, and they are formally presented to the

French king, Louis XV, at the palace of Versailles. Daughter Sally is married in Philadelphia to Richard Bache against her father's wishes.

1768 Identifies lead poisoning and its causes. Develops a new phonetic alphabet. Publishes the first map of the Gulf Stream giving its direction, course, and size. Appointed agent for Georgia, in addition to Pennsylvania.

1769 Also appointed agent for New Jersey in Britain. Writes position paper on taxation of the American colonies for circulation among members of parliament. Wife suffers a stroke which handicaps her for the rest of her life. In his absence he is elected president of the American Philosophical Society in Philadelphia and is reelected every year for the rest of his life. Helps form the Ohio Company to obtain land grants in the Ohio territory for sale to potential settlers. His grandson, Benjamin Franklin Bache, is born to his daughter.

1770 Elected agent for Massachusetts. Mrs. Stevenson's daughter is married.

1771 British Secretary for Colonial Affairs Lord Hillsborough refuses to recognize Franklin as colonial agent, claiming that the governors, not the legislatures of the colonies, can appoint official agents. Franklin ignores him. He visits his good friend Bishop Shipley and his family at their country estate, where he begins work on his autobiography. He visits Ireland, where he witnesses the opening of the Irish parliament and is guest of Lord Hillsborough on his vast estate. He also visits Scotland, where he stays with Lord Kames and David Hume. Meets son-in-law Richard Bache and his family and makes peace with him. He donates books to Harvard University.

1772 Ohio Company deal falls through. Elected one of eight foreign members of the French Royal Academy of Sciences. Makes first written denunciation of slavery and the slave trade in response to the Sommerset case. Receives secret correspondence of Massachusetts Governor Hutchinson to English government advocating repressive measures against the protesting colonists; he sends it to the Massachusetts speaker with instructions that it should not be made public. Performs experiments with oil on water. Descends one mile underground in a coal mine.

1773 Hutchinson's letters are made public by Massachusetts's legislature with angry protest against Governor Hutchinson. Franklin petitions for the removal of Hutchinson. He writes a satiric hoax, "Rules by which a great empire may be reduced to a small one," and another, "Edict by the King of Prussia." His oil-on-water experiment is tested in the ocean.

1774 News of the Boston Tea Party reaches London. Franklin is accused of stealing the Hutchinson letters and is officially denounced and stripped of his position as deputy postmaster general of North America. Publishes a paper, "Hints for a Durable Union between England and America."

Delivers colonies' petition to the king on the tax problem, but negotiations between Franklin and the British government prove futile. Deborah Franklin has another stroke and dies in Philadelphia while he remains in London. The First Continental Congress opens in Philadelphia.

1775 Parliament declares Massachusetts in rebellion. Rumors abound of Franklin's impending arrest. He leaves for Philadelphia. On the voyage he conducts experiments on the Gulf Stream. At Philadelphia he is chosen as a delegate to the Second Continental Congress, where he drafts the Articles of Confederation, the first U.S. Constitution. Congress delays its approval. He designs paper money and proposes free trade among the colonies. The king of England declares all colonies in rebellion. Franklin is sent to Cambridge, Massachusetts, to confer with General Washington on the needs of the Continental army. Takes his sister to Rhode Island to evade British occupation of Boston. Appointed to committee of secret correspondence to deal with foreign policy. Elected postmaster general of the colonies and serves on ten congressional committees.

1776 Son William, royal governor of New Jersey, is arrested and imprisoned as a leading loyalist. Franklin does not attempt to intercede for him. Joins delegation going to Canada to attempt to bring it into the rebellion. Attempt fails. Franklin becomes very sick on trip and is nursed by John Carroll of Maryland, who Franklin later helps to become first Catholic archbishop of America. Helps write and signs the Declaration of Independence. With John Adams, he meets British Admiral Lord Howe in an unsuccessful last attempt to find reconciliation with England. Lends almost 4,000 pounds to Congress, hoping others will do likewise. Elected commissioner to the court of France to obtain aid for America in the struggle against Britain. Is in France on his seventieth birthday, accompanied by his two grandsons.

1777 His older grandson serves as his secretary; the younger one is sent to school to become a printer. A request for French aid results in the king's secretly lending two million livres. War is going badly for Americans, and French are afraid of making a formal commitment. American privateers capture British ships. Britain accuses France of harboring the privateers. Franklin is very popular in Paris, where he is recognized as an outstanding philosopher, scientist, and personality. He is active in French society and in intellectual and scientific circles, where he is a living billboard for America and its ideals. At his house near Paris he sets up a private printing press where he prints propaganda for the American cause. He makes friends with Madam Houdetot and Madam Helvetius. The latter holds salons attended by influential men, and Madam Brillon, a beautiful and gifted musician. The American victories at the battles of Trenton, Princeton, and Saratoga bring a change in the attitude of the cautious French toward America.

1778 The French sign the Treaty of Amity and Commerce with America and grant six million livres. Franklin becomes sole minister plenipotentiary (ambassador) to France. France goes to war with Britain. Franklin and Voltaire meet. Franklin is formally presented to King Louis XVI. John Adams joins Franklin in Paris.

1779 Spain declares war on England. Franklin announces another three-million-livres loan from France. In London his nonscientific writings, "Political, Miscellaneous, and Philosophical Pieces," are published. He proposes marriage to Madame Helvetius and of his older grandson to the daughter of Madame Brillon. In both instances he is politely turned down. He arranges the first exchange of prisoners between England and America.

1780 Secures another loan of four million livres from France. Adams, now commissioner to seek peace with Britain, offends the French by repeated insults in letters to French foreign minister Vergennes. At the request of Vergennes, Franklin sends Adams's letters to Congress, thus antagonizing Adams and making him hostile to France and Franklin. The Spanish government demands that America give up all land claims to the Mississippi Valley in exchange for aid. Franklin refuses and responds that he would rather give up his street door. A book of his works is published in Germany.

1781 Appointed to a commission to seek peace with Britain, along with Adams, Jefferson, John Jay (ambassador to Spain), and Henry Laurens, and to act only with the knowledge and concurrence of France. Jefferson is unable to take part due to his wife's serious illness. English General Cornwallis surrenders to Washington, ending hostilities. Franklin suffers disabling attacks of gout and informs Congress that he wishes to resign and go home because of age and health. Congress does not approve his request.

1782 Meets secretly with English peace commissioners in Paris, requesting that Canada be ceded to the United States. Informally lays out necessary terms for peace settlement. Does not inform Vergennes of negotiations as required by Congress. Jay insists on English recognition of American independence for formal negotiations to proceed. English commissioners agree, and draft articles are sent to London, but without consulting Vergennes. Franklin suffers severe attack of gout and misses a few meetings. Jay takes over for the Americans. Adams, who has been in Holland, joins the negotiations. English and American commissioners sign preliminary articles of peace. Vergennes complains of the Americans' failure to consult him. Franklin admits his diplomatic impropriety but then has the temerity to request a further loan of 6 million livres, which he is granted. A lifelong Mason, Franklin is elected head of the prestigious Masonic Lodge of the Nine Sisters in Paris.

1783 At Versailles Franklin and Adams attend signing of the preliminary Anglo-French and Anglo-Spanish articles of peace. Franklin requests and obtains another 6 million livres, making a total of 20 million, which eventually gets paid back in full. Prints translation of American state constitutions, the Articles of Confederation, and Treaty with France, which he sends to all foreign ministers. Consulted by papal nuncio about organizing the Roman Catholic Church in the United States. Recommends his friend John Carroll, who is then appointed first U.S. archbishop. Observes and reports on first manned balloon flights. Franklin, Adams and Jay sign definitive treaty of peace. Franklin signs treaty of amity and commerce with Sweden.

1784 Appointed by king to investigate Dr. Mesmer's theories and practices of animal magnetism. After considerable consideration, Franklin and distinguished French scientists conclude that animal magnetism does not exist and its practice is fraudulent. Formal ratification of peace treaty with Britain. Franklin again requests to be relieved to go home. Congress names Franklin, Adams, and Jefferson (now in France) as commissioners to negotiate treaties with European nations and the Barbary states. At insistence of friends writes second part of autobiography.

1785 Congress finally gives Franklin permission to go home. Jefferson succeeds him as ambassador. Adams becomes ambassador to Britain. Franklin invents bifocal eye glasses so he won't have to change glasses for distant and close viewing. On his way home he stops briefly in England, where he meets with son, William, and a few close friends. On the ocean voyage home he again studies temperature, velocity, and plants of the Gulf Stream, as well his new ideas on improving the sails and rigging of ships to improve their speed and safety in rough weather. When his ship reaches Philadelphia he is met by a cheering crowd. He is immediately elected president (governor) of Pennsylvania.

1786 To the home which he had built while he was in England and which is now occupied by his daughter and her family with six children. He builds an addition which includes a large dining room for meetings and banquets and also a library to house his 4,000 books, the largest library in America.

1787 Just as he had founded the American Philosophical Society to study and understand science, he now organizes the Society for Political Enquiries to study government and serves as first president. He also becomes president of the Pennsylvania Society for the Abolition of Slavery, the first abolitionist organization in the United States. Is elected a representative from Pennsylvania to the Constitutional Convention, which he attends regularly from May to September although he suffers from the bladder stone; he can't walk or ride, so he is carried in a sedan chair. At the convention, he appeals for unity, arranges important compromises, and serves as the elder statesman. His great compromise, which solves the problem between the large and small states, allows for proportional representation in the House and equal by states in the Senate. His final speech to the convention is considered a masterpiece and convinces most of the delegates to vote for the Constitution.

1788 Writes will leaving bulk of his estate to his daughter, who has been caring for him since he has been home, and something for grandsons, but nothing to his son, who had opposed him in the war. Also makes bequests to the cities of Boston and Philadelphia. Ends service as president of Pennsylvania. Commences work on the third part of autobiography but does not live to complete it. Now too weak to write, he dictates to his grandson.

1789 As president of the abolition society, he writes an address to the public, which is sent to Congress, opposing slavery and the slave trade. It is vigorously opposed by the southerners and sent to a committee, which determines that slavery is regulated by the states and the federal government cannot interfere. Sends copies of his autobiography to friends in England and France. He is committed to bed, where he spends the last two years because of the pain from the bladder stone. He receives an opiate to relieve the pain, but this upsets his digestion and makes him weaker. He writes a friend, "I am nothing but a skeleton covered by a skin." Anticipating the future, he writes, " In this world nothing can be said to be certain except death and taxes."

1790 Petitions Congress to do away with slavery and the slave trade. He then answers the opposition in a satirical hoax he writes but purportedly was written by an official in the government of Algiers, in which the same arguments and justifications used by the southerners are given by the Algerian. Instead of referring to Negro slaves, the Algerian refers to white Christians who are being captured and kept as slaves by the Algerians, as actually occurred in those days. Franklin is visited by Jefferson, who is just back from France. Gives Jefferson a copy of the autobiography. Replies to a letter from the president of Yale as to his religious beliefs. Dies at home on April 17 of pleurisy resulting from his weakened condition. Buried beside wife Deborah and son Francis in Christ Church burial ground, Philadelphia.

1

Benjamin Franklin's Greatest Invention

What was Benjamin Franklin's greatest invention? Was it the lightning rod, the Franklin stove, or the bifocal eyeglasses? No, it was none of these; Franklin's greatest invention was the United States of America. Of course, he didn't create this one all by himself, but he started it, and he saw it through to completion.

Franklin didn't invent America; it was already there. And he didn't invent the states; they were also there, but they were then called colonies. What wasn't present was the union, the cement that united the colonies, binding them together into a nation. When Franklin began on the problem, a quarter of a century before the Declaration of Independence, the colonies were anything but united. The only thing they had in common was a common language and a loose attachment to England, the mother country. As shall be seen, they had little interest or desire to be united.

Franklin's was not the earliest attempt at making a union of the American colonies: the first attempt came in 1643, just 20 years after the Pilgrims landed, with representatives of the colonies of Massachusetts Bay, Plymouth, New Haven, and Connecticut, to give them protection from Indian attacks.[1] But this and other attempts did not last. Franklin's was the only attempt that finally led to a successful conclusion.

In 1751 trouble was brewing for the English colonies of America. In a few years Britain and France would be at war for the mastery of the continent of North America. France had forces in Louisiana, along the Mississippi River, in Canada, and in the Ohio territory and had alliances with many Indian tribes. The British colonies needed protection as they were totally unprepared for war, without an organized military establishment. Without a union to knit them together the separate colonies could be picked off one by one.

Indian Affairs

In addition to protection against the French, Franklin saw unification of the separate colonies as necessary for better regulation of trade between them and also for uniform, fair dealings with the Indians. The Indians played an important part in this balance of forces between the English and the French. They controlled the territory between the two European occupiers and served as a buffer for them. Each side vied for their friendship and loyalty. On the English side was the large Iroquois federation known as the Six Nations, with whom the colonists had traded for many years, and it was essential that their loyalty be retained. These Indians were known to be fierce fighters, and historians have declared that without their allegiance Americans today might be speaking French. However, there were problems because the English traders often cheated the Indians, giving them liquor to drink before making a deal and then taking advantage of them when they were drunk.

In 1750 Conrad Weiser, the Indian interpreter for Pennsylvania, reported to the governor very disagreeable news: Through the indefatigable industry of the French the Six Nations were much shaken in their affections for the English and were inclining to go over to their rivals. Weiser told of the Indians' suspicion of the English because of the shady dealings of the traders. He illustrated his point with a story told to him by the Iroquois chief Canasatego. The chief had noticed that the white men had worked hard for six days, then shut up their shops on the seventh day, and all assembled to a great house. He asked Weiser, "What is it for? What do they do there?" Weiser thought for an answer that would explain it simply to the Indian: "They meet in the great house to learn and hear good things." Canasatego indicated that this was what they might have told Weiser, but he had his doubts. He explained that he had taken a batch of beaver skins to a merchant named Hans Hanson, for which he was offered four shillings per pound. Canasatego considered this price was so low as to be insulting. But Hanson said he could not discuss business further as it was the day when all the Europeans gather at the great house to learn "good things."[2]

Curious to know what was going on in the great house, Canasatego went inside and saw everybody seated listening to a man in black standing in front who was speaking rapidly in an angry voice. Canasatego could not understand what was being said, but when the man in black looked at him angrily he went outside and smoked his pipe, waiting for the meeting to break up. Then Hanson emerged, and Canasatego told him that his offer of four shillings was too low. Hanson replied, "I'm sorry. I cannot give more than three shillings and sixpence." Canasatego then went to the other merchants and was surprised that every buyer quoted the same price of three shillings sixpence. From this he concluded that when they pretended in the meeting to learn "good things," the real purpose was to learn ways to cheat Indians in the price of beaver skins.

Franklin couldn't understand how the Indian tribes of the Six Nations had formed a union, whereas the colonies had shown no interest in doing so. He wrote, "it would be a very strange thing, if six nations of ignorant savages should be capable of forming a scheme for such an union, and be able to execute it in such a manner that it has subsisted ages, and appears indissoluble; and yet that a like union should be impracticable for ten or a dozen English colonies, to whom it is more necessary."[3]

Franklin referred to the Indians as ignorant savages, but it should be understood this was the common term used by the white people of the time in regard to the Native Americans. As Franklin had commented, "Savages, we call them, because their manners differ from ours."[4] Indians didn't wear clothes or live in houses as "civilized" people did, and when they drank the whiskey that the settlers gave them, they simply went berserk. But Franklin had great respect for the Six Nations: "I would only observe that the Six Nations as a body, have kept faith with the English ever since we knew them now a hundred years; and these people had notions of honor."

In 1751 Franklin wrote, "I am of opinion ... that securing the friendship of the Indians is of the greatest consequence to these colonies; and that the surest means of doing it, are to regulate the Indian trade, so as to convince them by experience that they may have the best and cheapest goods and the fairest dealing from the English."[5] He went on, "And to unite the several governments so as to form a strength that the Indians may depend on for protection in case of a rupture with the French.... Such an union is certainly necessary to us all."

But how to bring about this union? He anticipated practical difficulties. The colonial governors of the colonies were appointed by London and represented the proprietors abroad. The councils, or legislatures, represented the local people, who expected the proprietors to pay their fair share of the taxes on their vast land holdings, which the proprietors were reluctant to do. Thus, as Franklin saw it, if the governor should propose unification, it would only arouse suspicion and opposition in the assembly. On the other hand, it was unlikely that the governors would favor unification, for while they might appear outwardly to do so, in private, Franklin indicated, they would throw cold water on it since they had no disposition to give up any of their authority or perquisites that a union might require. The colonies themselves were also loath to give up their privileges or independence.

Franklin therefore proposed an indirect approach, namely that a "half dozen men of good understanding and address ... in the nature of ambassador" be sent to other colonies to convince their leading men to promote the scheme. He visualized a voluntary union of the colonies preferable to one that might be imposed by Parliament, presaging what was to come about some 25 years later under quite different circumstances.

His blueprint for the government of such a union would have a general council representing all the colonies and a governor to be appointed by the Crown to preside and execute the council's legislation. Their responsibility would cover everything related to Indian affairs and defense, such as the building of forts. There would also be public trading houses with a superintendent of trade to regulate private trading and prevent the dishonest practices of some of the merchants. In times a peace, the men who manned the forts might go on hunting expeditions with the Indians and thus become well acquainted with them and the countryside. He considered this to be very valuable, as the Indians knew the terrain and were excellent hunters and warriors. He said,

> Every Indian is a hunter; and as their manner of making war, viz. by skulking, surprising and killing particular persons and families, it is the same as their manner of hunting, only changing the object. Every Indian is a disciplined soldier [and] soldiers of this kind are always wanted in the colonies in an Indian war, for the European military discipline is of little use in these woods.[6]

This is a lesson the British general Braddock was soon to learn in the French and Indian War, when he was mortally wounded and 1,000 of his men were killed or wounded in a massacre by the Indians. He had boasted, "These savages may indeed be a formidable enemy to your raw American militia, but upon the King's regular and disciplined troops, sir, it is impossible they should make any impression."[7]

Franklin had plans for a common treasury for the union into which each colony would pay an amount depending on the number of representatives it would send to the council. The treasury would also be funded by an excise tax on strong liquors, which were used in an equal amount per capita in all the colonies. To prevent jealousy among the colonies, he would not specify any colony as the capitol of the union but would have the council moved successively to different colonies.[8]

In 1751, Governor Clinton of New York had invited representatives of the neighboring colonies to an Indian conference at Albany, but nothing came of it: There was no war, and the colonies had other matters to attend to. By 1753, the French were instigating raids on the pro-English Indians, including the Indians of the Six Nations, who had just conferred with the governor of Virginia and asked him to notify the governor of Pennsylvania that they wanted to meet with him at the frontier town of Carlisle, Pennsylvania, about 20 miles from Harrisburg. The Pennsylvania governor sent a delegation of three men, which included Franklin, to meet with the Indians. The conference lasted four days, and Franklin was a witness to the manner in which the Indians conferred. He had previously printed a treaty between the governments of Virginia, Maryland, Pennsylvania and the Indians of the Five Nations (who were later joined by a North Carolina tribe to become the Six Nations). Of all the works of Franklin's print shop, which included religious books, legislative records, as well as his newspaper and almanacs, his reports of the Indian treaties are considered unique and most memorable as a record of a culture and a time gone by.

The delegation did not know why the Indians wanted this conference, but they were soon to find out. In Indian fashion, however, before they would agree to get down to business, certain ceremonies had to be performed, including the laying out of the gifts of English goods the colonists were expected to bring them. These gifts included blankets, knives, shovels, rifles, gunpowder, lead, flour, and rum. All of these were carried separately in a wagon, and since the wagon had not yet arrived, the ceremonies had to be delayed. When it arrived, the presents were spread on the ground, and, the colonists, knowing that the conference would be a total loss if the Indians got the liquor before the business was done, told the Indians that the rum would not be given out until the conference was over.[9]

The Indians selected as their spokesman a chief named Scarrooyady. He explained that his Indians had lost several warriors killed in skirmishes with the French and their Indian allies. According to their custom, proper condolences would have to be performed before the business matters could begin. When those warriors were properly wrapped in blankets and put in their graves, Scarrooyady accepted a string of wampum from the colonists and expressed the hope that the chain of friendship with the English would last and not be rusted and broken. He then explained the purpose of the meeting: The French governor of Canada had blamed the English for their incursions into the whole Ohio region, but Scarrooyady was not to be fooled, saying "He speaks with two tongues." Scarrooyady was concerned, however, that the English coming into that area from the east was making matters worse. He also complained that the English goods the traders brought were too expensive and were not what they wanted. The Indians wanted gunpowder and lead, but the merchants brought flour and rum. He said, "These wicked whiskey sellers, when they have got the Indians in liquor, make them sell their very clothes from their backs."[10]

The Indians also remarked that there were too many English traders coming into the area, which disturbed the French and caused trouble for the Indians. They wanted there to be only three trading posts. The delegates agreed to bring these matters to their government, and the business now being over, they dispensed the alcohol as promised. Franklin related what followed: "They all got drunk that night, made a great bonfire and all, men and women, were quarreling and fighting, their dark-colored, half-naked bodies could be seen in the flickering light of the bonfire as they ran and beat one another with firebrands." This sight, accompanied as it was with horrid yelling, was a scene that Franklin speculated was as closely "resembling a vision of hell as one could imagine."

At midnight some of the Indians came thundering to the door of the colonists, demanding more rum, but they did not get it. The next day the Indians sent three of their old counselors to apologize for their misbehavior. The orators acknowledged the fault but blamed it on the rum by saying, "The Great Spirit who made all things made everything for some use, whatever use he designed everything for, that use it should always be put to. Now, when he made rum, he said, 'Let this be for the Indians to get drunk with. And it must be so.'"[11]

In March 1751 Franklin wrote:

> I am of opinion ... that securing friendship of the Indians is of the greatest consequence to these colonies; and that the surest means of doing it, are to regulate the Indian trade, so as to convince them by experience, that they may have the best and cheapest goods, and the fairest dealing from the English; and to unite the several governments, as to form a strength that the Indians may depend on for protection in case of rupture with the French; or apprehend great danger from, if they should break with us.[12]

Virginia as well as Pennsylvania had claims on western territories, and in 1754 Virginia sent young Major George Washington with two companies of militia to dislodge the French military from the Ohio territory. He was miserably defeated and had to surrender.[13] Virginia had requested military assistance from Pennsylvania, but the Pennsylvania legislature, jealous of Virginia and controlled by pacifist Quakers, refused. The hostilities between the French and English in America ushered in what we call the French and Indian Wars, which were to last off and on from 1754 to 1763 and were just part of the European struggle between England and France known as the Seven Years War.

Albany Plan of Union

In 1754 Franklin reported in his newspaper the defeat of Washington and commented:

> The confidence of the French in this undertaking seems well grounded on the present disunited state of the British colonies, and the extreme difficulties of bringing so many different governments and assemblies to agree in any speedy and effectual measures for our common defense and security; while our enemies have the very great advantage of being under one direction, with one council and one purse. Hence ... they presume that they may with impunity violate the most solemn treaties ... kill, seize, and imprison our traders ... murder and scalp our farmers with their wives and children, and take easy possession of such parts of the British territory as they find most convenient for them; which if they are permitted to do so, must end in the destruction of the British interest, trade, and plantations in America.[14]

This is a powerful statement. But Franklin had made it even more clear and emphatic with his cartoon, which he placed in his newspaper, the *Pennsylvania Gazette*, of May 9, 1754. This was the first political cartoon in America. It shows a snake disjoined in eight separate pieces and the pieces labeled with the initials of New England, New York, New Jersey, and South Carolina. The caption is: "JOIN OR DIE" (Figure 1.1). This caught the attention of every reader and made clear the urgency of its message.

The English colonies had traded with the Indian league of Six Nations for many years but were worried that the Indians might be enticed to join with the French against them. In June 1754, the government in London, finally taking notice of the troubles on the frontier and Washington's defeat, called a conference with the Six Nations, which was held in Albany, New York.[15] Now others besides Franklin saw the need for a common defense, and the conference was attended by representatives from New Hampshire, Massachusetts, New York, Rhode Island, Connecticut, Pennsylvania, and Maryland. Virginia and New Jersey had been invited but did not show up. The meeting at Albany, nevertheless, was the best-attended meeting of its kind to date, and much progress was expected of it.

Franklin was one of the delegates selected by Pennsylvania to the conference at Albany, and he went to the meeting primed with a plan for union of the colonies. On his way to Albany he promoted it with friends and influential people that he met. He modestly called his plan "Short Hints Toward a Scheme for Uniting the Northern Colonies."[16] He discussed the plan with the representatives of other colonies at Albany and asked for their suggestions to improve the plan. They all agreed that a union was necessary, and they formed a committee of one representative from each colony to consider the matter.

Meanwhile, the Indians of the Six Nations arrived, and now it was even more important, as the Indians said, to keep the chain of friendship with them bright and shiny. After the usual ceremonies and dispensing of the presents, the Indian sachem, Hendrick, addressed the representatives, haranguing them with the injustices the English had perpetrated on the Indians by invading and taking their lands. This was true. The English in 1747 had chartered a private company, the Ohio Company of Virginia, for the purpose of trading and selling land cheaply to settlers. In addition, both Virginia and Pennsylvania competed for land in that area, which was on their western boundaries. The Indians felt themselves squeezed by the advances of the British from the east and the French from the west. Hendrick spoke with brutal frankness. Virginia and Pennsylvania, as well as the French, had all invaded the territory of the Six Nations. Yet, toward the French, the English were,

Figure 1.1 Franklin cartoon in 1754 illustrating the necessity for the American colonies to unite for their defense.

according to Hendrick, slack and craven. "Look about your country and see. You have no fortifications about you ... and the French may easily come and turn you out of doors, using their utmost endeavors to seduce and bring our people over to them.... Look at the French; they are men, they are fortifying everywhere. But we are ashamed to say it, you are all like women, bare and open, without any fortifications."[17]

Franklin had a small suggestion Indians might have liked. Since their whole subsistence, whether fighting or hunting, depended on keeping their guns in order, and because they had to make a journey of two or three hundred miles to an English settlement to get a gun lock repaired, they could lose a whole hunting season for that purpose. He proposed having a number of sober, discreet, English smiths reside with the Indians. Since the Indians were a practical people with few spiritual interests, he thought, "A smith is more likely to influence them than a Jesuit."[18] (In addition to saving souls, the French Jesuits were trying to influence the Indians to come over to the French side.)

While the Indian affairs were going on, the committee studying the various plans for unification that had been submitted decided on Franklin's plan. There was debate on it, resulting in some amendments that Franklin accepted against his judgment in order to carry the main points. It was his experience when drafting documents to make necessary concessions: "When one has so many different people with different opinions to deal with in a new affair, one is obliged sometimes to give up some smaller points in order to obtain greater."[19]

The representatives appointed Franklin to draw up a concrete proposal to be acted upon by Parliament. Franklin's plan of union was a detailed extension of his 1751 ideas.[20] It provided for a federal system with two branches; the first, an executive, the governor general, a military man appointed and paid by the Crown. He would execute measures adopted by the other branch, the Grand Council, which was to be made up of the elected assemblies of the colonies. The smaller colonies would send one member to the Grand Council; the larger colonies were allotted two members. The treasury would be funded by an excise tax on liquor and tea, which were consumed equally per capita in the colonies, and would represent the population. The duties of the union would be to provide for defense, deal with the Indians, make new settlements, raise and pay soldiers, and construct forts and naval vessels to be available in case of war.

The plan was a detailed constitution of the union, with such considerations as the powers of the governor general and the Grand Council in peace and war, the powers to make laws, actions to be taken in case of the death of the governor general, and so on. The colonies to be members of the union included all of the original thirteen with the exception of Delaware and Georgia. In addition to this constitution, Franklin wrote a lengthy document, "Reasons and Motives for the Albany Plan of Union," in which he explained and justified all of the articles in the constitution.[21] For example, he explained that Philadelphia was selected as the site of the first meeting of the government since it was centrally located, being only two days from New York, four days from Rhode Island and Charleston, South Carolina, by water, but if the whole journey had to be made on horseback, the most distant members, New Hampshire and South Carolina, could make it in just 15 to 20 days.

On the subject of taxation, Franklin made a statement that foreshadowed future history, namely, "That it is essential to English liberty, that the subject should not be taxed but by his own consent or the consent of his elected representatives."[22] Here in 1754 he was enunciating what would be the war cry of the colonies in 1776 in their rebellion against Britain, "No taxation without representation."

In his plan Franklin had reluctantly conceded to amendments that he hoped would make it easier for the colonies to accept; however, when the plan was transmitted to the assemblies of the colonies for ratification, not one of the 11 colonies to which it had been sent was willing give up its independence by yielding power to a central authority. Even the Pennsylvania assembly, having purposely taken it up in Franklin's absence, rejected it, much to his mortification. The home government in London didn't even consider it, having good reasons, as history was to demonstrate, why it didn't wish to encourage unification of the colonies. This plan, however, was strictly for the benefit of the colonies with no intent of making them independent of the home government.[23]

Reflecting on the Albany Plan 35 years later, Franklin summarized its fate: "The Assemblies did not adopt it, as they all thought there was too much prerogative in it; and in England it was judged to have too much of the democratic." So it was totally rejected. In his autobiography, he says, "I am still of opinion it would have been happy for both sides [of] the water if it had been adopted. The colonies so united would have been sufficiently strong to have defended themselves; there would then have been no need of troops from England; of course the subsequent pretense for taxing America, and the bloody contest it occasioned would have been avoided." Then he began to philosophize: "But such mistakes are not new; history is full of errors of states and princes. Those who govern, having much business on their hands, do not generally like to take the trouble of considering and carrying into execution new projects. The best measures are therefore seldom adopted from previous wisdom, but forced by occasion."[24]

Richard Bernstein in "The Making of the Constitution" states,

> The Albany Plan of Union was the most detailed proposal to create a union among the American colonies ever attempted. It contemplated a government with the authority to operate directly on the citizens of the several colonies and with unchallenged authority in the matters assigned to it by the plan. Indeed the plan's provisions checked the powers of the British government over the colonies as much as it did the powers of the colonies over the matters committed to the proposed union's authority. Many scholars regard this document as the ancestor of both the American idea of federalism and the British Commonwealth.[25]

Long before he had any idea of America separating from Britain, Franklin persisted in his goal of unifying the colonies. As well as his "Join or Die" cartoon, he showed his strong advocacy of union with the expressions "Our safety depends on our union" and we are like "a cask with thirteen stout staves without a single hoop to hold them together." Later, there came the statement, "We Are One" on the first United States currency, which was designed by Franklin when the Revolution had begun.[26]

Governor Shirley

On a trip to Boston in December 1754, Franklin met William Shirley, the governor of Massachusetts, and began a correspondence with him on the Albany Plan, which, 22 years before the Declaration of Independence, gave a statement of the principles that resulted in the rupture with England that was to ensue.[27] Governor Shirley had proposed an alternative to the Albany Plan that excluded representatives of the colonies on the Grand Council. Franklin replied that this was just taxing the colonies by an act of Parliament, where they have no representative, would produce extreme dissatisfaction in the colonies and wouldn't work:

> I apprehend that excluding the *People* of the Colonies from all share in the choice of the Grand Council, will give extreme dissatisfaction, as well as the taxing them by act of Parliament where they have no representative. ... Where heavy burdens are to be laid upon them, it has been found useful to make it, as much as possible, their own act; for they bear better when they have ...

some share in the direction; and when any public measures are generally grievous or even distasteful to the people, the wheels of government must move more heavily.

Speaking freely, Franklin told Governor Shirley of his low opinion of the governors that England had sent to the colonies. The "governors often come to the colonies merely to make fortunes ... are not always men of the best abilities and integrity ... [and] the Parliament of England is at a great distance subject to being misinformed by such governors." He then argued that with no representatives in Parliament the colonials were being treated as a conquered people, not as true British subjects. Since they were defending the frontiers in America and must bear the expense, they should be allowed to have a share in the voting for the money to be expended. He complained that although they must pay a considerable part of English taxes, they suffered unfairly from restraints of trade. They were prohibited from purchasing supplies from foreign nationals but were required to buy them from English merchants at higher prices. They had to export their raw materials to Britain at lower prices than could be received in other markets. Further, they were forbidden to manufacture many products, like ironware and shoes, so as not to compete with English merchants.

Although Franklin didn't say so in so many words, Britain looked upon the colonies as a source of wealth to be exploited for the benefit of the home country. Britain was then doing this in Jamaica and the Caribbean Islands and later did it in India and Africa. But those people were natives of other races and cultures. The American colonials considered themselves to be transplanted English people who deserved to be treated with the same rights and privileges as the people in England. Franklin offered an analogy: There was an island close to the coast of England called Goodwin Sands, which at low tide was connected to the mainland. It then increased the size of the population of England and was part of that country as any other part. At high tide, when it was separated by the ocean, as was America, would it be right to deprive the inhabitants of the common privileges enjoyed by other English people, such as the right of selling their produce in the same ports or making their own shoes? "Now, I looked upon the colonials as so many counties gained to Great Britain" with the advantages of "being in different climates, they afford greater variety of produce and materials for more manufactures; and being separated by the ocean, they increase much more the shipping and seamen."

To emphasize the unequal treatment of the colonies, Franklin closed the correspondence with the following emphasis: "Those who have contributed to enlarge Britain's empire and commerce, increase for strength, her wealth, and the numbers of her people, at the risk of their own lives and private fortunes in new and strange countries" ought to expect not only equality but "some preference."[28]

Military Matters

With Washington's defeat and the French military actions, the British government became aroused and in 1755 sent two regiments of British regulars under General Edward Braddock of the Coldstream Guards to capture the French strongholds in the Ohio territory. Franklin met with Braddock and tried to acquaint him with Indian-style fighting and their expertise in laying ambushes. He explained that "the slender line, near four miles long, which your army must make [in going through the woods] may expose it to be attacked by surprise in its flanks, and to be cut like a thread into several pieces."[29] Braddock was not to be convinced and suffered a disaster, exactly as Franklin had warned. The only benefit of this catastrophe was that Washington, who joined Braddock in this venture, escaped with his life and gained practical experience that would be of use later on. Braddock had been able to obtain only 25 wagons to transport his supplies to the battlefront. Franklin, who had offered to help, was able to round up 150 wagons and 259 packhorses for him. However, the farmers who lent the wagons and horses, did not know or trust Braddock and insisted that Franklin put up his own bond, for which he had to make good upon Braddock's defeat and loss of the wagons.

That year, using his influence with the Pennsylvania assembly, Franklin had it pass his militia bill, which approved 60,000 pounds for defense. He was chosen colonel of a Pennsylvania regiment and traveled to the Pennsylvania frontier building forts and organizing defenses. In the following years, under the strong leadership of British Prime Minister William Pitt, Britain gained the upper hand in its military contest with the French and was able to drive the French off the entire North American continent.

When Franklin gave Governor Shirley his opinion of the governors who came from Britain to the American colonies, he knew from experience what he was saying. The governors of Pennsylvania had been selected by the proprietors of that colony, the sons of William Penn, the founder of Pennsylvania. The elder Penn was an honest man who treated everyone fairly, including the Indians. His sons, however, cheated the Indians and refused to pay taxes on their great estates in Pennsylvania. In 1757, the

Pennsylvania assembly dispatched Franklin to London to try to make the proprietors pay up. That turned out to be a much more difficult task than had been assumed. Franklin served in that capacity until 1762, when he came home for two years, but in 1764 he was again sent to London as agent for Pennsylvania to represent the grievances of that colony to the British government. He remained there until 1774, becoming agent also for three other colonies, Massachusetts, New Jersey, and Georgia. In effect, he was the unofficial ambassador of America, pleading and lobbying for American causes.

Taxes, Taxes, Taxes

After the defeat of the French, the British government reasoned that since the war in America was very costly and was to the benefit of the colonies, they should pay the cost through additional taxes. First, there was the Stamp Act, which put a tax on all legal documents and printed matter including newspapers and other printed material, even playing cards. Franklin had opposed this act, but when it passed he was reluctantly reconciled to live with it. However, he had grossly misjudged the sentiments of his fellow Americans, who erupted violently in opposition to the act. When a rumor spread that he had written this act, a mob attacked his house in Philadelphia, threatening to burn it down, with his wife inside, rifle in hand, bravely defending it. The colonists were incensed because they believed this act was an infringement of their rights as British citizens. When Franklin heard about the riots in America, he sprang into action, skillfully organizing and leading an opposition which successfully removed the Stamp Act.

While opposing the Stamp Act and also the 1764 Colonial Currency Act, which prevented the colonists from paying their debts to England in colonial currencies (some of which had depreciated) and from issuing more paper money, Franklin made yet another attempt to unify the colonies, by proposing one uniform paper currency for all the colonies (as now Europe has done with the Euro) instead of separate paper money as was then printed by each colony. This new paper currency would be backed by mortgage loan security and printed in England as official currency by act of Parliament, bearing six percent interest for ten years. This was Franklin's substitute for the Stamp Act, which he introduced anonymously. The plan was presented to the British ministers, but, as Franklin said, they "paid little attention to it, being besotted with the Stamp Scheme." He noted that it was considered too radical by the representatives of the

Crown, and it was then rejected by his fellow Americans as too conservative. By 1767 his authorship of the proposal was revealed, but none of his efforts came to fruition until 1776 with the Revolution, when he designed and supervised the printing of the first paper money of the new United States of America.[30]

America's troubles did not end with the defeat of the Stamp Act. Parliament substituted other taxes to produce the same effect: the Townsend Acts, which put duties on tea, glass and paper; and the Tea Act, which resulted in the Boston Tea Party, in which Bostonians masquerading as Indians seized a shipload of British tea in Boston harbor and dumped it into the ocean. There was the Quartering Act, in which British troops were housed in America at the Americans' expense. There were also the Intolerable Acts, in which Britain blockaded Boston harbor in retaliation for the tea incident. Each act produced greater resentment and an escalation of retaliatory action, leading to violence.

Franklin tried his best to defuse the situation by pleading America's case. He obtained the aid of powerful British friends who spoke in Parliament for the American cause. The famous statesman Edmund Burke spoke eloquently on the need for reconciliation, and the former prime minister, William Pitt, personally called on Franklin at his residence to do his best to prevent the imminent split. Franklin, who rose from humble beginnings, was greatly flattered by the visit from this great man, but Lord North, the prime minister, the king, and Parliament were in no mood to make concessions to their wayward offspring in America. Jefferson described Lord North's answers to all attempts at reconciliation as "dry, unyielding, in the spirit of unconditional submission, and betrayed an absolute indifference to the occurrence of a rupture."

In 1774 Franklin wrote Joseph Galloway, a friend in Philadelphia, suggesting that he prepare a constitution that would specify American rights and duties. In response, Galloway drew up a plan that closely followed the Albany Plan except that it included the union between the colonies and Great Britain, with the colonies having representation in Parliament. Franklin had discussed such a similar aspiration of his own in 1754 when writing to Governor Shirley, saying that a government in which the colonies would have fair representation in Parliament would be desirable, and he expressed the hope that with "such an union, the people of great Britain and people of the colonies could learn to consider themselves, not as belonging to different communities with different interests, but to one community with one interest, which I imagine would contribute to strengthen the whole, and greatly lessen the danger of future separations."[31]

Franklin had been a loyal and even enthusiastic citizen of Britain and

Figure 1.2 Franklin cartoon in 1766 after the Stamp Act, to show Britain what the loss of the American colonies could mean to her.

its empire, but as early as 1758, when in London trying to get economic justice for Pennsylvania, he was disillusioned by the kind of people in the British government. He wrote a friend in America that "you may conjecture what reception a petition concerning privileges from the colonies may meet with those who think that even the people of England have too many." And when an Englishman questioned the loyalty of Americans, saying that the Americans, for all they said of their loyalty and affection, would move for independence, Franklin replied that no such idea was ever entertained by Americans, "nor will any such enter their heads, unless you abuse them." In 1760, in London, he foresaw that "the most grievous tyranny and oppression" could drive the colonies into union. In 1774, after observing the conduct of the British government for 16 years and suffering all the rebuffs from it, he was then considering independence not as a possibility but a probability. He wrote Galloway of the corruption in the British government, indicating that a closer association would also corrupt America:

> When I consider the extreme corruption prevalent among all orders of men in this old rotten state, and the glorious public virtue so predominant in our rising country, I cannot but apprehend more mischief than benefit from a closer union. I fear they

will drag us after them in all their plundering waste ... injustice and rapacity.... Here [there are] numberless and needless places [employees], enormous salaries, pensions, perquisites, bribes, groundless quarrels, foolish expeditions, false accounts or no accounts. Contracts and jobs devour all revenue and produce continual necessity in the midst of natural plenty. I apprehend therefore that to unite us intimately will only be to corrupt and poison us also.[32]

It is obvious that Franklin didn't have a high opinion of the British government, yet he would not close off discussion if there were any chance of preventing a war: "However, I would try anything, and bear anything that can be borne with safety to our just liberties, rather than engage in the war with such near relations, unless compelled to it by dire necessity in our own defense."

He created a cartoon that he hoped would show the government the folly of their treatment of the colonies and where it could lead. It shows a young woman looking mournfully to heaven (Britannia defenseless, Figure 1.2), with her arms and legs severed, the sections lying on the ground labeled with the names of American colonies (Figure 1.2). He even had the temerity to write a speech for the king, supposedly to be delivered to the members of Parliament castigating them for their mistaken, ruinous policies toward the American colonies. As might be expected, none of these things had any effect. When a nobleman asked him what would satisfy the Americans, Franklin replied that it might easily be described in a few "Re's":

Re

call your forces,
store Castle William [an island in Boston harbor] and
pair the damage done to Boston,
peal your unconstitutional acts,
nounce your pretensions to tax us,
fund the duties you have exhorted; after this
quire and
ceive payment for the destroyed tea, with the voluntary grants of
  the colonies. And then
joice in a happy
conciliation.[33]

In 1775, Franklin decided that he could be of no further use in London and set sail for home. While he was still on the ocean, the battles at Lexington and Concord broke out in America. British General Gage, stationed in Boston, in a surprise move to forestall a rebellion by New England patriots, sent his troops in the night to Concord to seize the patriots' gunpowder and shot. The embattled farmers, however, were alerted and ready, upsetting the British regulars, who lost 273 of their 1,000 men in their hurried march back. When he departed from London, Franklin expressed to Burke his deep regret for the impending break with Britain, saying, "America would never again see such happy days as she had passed under the protection of England." But he saw no hope for relations to return to the way they had been before the troubles began. Burke reported that Franklin's mind was "soured and exasperated" and was made up. After Lexington and Concord, Franklin wrote to Burke, "You will see by the papers that General Gage ... drew the sword and began the war. His troops made a most vigorous retreat, 20 miles in three hours, scarce to be paralleled in history: the feeble Americans, who pelted them all the way, could scarce keep up with them."[34]

In 1774 representatives of the colonies had gathered in Philadelphia for the First Continental Congress, in which they attempted to formally declare their rights (the Declaration of Rights and Grievances). In 1775, with no reply from London and things getting worse, they held the Second Continental Congress to confront the precarious military situation. On the day that Franklin landed in Philadelphia he was chosen a representative from Pennsylvania to this Congress. Franklin said that in Congress he was busier than in any time of his life. He was elected America's first postmaster general and was appointed to ten congressional committees. One of the committees was to provide munitions for the Continental Army, another to arrange for the printing of paper money, and a third, called the committee of secret correspondence, was to deal with foreign policy. He was also elected to the Pennsylvania assembly and appointed to the committee of safety for protecting Philadelphia from attack by British warships navigating the Delaware River. As president of the American Philosophical Society, he had to find time to preside at its meetings. And Congress sent him to Cambridge, Massachusetts, to meet General Washington in order to help provide supplies for the Continental Army.

However, nothing he did was more important than his presentation to the Congress of his plan of union, titled "The Articles of Confederation and Perpetual Union." This was the first draft of what would be the first Constitution of the United States. These articles carried this new nation for 11 years, through the War of Independence and afterward until 1787, when the present federal Constitution was adopted. The encyclopedias will tell you that the first draft of the Articles of Confederation was written in 1776, not 1775, and its author was John Dickinson, not Benjamin Franklin.

The apparent anomaly is explained by James Madison in his preface to his "Notes of Debates in the Federal Constitution of 1787." Franklin presented his "Articles" to the Congress in July 1775, but there were many members who were not yet ready for a break with England and felt Franklin's draft too radical. Thus, it was not acted upon or recorded so as not to cause dissension within the membership. One year later, the mood had changed, and John Dickinson, a friend of Franklin and a lawyer, was given the assignment, but as Madison notes, Franklin's draft was the basis for the later version.[35] Dickinson's was considered the first draft because it was voted upon and approved, even though it was not accepted by all the states until 1781. According to the editors of the Franklin Papers at Yale University, Franklin's proposed "Articles," although not directly implemented, "became part of the intellectual store from which the Articles of Confederation and even the Federal Constitution were derived."[36]

In his 1751 plan of union, Franklin had proposed a voluntary union of the colonies rather than one imposed by Parliament, but in his Albany Plan, in 1754, he concluded that the colonies would not act on their own and called for Parliament to take action in establishing the union. Now, in 1775, with the political climate very different, the document no longer included Parliament. Franklin used the Albany Plan as the basis for his articles, with modifications to bring it up to date. Franklin's plan was approved by Jefferson and others who had given up hope of reconciliation, but it antagonized those who still fostered that hope. To satisfy the latter and not shatter the fragile consensus in Congress, Franklin added a final paragraph allowing for the return of the colonies to their former relationship with Britain should the mother country repeal all the injurious acts and pay reparations "for the injury done to Boston by shutting up its port, for the burning of Charleston; for the expense of this unjust war" and if all the British troops were withdrawn from America. It concluded with a final caveat: "but on failure thereof, this Confederation is to be perpetual."[37]

With the extremely remote chance that Parliament would meet these demands, it should be no surprise that the conservatives in Congress were not mollified, and Franklin's articles were set aside and not voted on. An interesting inclusion of Franklin's articles is his open invitation to other colonies of Great Britain, namely Ireland, the West Indies, Quebec, St. John's (Prince Edward Island), Nova Scotia, Bermuda, east and west Florida, to join the confederation. This certainly could not have pleased the English government. In regard to Canada, in February of 1776 Congress dispatched Franklin to Montreal to determine whether the Canadians would join the alliance of American colonies in opposition to Britain. They wouldn't, and Canada did not become part of the United States.

In comparing the Franklin and Dickinson articles of confederation, the first article of each, which gives the name of the confederation, indicates a major difference.[38] In Franklin's articles the name is "the United Colonies of North America." Dickinson's articles, issued a week after the Declaration of Independence, is titled "the United States of America" (this undoubtedly was a last-minute change because in the individual articles the words "United Colonies" rather than "United States" were used). Because it was written for a now independent nation currently engaged in war, and perhaps because Dickinson was a lawyer, his plan is much more detailed than Franklin's. Both plans recognized the confederation as "a firm league of friendship" of the colonies, each colony being autonomous with few restrictions imposed by Congress. In both plans the confederation provides for the common defense against enemies, the power to declare war and make peace, to enter into alliances with foreign powers, to settle disputes between colonies, to create new colonies, to regulate treaties with Indians, and to establish and regulate a general currency. In each plan the confederation would ensure the safety, security, and liberty of the people and their property as well as their general welfare.

A significant difference in the plans is found in the method to amend the articles. In Franklin's plan a majority of the colonies could vote amendments, whereas in Dickinson's document the vote had to be unanimous. This resulted in Dickinson's articles of Confederation not being officially adopted until five years later, 1781, because one state, Maryland, would not sign until its disagreement about western boundaries was settled. Another important difference was based on the method of determining representation of the states in Congress. In Franklin's articles, the number of votes allotted each state in Congress was based upon its population, but Dickinson's allowed only one vote for each state. Franklin's plan was favored by the states with larger populations and Dickinson's by those with fewer people. Dickinson's plan for voting made for considerable controversy among the states and was settled only when the new Federal Constitution took over in 1787.

Accommodation or Separation?

The advent of both independence and the Revolutionary War was very difficult for Franklin. Many of his friends both in England and America, and even his own son, were on the other side of the battle. Once he had been a loyal, even enthusiastic, subject of the British Empire, although aware of its shortcomings in its treatment of the American colonies, and had done his best to reconcile the problems. But having failed in diplomacy in England, he was resolute in the course of separation. He had met Thomas Paine in England and had arranged for him to come to America. When Paine wrote his pamphlet, "Common Sense," which convinced America to choose independence, he showed it first to Franklin and got his approval before publishing it. Franklin was on the committee appointed by Congress to draw up the Declaration of Independence, to which he affixed his signature. There was no question, therefore, as to where he stood on this delicate issue of independence, yet even after the war had begun he was still hopeful of the possibility for reconciliation and peace. In September 1776, with Washington's troops embattled with the British redcoats in Manhattan, Franklin met with British Admiral Lord Richard Howe on the latter's battleship off Staten Island in a last-ditch, but futile, effort for peace. Admiral Howe was a personal friend whom Franklin had known in England. He had written Howe: "Long did I endeavor with unfeigned and unwearied zeal to preserve from breaking that fine and noble China vase, the British Empire."[39] Now, it was too late; the vase had been broken and could not be repaired.

Franklin had great expectations for America. Even when he was an enthusiastic booster of the British Empire, he envisioned America as the greater partner, exceeding the British Isles not only in geographic size but eventually in population and production as well. Now, with independence, he referred to America as "a rising state which seems likely soon to act a part of some importance on this stage of human affairs." He looked forward to the growth of the new country, adding new states in westward expansion, by buying land from the Indians in the Ohio territory and along the Mississippi River. When the Spanish government suggested that it might enter the war on the side of America if America would renounce her claim to the lower Mississippi, then owned by Spain, Franklin adamantly refused to consider it.

It should have been clear at the outset of the war that this new, self-declared country could not stand up against the then mightiest empire on earth without outside assistance. In November 1776, recognizing this fact, Congress reacted by sending Franklin to France, England's traditional enemy, to obtain the necessary money and war supplies that America so badly needed. There was just one problem: Washington had been losing battle after battle to the better-trained, better-equipped British regulars, and the French didn't want to be backing a loser. However, Franklin was very hard to refuse. This famous scientist-philosopher with his beaver-fur cap and Quaker clothes became an instant folk hero in France, popular with the aristocracy, the intelligentsia, and the common people as well.

He was received at court by the king and queen and by the diplomats in the government. He suggested to the diplomats that if America won, France could look forward to the trade that Britain had been allotting all to herself. France surely did not want her enemy to win and secretly made a loan to America that was used by Franklin to buy munitions through phantom companies.

After Washington won some battles, the French openly recognized America, and Franklin was able to obtain more money and the aid of the French army and navy, without which America could never have won its revolution. Vergennes, the foreign minister, through whom all the money was funneled, would talk to no American other than Franklin. Franklin would plead his case in a quiet, patient manner which was persuasive with the polished French diplomat. Franklin said, "This Court [France] is to be treated with decency and delicacy." Jefferson, who succeeded Franklin as ambassador to France, indicated that Franklin had the confidence of the French ministers to such a degree "that it may truly be said that they were more under his influence than he under theirs."[40]

In 1783, the war having been won with French assistance, Franklin signed the peace treaty with England and was ready to come home. Congress, however, found him too valuable in Europe and kept him in his post as American ambassador to France until 1785. Coming home at the age of 79, after nine years in France, Franklin intended to retire from public life and spend his remaining years in scientific activities. But as soon as he returned he was made president (governor) of Pennsylvania. It was in that capacity two years later that he found himself host to the other delegates at the Constitutional Convention in Philadelphia. The articles of confederation had, in practice, served from 1776 to 1787 as the Constitution of the United States, but it had so many faults and weaknesses that the country could not have continued to survive without a stronger binding charter. In fact it was remarkable that the country did survive that long with this weak structure, but that was all the states would approve up to that time.

Under the articles, the army was always starved for funds, unable to pay the soldiers or pay for supplies. The Congress had no power to force the states to pay what they owed, and they were usually in default. Under the articles the states were sovereign, like separate nations in Europe, without any effective national executive and no national judiciary at all. Congress could not regulate commerce; it had no taxing power; and amendments to correct these defects required the unanimous vote of the states, which was never possible. The states constrained trade by setting up tariffs against each other, and Congress had no power to set up national tariffs to protect America's emerging industries from foreign competition. Washington, Hamilton, and other leaders, realizing that something had to be done, called upon the states to send delegates to Philadelphia in May 1787, for a convention to write a new constitution, assuring the states that whatever was adopted would be submitted to them for their approval. The states all realized that a better arrangement was necessary, but they all had different interests and could not commit themselves to agreeing to what others approved. Nevertheless, they sent delegates, and a convention was held, which lasted four months, from May to September, and produced a constitution for a functioning federal government of all the states, with executive, legislative, and judicial branches, which has served the nation all the years from 1787 to the present.

At the Constitutional Convention, Benjamin Franklin's position was unique. At 81, he was the oldest member, 20 years older than the next in age; he was the elder statesman, a respected sage. His mind was clear and sharp, but he suffered from a bladder stone, which gave him terrible pain when he walked or rode in a carriage. Thus, he was carried to the meetings seated in a sedan chair held by four strong men, like an oriental potentate. Despite his ailment, he attended the meetings more regularly than most of the other delegates, yet he let the younger men carry the major burden, making only occasional suggestions and proposals to keep the sessions moving in a productive way. Dr. Benjamin Rush, a Philadelphia physician and fellow signer of the Declaration of Independence, observed that during the sessions, "Dr. Franklin exhibits daily a spectacle of transcendent benevolence by attending the convention punctually and even taking part in its business and deliberations." James Madison, who kept a record of the convention, noted: "In the convention Dr. Franklin seldom spoke but when he did, he would make short, extemporaneous speeches with great pertinancy and effect."[41]

Unlike many of the members, who were provincial, representing in a partisan manner only their own state or region with its special interests, Franklin was first an American and then a Pennsylvanian. He had served his country in so many ways: on the city council of Philadelphia, in the Pennsylvania assembly, as postmaster general, where he had traveled the country setting up post offices and meeting the people, and in London and Paris, as agent and ambassador, where he had represented all Americans. He looked toward this convention with great expectations, as the final chance to succeed in the unification of the nation, a task he had so devotedly worked to bring about for the past 36 years.

When Washington and several other delegates arrived early for the convention, Franklin invited them to his house for dinner. He opened a cask of porter sent to him by a London brewer, which they agreed unanimously "was the best porter they had ever tasted." He regarded the delegates as the most august and respectable assembly he was ever in in his life. He wrote to Jefferson in France that the delegates were men of character, prudence, and ability, "so that I hope good from their meeting. Indeed if it does not do good it must do harm, as it will show that we have not wisdom enough to govern ourselves and ... that popular governments cannot long support themselves."[42] Lincoln, in his famous Gettysburg Address in 1863, would eloquently echo this concern, "whether this nation or any nation ... of the people, by the people, for the people shall not perish from the earth."

With his experience in diplomacy, Franklin expressed his talent for finding a compromise for difficult problems, injecting humor into the situation, and cooling hot tempers. When members clashed angrily, Franklin reminded them, "We are sent here to consult not to contend with each other.... [H]armony and union are extremely necessary." He noted that the members responded to his plea and picked up their debates "with great coolness and temper." When angers flared up again, Franklin proposed prayers for each session declaring "Except the Lord build the house they labor in vain to build it. I firmly believe this." Hamilton was reported to have said that the delegates were competent and jested, "We have no need for foreign aid." After discussion, prayers were not voted, but Franklin thought that the mere discussion produced a soothing effect.[43]

When the method of appointing federal judges came up, the members disagreed on whether they should be appointed by the president or the legislature. Franklin suggested that the members consider a method he understood was practiced in Scotland. There the judges were selected by the lawyers, who always selected the ablest of their profession, "in order to get rid of him and share his practice among themselves." Franklin's stories added a touch of levity that relieved the strain and lightened the mood of the sessions. The delegate from Georgia wrote of Franklin, "He is a most extraordinary man, and tells a story in a style more engaging than anything I've ever heard.... He is 82 and possesses an activity of mind equal to a youth of 25 years of age."[44]

The most severe test of the convention was the dispute over representation of the large and small states in Congress. The large states demanded representation based upon the number of their people, whereas the small states argued for equal representation regardless of population. Franklin noted, "if a proportional representation takes place, the small states contend their liberties will be in danger. If an equality of votes is to be put in its place, the large states say their money will be in danger." Then he appealed for a compromise: "When a broad table is to be made and the edges of planks do not fit, the artist takes a little from both and makes a good joint." He made a compromise motion which provided that in one branch (the House) representation would be proportioned on population, and it would originate all money bills, and in the second branch (the Senate) each state would have an equal vote. After a long debate the motion passed by a vote of five states to four. This was called "the Great Compromise" of the Constitution and was Franklin's great contribution to it because without it the convention might well have broken up without producing any document.

There was a subject before the convention that was even more basic to the future government of the United States. This was whether the new country was going to be a representative democracy or an aristocracy. It is hard to imagine now that this was the question to be decided, but in 1787 it was not at all clear which would win out. Elbridge Gerry, the delegate from Massachusetts, said that democracy was "the worst of all political evils," and he feared power in the hands of the people. The great landholders of Virginia and New York were staunch advocates of aristocracy and were fearful of the landless multitudes getting control of the government. Even their great leader, George Washington, was an aristocrat with great land holdings and many slaves. Gouverneur Morris of New York argued for making one branch of the legislature an aristocracy, "to be composed of men of great and established property ... chosen for life." Such an aristocratic body was necessary, he explained, "to keep down the turbulency of democracy." After all, we should not be surprised at these feelings since at that time aristocracies governed all the countries of the world.

This matter came up to the convention on the decision of who should have the right to vote. Many of the delegates held that only those who owned property should be eligible to vote. Franklin vigorously contested this position, saying that he was afraid such a restriction would "depress the virtue and public spirit of our common people.... I am sorry to see the signs of a disposition among some of our people to commence an aristocracy by giving the rich a predominance in government.... [I]s it supposed that wisdom is the necessary concomitant of riches[?]... [W]hy is property to be represented at all?"

When property qualifications for holding office were proposed, Charles Pinckney of South Carolina said he did not want "an undue aristocratic influence," but he "thought it essential that the members of the legislature, the executive, and the judges should be possessed of competent property to make them independent and respectable." Franklin rose in opposition saying, "If honesty were often the companion of wealth, and poverty was exposed to peculiar temptation, it was not less true that the possession of property increased the desire of more property. Some of the greatest rogues I ever was acquainted with were the richest rogues.... The personal securities of life and liberty, these remain the same in every member of the society, and the poorest continues to have an equal claim to them with the most opulent."[45]

The delegates worked from the end of May until the middle of September to forge a constitution for the United States of America. They had worked through the hot summer in a room in the Pennsylvania State House (now Independence Hall) with the windows shut and draped because the deliberations were strictly secret, so as to be free from outside influence. They were tired and frustrated because they were all on the losing side of some compromise votes. Yet they had a document, and it was now time to vote on it. It was a critical moment.

Franklin arose with a speech he had written. He handed it to James Wilson of Pennsylvania to read for him because standing was so painful to him. While Wilson was reading, Franklin reflected on his years of laboring to create a union of the states—from the first expression of his ideas in 1751, when most of the delegates were still children and some were not even born, to the Albany Plan in 1754, to the Articles of Confederation in 1775, and here in 1787 at the Constitutional Convention. Everything depended on this speech, which he addressed to the president of the convention, George Washington:

> Mr. President, I confess there are several parts of this constitution which I do not at present approve, but I am not sure I will never approve them. For having lived long, I have experienced many instances of being obliged by better information or fuller consideration to change opinions, even on important subjects, which I once thought right but found to be otherwise. It is therefore that the older I grow, the more apt I am to doubt my own judgment and to pay more respect to the judgment of others. Most men indeed, as well as most sects in religion, think themselves in possession of all truth.... Steele, a Protestant ... tells the Pope that the only difference between our churches ... is that the Church of Rome is infallible and the Church of England is never in the wrong. But though many private persons think almost as highly of their own infallibility as that of their sect, few express it so naturally as a certain French lady, who in a dispute with her sister, said, "I don't know how it happens, sister, but I meet with nobody but myself that's always in the right."[46]

It is said that Jefferson was given the job of writing the Declaration of Independence instead of Franklin because the Founding Fathers were afraid that Franklin would put a joke in it. Apparently, this little story about the French lady helped to relieve the tension and put the members at ease. One of them wrote to Jefferson in Paris and repeated Franklin's story about the "French girl." Franklin continued:

> In these sentiments, Sir, I agree to this constitution with all its faults, if they are such; because I think a general government necessary for us, and there is no form of government but what may be a blessing to the people if well administered ... and can only end in despotism ... when the people shall become so corrupted as to need despotic government, being incapable of any other. I doubt too, whether any other convention we can obtain may be able to make a better constitution. For when you assemble a number of men to have their joint wisdom, you inevitably assemble with those men all their prejudices, their passions, their errors of opinion, their local interests, and their selfish views. From such an assembly can a perfect production be expected? It therefore astonishes me, Sir, to find this system approaching so near to perfection as it does.... Thus I consent, Sir, to this constitution because I expect no better, and because I am not sure that it is not the best....
>
> On the whole, Sir, I cannot help expressing a wish that every member of this convention who may still have objections to it would, with me, on this occasion doubt a little of his own infallibility, and to make manifest our unanimity, put his name to this instrument.

With his speech completed, Franklin moved that the Constitution be signed by the members of the convention. The speech had a solidifying effect. It settled the doubts of the sincere but troubled delegates as to how to accept a document to which they had so many objections. Of the 12 states represented, all voted approval except South Carolina. A member from Maryland, who confessed he opposed many parts of the Constitution, explained why he had signed it, using almost the same words Franklin had used in his speech. This speech was considered the literary triumph of the convention, and members requested copies so they could circulate them in the further struggle to get the Constitution ratified by the states.

Benjamin Franklin died in 1790 at the age of 84, but he lived just long enough to see the new government in operation with the first Congress seated in 1788 and President Washington inaugurated in 1789. At the close of the Constitutional Convention, with the signing ceremony, Madison reported in his records: "The members then proceeded to sign the instrument. While the last members were signing it, Dr. Franklin, looking towards the President's chair at the back of which a rising sun happened to be painted, observed to a few members near him that painters had found it difficult to distinguish in their art a rising from setting sun. 'I have,' said he, 'often in the course of the session, and the vicissitudes of my hopes and fears as to its issue, looked at that behind the President without being able to tell whether it was rising or setting. But now at length I have the happiness to know that is a rising and not a setting sun.'"[47]

During the dark days of the Revolutionary War, Franklin wrote to Washington from France expressing in poetic prose his great hopes for the future of his country:

> I must soon quit the scene, but you may live to see our country flourish, as it will amazingly and rapidly after the war is over. Like a field and of young Indian corn, which long fair weather and sunshine have enfeebled and discolored, and which in that weak state, by a thunder gust, of violent wind, hail, and rain, seemed to be threatened with absolute destruction; yet the storm being passed, it recovers fresh verdure, shoots up with double vigor, and delights the eye, not of its owner only, but of every observing traveler.[48]

In the more than 200 years since the Constitutional Convention, the United States of America has proved to be the greatest advance in the history of political democratic government, serving as a model for nations around the world.

And Benjamin Franklin started it.

2

The Mystery
of Polly Baker

The greatest revolution in modern times is the liberation of women —
half of the human race. When George Washington married Martha Custis,
a wealthy widow, he gained legal possession of all her wealth. She retained
only ownership of the clothes she was wearing. While John Adams was in
Philadelphia working for independence, his spunky wife Abigail had ideas
of independence of another sort. She wrote to John, "Do not put such
unlimited power into the hands of the husbands. Remember all men would
be tyrants.... If particular care and attention is not paid to the ladies, we
are determined to foment a rebellion." To this John replied, "As to your
extraordinary code of laws, I cannot but laugh."[1]

In Britain too, lacking rights, women were subject to submission.
Among the lower classes, wives were frequently bought and sold in the
open market. The *Doncaster Gazette* of March 25, 1803, describes such a
sale: "A fellow sold his wife, as a cow, in Sheffield market-place a few days
ago. The lady was put into the hands of a butcher, who held her by a hal-
ter fastened round her waist. 'What do you ask for your cow?' Said a
bystander. 'A guinea', replied the husband. 'Done', cried the other, and
immediately led away his bargain. We understand (the reporter had a sense
of humor) that the purchaser and his 'cow' live very happily together."[2] In
the sales of wives that occurred between 1766 and 1832, the prices ranged
from 1 shilling up to 100 guineas (2,100 shillings), no doubt depending

upon the estimated quality of the product and the market conditions. There were reports of the sale of wives as late as 1882, when the *South Wales Daily News* for May 2 noted that at Alfreton, a woman was sold by her husband in a public house for a glass of ale, and in the *Pall Mall Gazette* of October 20, at Belfast a certain George Drennan sold his wife to one O'Neill for one penny and a dinner.

On April 15, 1747, one of London's leading newspapers, the *General Advertiser*, printed a courtroom speech of a woman who was prosecuted for the crime of bearing a bastard child, the penalty for which was whipping, a fine, jail, or all three.[3] The story is a sordid account of innocence, deception, and punishment. The newspaper said the trial had taken place "at Connecticut near Boston in New England." The defendant's name was Polly Baker. This publication produced an explosive chain reaction in the British press. In the next few days "The Speech of Miss Polly Baker" appeared in five London newspapers and was copied in papers of other British cities. By the end of the month, three monthly magazines followed suit, as well as one in Edinburgh and another in Dublin (Figure 2.1). By July, this news had traversed the ocean and was printed in newspapers in New York, Boston, and Annapolis. It didn't appear in any American magazines for a very good reason — there weren't any.

The interest in this sensational trial finally abated but, phoenixlike, came back to life about a quarter of a century later to satisfy the "supermarket tabloid" tastes of a new generation of readers. In 1768, a translation from the *London Magazine* appeared in a Swedish periodical, and in 1773, a newspaper in Salem, Massachusetts, picked up the story, which was followed soon after by a paper at Williamsburg, Virginia. It then took a turn and attracted the attention of serious writers, including French intellectuals: the Abbé Raynal, Denis Diderot, and Brissot de Warville.

One may ask what was so intriguing in poor Polly's affair to capture the attention and interest of the lowbrows and highbrows alike? Perhaps Polly's speech, first presented in the London newspaper will help to explain.[4]

> *The Speech of Miss Polly Baker*, before a court of judicature at Connecticut near Boston in New England; where she was prosecuted the fifth time, for having a bastard child: which influenced the court to dispense with her punishment, and induced one of her judges to marry her the next day.
>
> *Polly Speaks*: May it please the Honorable Bench to indulge me in a few words: I am a poor unhappy woman who have no money to fee lawyers to plead for me, being hard put to get a tolerable living. I shall not trouble your Honors with long speeches; for I

have not the presumption to expect, that you may, by any means, be prevailed on to deviate in your sentence from the law in my favor. All I humbly hope is, that your Honors would charitably move the Governor's goodness on my behalf, that my fine may be remitted. This is the fifth time, gentlemen, that I have been dragged before your court on the same account; twice I have paid heavy fines, and twice have been brought to public punishment, for want of money to pay the fines.

This may have been agreeable to the laws, and I don't dispute it; but since laws are sometimes unreasonable in themselves, and therefore repealed, and others bear too hard on the subject in particular circumstances; and therefore there is left a power somewhat to dispense with the execution of them; I take the liberty to say, that I think this law, by which I am punished, it is both unreasonable in itself, and particularly severe with regard to me, who have always lived an inoffensive life in the neighborhood where I was born, and defy my enemies (if I have any) to say I have ever wronged man, woman, or child.

Abstracted from the law, I cannot conceive (may it please your Honors) what the nature of my offense is. I have brought five fine children into the world, at the risk of my life; I have maintained them well by my own industry, without burdening the township, and would have done it better, if it had not been for the heavy charges and fines I have paid. Can it be a crime (in the nature of things I mean) to add to the number of the King's subjects, in a new country that really wants people? I own it, I should think it a praiseworthy, rather than a punishable action.

I have debauched no other woman's husband, nor enticed any youth; these things I never was charged with, nor has anyone the least cause of complaint against me, unless, perhaps, the minister, or justice, because I have had children without being married, by which they have missed a wedding fee. But, can ever this be a fault of mine? I appeal to your Honors.

You are pleased to allow I don't want sense; but I must be stupified to the last degree, not to prefer the honorable state of wedlock, to the condition I have lived in. I always was, and still am willing to enter into it; and doubt not my behaving well in it, having all the industry, frugality, fertility, and skill in economy, appertaining to a good wife's character.

I defy any person to say I ever refused an offer of that sort; on the contrary, I readily consented to the only proposal of marriage that ever was made me, which was when I was a virgin; but too easily confiding in the person's sincerity that made it, I unhappily lost my own honor by trusting to his; for he got me with child and then forsook me:

That very person you all know; he is now became a magistrate of this country; and I had hopes he would have appeared this day on the bench, and have endeavored to moderate the court in my favor; then I should have scorned to have mentioned it; but I must now complain of it as unjust and unequal that my betrayer and undoer, the first cause of all my faults and miscarriages (if they must be deemed such) should be advanced to honor and power in the government, that punishes my misfortunes with stripes and infamy.

I should be told, tis like that were there no act of assembly in the case, the precepts of religion are violated by my transgressions. If mine then is a religious offense, leave it to religious punishments. You have already excluded me from the comforts of your church communion. Is that not sufficient? You believe I have offended heaven and must suffer eternal fire: Will that not be sufficient? What need is there then of your additional fines and whipping?

I own I do not think as you do; for if I thought what you call a sin was really such, I could not presumptuously commit it. But, how can it be believed that heaven is angry that my having children when to the little done by me towards it. God has been pleased to add his divine skill and admirable workmanship in the formation of their bodies and crowned it by furnishing them with rational and immortal souls. Forgive me, gentlemen, if I talk a little extravagantly on these matters; I am no divine but if you gentlemen must be making laws, do not turn natural and useful actions into crimes by your prohibitions.

But take into your wise considerations, the great and growing number of bachelors in the country, many of whom from the mean fear of the expenses of family have never sincerely and honorably courted a woman in their lives; and by their manner of living, leave unproduced (which is little better than murder) hundreds of their posterity to the thousandth generation. Is this not a greater offense against the public good than mine?

Compel them by law, either to marriage or to pay double the fine of fornication every year. What must poor young women do, whom custom have forbid to solicit the men, and who cannot force themselves upon husbands, when the laws take no care to provide them any; and yet severely punish them if they do their duty without them; the duty of the first and great command of nature and of nature's God, *increase and multiply.*

A duty from the steady performance of which nothing has been able to deter me; but for its sake I have hazarded the loss of the public esteem, and have frequently endured public disgrace and punishment; and therefore ought, in my humble opinion, instead of a whipping, to have a statue erected to my memory.

Responses to the Trial

LETTERS TO THE EDITOR

It should be evident that Polly's stirring declamation had something for everyone. But the elegance of her rhetoric led readers to become skeptical of this performance coming from a woman of her low station in life, at a time when most women received little or no education. But in May a letter to the editor of *Gentlemen's Magazine* responded to the doubters: "When I was in New England in the year 1745, I had the pleasure of seeing the celebrated Polly Baker, who was then, though near 60 years of age, a comely woman, and the wife of Paul Dudley, Esq. ... who married her ... and had 15 children by her. I send you this information, because it has been insinuated that the speech published in her name was entirely fictitious."[5]

The newsy item about the 15 children was not in the earlier account in the London newspaper but was added to this story in the *Gentlemen's Magazine*. The writer of this letter, who signed himself William Smith, then went on to describe an irrelevant subject, namely that of bundling (which existed at that time in New England), apparently just to titillate the English readers who knew nothing about bundling: "It is the custom in this country [New England] for young persons between whom there is a courtship or treaty of marriage, to lie together, the woman having her petticoats on, and a man his breeches. And afterwards if they do not fall out, they confess the covenant at church, in the midst of the congregation, and to the minister, who declares the marriage legal. And if anything criminal has been acted, orders a punishment accordingly, sometimes of 40 stripes save one."

The news of Polly Baker having been married to Paul Dudley was indeed sensational since Dudley was the chief justice of Massachusetts. He was then 72 years old and one of the most distinguished men in New England, whose father and grandfather had been governors of Massachusetts. This information had answered those who doubted the authenticity of the Polly Baker story but left them amazed. Just one month later the mystery deepened when the same magazine published another letter on the subject, this time by someone who signed himself L. Americanus.[6] (In the eighteenth century it was common for people to write under fictitious names.)

> The author of the letter in your magazine for May, signed William Smith, is egregiously imposed upon, for it is well-known that Paul Dudley, Esq. never acted in any judicial capacity in Connecticut,

The *Gentleman's Magazine:*

St JOHN's GATE

Lond Gazette
Read's Journ
Craftsman
Daily Adver-
tiser.
St James's E
vening Post
London Even-
ing Po;
Gen. Evening
Post
Daily Gazet-
teer
Gen. Adver-
tiser.
Westminster
Journal.
Old England
Anatomist.
Lon.Courant
Whitehall Eb
Post

Lon. 3 News
Dublin 4
Edinburgh 2
Bristol :: 2 :
Norwich 2
Exeter 2
Worcester
Northampton
Gloucester 3
Stamford :
Nottingham:
Chester Jour
Derby ditto
Ipswich 1 1
Reading 1 1 2
Leeds Mercr.
Newcastle 3
Canterbury
Colchester.
Sherborn
Birmingham
Manchester
Bath
Cambridge

For A P R I L 1747.

C O N T A I N I N G,

[More in Quantity and greater Variety than any Book of the Kind and Price.]

I. ACCOUNT of the behaviour and execution of lord *Lovat*, with further particulars of his life.

II. HISTORY of *Genoa*, an account of the expulsion of the *Austrians*, and the ostentatious inscription on ý occasion.

III. REMEDY for sizy blood.

IV. METHOD to prevent ships from leaking.

V. METHOD of warming all the rooms in a house by the kitchen fire, with a cut.

VI. DESCRIPTION of *Iseland* and manners of its inhabitants.

VII. SPEECH of *Polly Baker*.

VIII. The abbe *de la Ville*'s memorial, and the *French* king's curious declaration at length to the *Dutch* states.

IX. ESSAY on female education.

X. Emendation of a passage in *Shakespear*.

XI. OFFICE of a Stadtholder.

XII. DESCRIPTION of *Dutch Brabant*, and *Dutch Flanders*.

XIII. LETTER from the master of *Lovat*, Mr *Painter*'s letters, with lord *Lovat*'s remarks on him.

XIV. ELECTRICAL experiments proposed, and problems answered.

XV. An account of the taking fort St *George* and *Madrass*.

XVI. CHARGE against *Milton* continu'd.

XVII. LIST of ships taken.

XVIII. POETRY. Specimen of a new translation of *Tasso*; the father, a tale; to the duke of *Cumberland*, *French* and *English*; in memory of Mr *Chubb*.

XIX. HISTORICAL chronicle.

XX. LIST of births and marriages.

XXI. EACH day's price of stocks.

XXII. FOREIGN history.

XXIII. REGISTER of books.

With a PLAN of G E N O A, shewing its remarkable places by above 100 references, also another curious Plate.

By *S Y L V A N U S   U R B A N*, Gent.

LONDON: Printed by E. CAVE, jun. at St *John's Gate*.

SOCIAL BLISS

CONSIDERED:

In MARRIAGE and DIVORCE; COHABITING UNMARRIED, and PUBLIC WHORING.

CONTAINING

Things neceſſary to be known by all that ſeek mutual Felicity, and are ripe for the Enjoyment of it.

WITH

The SPEECH of Miſs POLLY BAKER; and Notes thereon.

————*Man when created,*
At firſt alone, long wandered up and down,
Forlorn and ſilent as his Vaſſal Beaſt;
But when a Heav'n-born Maid to him appear'd,
Strange Paſſion fill'd his Eyes, and fir'd his Heart,
Unloos'd his Tongue, and his firſt Talk was Love.

OTWAY.

By GIDEON ARCHER. *P. Annet*

LONDON:

Printed for and ſold by R. ROSE, near St. *Paul's.*

M. DCC. XLIX.

(Price Two Shillings.)

Above: *Figure 2.2* Title page of "Social Bliss Considered" with speech of Polly Baker. (From Hall.)

Opposite: *Figure 2.1* Title page of the *Gentleman's Magazine* (London), April 1747, with the speech of Polly Baker (vii) along with remedy for fizy blood (iii) and method for keeping ships from leaking (iv). (From Hall.)

but is chief justice of the province where he has always resided, and has been long married to a daughter of the late Governor Winthrop, by whom he never had any children. As they are of very good families, and he is one of the first rank in the country, is a pity their names should be ignorantly or wantonly used in support of a fictitious speech.

Strike one in favor of the honor of Judge Paul Dudley and against William Smith. L. Americanus also wants you to know that the well-respected people in America do not practice bundling: "The scurrilous description of the customs of young persons, if in use at all, is among the lowest sort of people only."

What is the truth here? The facts given by L. Americanus are essentially correct, except that Dudley was not married to the daughter of Governor Winthrop but to another woman, with whom he had six children, all of whom died in infancy. Since the papers with the trial of Polly Baker did not arrive in America until July, it is evident that the letter from L. Americanus had not been initiated by Justice Dudley, but when he did receive the news he must have been furious, for in a later issue of the magazine the publisher most humbly apologizes for the whole incident:[7]

> Whereas through the wicked contrivance of one William Smith, we unwarily published in our magazine for May 1947, a letter signed by him which we arc now fully sensible contains a groundless, vile and injurious slander and imputation upon the Honorable Paul Dudley, Esq. His Majesty's Chief Justice of the province of the Massachusetts Bay, the principal province in New England, and his lady, a person of the most unblemished reputation, and remarkable... for her great modesty, virtue, and other amiable qualities.

The publisher then tells us that the said William Smith had since absconded, so he cannot lawfully be punished for his malicious and gross abuse, so all that the publisher can do is to publicly confess his great concern for publishing so great a calumny and beg Dudley and his lady for their pardon. It is obvious that the publisher does not want the good judge to sue him for defamation of character.

While he is apologizing, the publisher includes his regret for printing the material about the nature of bundling in New England: "And whereas the said letter also contains a base and scandalous aspersion upon the inhabitants of the aforesaid province, by representing their customs in points of marriage as extremely irregular and indecent, contrary to the truth and to the standing laws of the province."

SOCIAL BLISS CONSIDERED

Although he apologizes for the contents of William Smith's letter, the publisher makes no apology for the Polly Baker story, and the saga of Polly Baker continues. The next episode appeared in the form of a book with the catchy title "Social Bliss Considered; in Marriage and Divorce; Cohabitating Unmarried, and Public Whoring"[8] (Figure 2.2). The title page says that it contains "Things necessary to be known by all that seek mutual felicity, and are ripe for the enjoyment of it." To top it off, the author offers us "The Speech of Miss Polly Baker" with his own notes on it. All of this for only two shillings.

The writer, Peter Annet, using the pen name Gideon Archer, had unusually liberal views for someone of his time. Although he advised young women to remain virgins until marriage, he advised young men to be moderate in their sex life. He also urged parents to forgive the indiscretions of their children. He believed that public whoring should be allowed under proper regulations as a means of preventing private whoring. He said, "Take away the law and you take away the sin; for there is none against nature."

With regard to Polly Baker, he felt it was irrelevant whether her speech was fact or fiction. He said that in matters of belief many people strain at a gnat and swallow a camel. "They cannot credit the truth of a story that has nothing improbable in it, but can credit stories reported by a credulous people to be done in distant ages, and in a strange country, which are impossible in nature." As a freethinker in religion, he no doubt was referring to the miracles in the Bible.

In his 24 notes on Polly Baker, he is firmly on her side, and his notes only go to amplify the points she makes in her speech. When Polly says that "abstracted from the law I cannot conceive what the nature of my offense is," Annet comments: "T'would be very hard by the laws of reason and nature, without the arbitrary authority of law, to prove her a criminal or offender."

When Polly complains that her betrayer is advanced to a position of honor and power in the same government that punishes her with stripes and infamy, Annet states that just as in Polly's case, "people do not suffer for their crimes but for their weakness, ignorance and poverty."

And when Polly finally decides that she deserves a statue instead of a whipping, for she had obeyed God's command to increase and multiply, Annet is wholly in agreement. He says, "This speech is beyond all statues that can be erected to eternalize her memory."

This book with Polly's speech and his 24 notes was reissued in 1766 as part of a collection of the author's works. Annet was constantly in trouble with the church and was first fired from his position as a schoolteacher and later was put in jail for a year at hard labor and sent to the pillory for his "irreligious and diabolical opinions." But Polly continued on. In 1768, Polly appeared in a Swedish periodical, and in 1773 she was introduced to a new generation of Americans, appearing in newspapers in Salem, Massachusetts, and Williamsburg, Virginia.

"Polly" Vous Français?

Another fertile land for the correction of injustice in the 1770s was the prerevolutionary kingdom of France. There, Polly had her greatest popularity. The Abbé Raynal, one of the most successful writers of the period, put Polly's speech in his best-selling book, *The History of the Indies.* This book, which was published in 1770 in six volumes and enlarged in 1781, was reported to be the most widely read book in France during that interval. It appeared in 20 official editions and 50 or more pirated editions across Europe. It related the history of the expansion of European countries into America and the Far East, with interesting stories and anecdotes, making it fascinating reading to people who knew nothing about these places. The Abbé Raynal was a social reformer, and Polly's spectacular trial gave him a wonderful opportunity to show the need for reform in what the Europeans regarded as backwoods America.[9]

Raynal presented the speech as unquestioned historical fact, as something that had not occurred long ago, although he did not give the date. He reported a footnote in Polly's speech with her final triumph, that the court had dispensed with her punishment and one of her judges had married her the next day. But, in his write-up, he said nothing about the 15 children that followed. Nor did he report her words about erecting a statue in her memory since that may have been considered a humorous or flippant remark, and he was a serious reformer. For his purpose, he "improved" on Polly by inserting words for her to speak that had never appeared in any previous publication. His insertions tended to be more emotional, as, for example: "Oh just and good God, God repairer of evils and Injustices, It Is to thee I appeal the sentence of my judges. Do not avenge me; do not punish them; but deign to enlighten them and soften them." In his "improvements" Raynal attempted to inject moral principles.

Raynal's Polly originally came from an English version, which he translated into French. An English publisher, not aware of the original English publications, translated Polly back into English to appear again in an English newspaper. She was to be resurrected again in further French works. Denis Diderot, the famous encyclopedist, a giant intellect of the eighteenth century, who was selected by Catherine the Great of Russia to be her private scholar and librarian, picked up the Polly story and put it in his novel, "Supplement to the Voyage of the Bougainville," published in 1780. Like Raynal, Diderot was a moralist who did not want humor to obstruct the serious message of the story; therefore he deleted the sentence about the statue. In his version of the story it was not one of her judges who married her but her original seducer, who was so remorseful that he married her two days after the trial.[10, 11]

A third French writer, Brissot de Warville, found Polly irresistible and included her in volume eight of his 1772 work on politics and the law. Brissot was a young, idealistic reformer who became involved in the French Revolution and lost his head in 1792 when the revolution took a turn and he was on the wrong side. In his comments on Polly's speech, he expressed his opinion that Polly was no less virtuous than a girl who had maintained her chastity because it was nature's law for women to have children, and marriage was just an arrangement of society which lacked precedence. By having children even though not married, Polly was vindicated in the grand scheme of things, according to Brissot.

Raynal, Diderot, and Brissot would perish in time, but Polly, the immortal, lived on. In 1785 Polly was home again in America, this time appearing in a newspaper in Springfield, Massachusetts, and in 1786 in a magazine in New Haven, Connecticut. Polly's story then appeared in a Philadelphia publication similar to the *Readers' Digest*, called *The American Museum*. This periodical was published by Matthew Carey, a young immigrant who had gotten in trouble with the British in Ireland and set up as a printer and publisher in Philadelphia. Carey added a comment of his own, namely that after Polly had married one of her judges she "supported an irreproachable character" and, as stated in the *Gentleman's Magazine*, had 15 children by her husband. As a footnote, he said that another account gives her name as Sarah Olitor. In 1798, a different Philadelphia magazine reprinted the speech verbatim from the *American Museum* and included the same footnote.[12]

The Intimate Details

All the previous appearances of Polly in newspapers, magazines, and books were only dress rehearsals for her debut on the great world stage. A magazine in Edinburgh, Scotland, in 1794 finally provided intimate details about Polly and her background, which apparently had eluded the earlier accounts. Titled "Interesting Reflections on the Life of Miss Polly Baker," it begins:

> Miss Baker was a beautiful, but unfortunate young woman of Connecticut, in New England; and daughter of a reputable mechanic, soberly and, as it is the custom of that town, religiously brought up; educated according to her rank in life, in reading, writing, and plain work and ... was instructed in the useful and domestic duties of life.
>
> She possessed that female grace and captivating softness of manners "in which the charm of woman principally consists." It was her fate, or rather her misfortune, to form an acquaintance with an agreeable young man, the son of one of the principal magistrates of the town. An intimacy quickly followed.... They experienced the usual difficulties of love, which are always increased by inequality of condition. She discovered too late that her affections were fixed on one whose family would never consent to their union.
>
> She was thrown off her guard by his promising to marry her, and in a fatal, incautious moment, undone. Rejected by her relations, perfidiously forsaken by her betrayer, pregnant, without fame, and without a friend, the pains of childbirth were added to wretchedness and loss of reputation — "and hissing infamy proclaimed the rest!"
>
> Her personal beauty being unimpaired, she attracted the loose desires of neighboring men and shocked the village with numerous instances of rapid progress from virgin innocence to undaunted turpitude. This unhappy woman, so lately the darling of her family, doted on by a lover ... was now an outcast from society. Reduced by necessity "to support herself and a helpless infant by illicit practices, she was forced to tread the odious and disgusting path of filthy infamy."
>
> In consequence of this and other natural children, she several times suffered whipping, fine, and imprisonment. Brought before a court of justice, she surprised her hearers by her address, which was taken down in shorthand by a person on the spot. Her judges were moved by the circumstances of her case and she was discharged without punishment. A handsome collection was directly made for her, and the original seducer married her shortly after.[13]

The author of this biography then added some thoughts of his own. He deplored the vulgar prostitutes in the streets of London, but he had a word of praise for a certain Mr. Beckford, who indulged his amorous nature in which he followed an ethical code of his own. He had an invariable rule "to make an ample provision for his natural children, as well as their mother." Beckford explained his moral principles in his affairs with women:

> In all my warfare with women, I never considered myself justified either to use violent force, intoxicating drugs, or to delude them by promising marriage. If I could work on their vanity, their passions, their hopes, and their fears, it was fair fighting on equal ground; but having recourse to the modes above mentioned, it is like fighting with infected weapons or poisoning the wells and springs, and contrary to the laws of war.

Polly Marches On

Without copyright laws it was a great temptation in those days for publishers to help themselves to good stories from other publications. Thus, as soon as it arrived in America in 1795, Polly's history was appropriated by a New York magazine. It then crossed the ocean again, back to London where it appeared in 1803 in a book titled *Eccentric Biography; or, Memoirs of Remarkable Female Characters, Ancient and Modern.*[14] These characters included actresses, adventurers, fortunetellers, gypsies, dwarfs, swindlers, and others who had distinguished themselves. The women who were honored in this book included Mary Queen of Scots, Madame du Barry, Lady Godiva, Catherine first and second, Joan of Arc, and last but not least, our own Polly Baker. Fifty-six years since she had first become known to the reading public, Polly hit the big time!

The peripatetic Polly then made another transatlantic voyage back to her home country, this time in an American edition of the *Eccentric Biography* issued at Worcester, Massachusetts. It proved to be so popular that the 1804 edition was sold out, and another edition was published in 1805. But this was not the height of her fame. The *American Law Journal*, along with legal documents such as the decisions of the United States Supreme Court, printed her speech as an example of a case from the Connecticut courts.[15] The bound volume appeared in 1813 and had one principal change from the original. Where Polly had said, "Can it be a crime to add to the number of the King's Subjects," the journal changed the words "King's Subjects" to "useful citizens." Thus, Polly had now become a citizen of the free and independent United States of America. Not only that, she was now securely ensconced in the legal literature of the sovereign state of Connecticut. Let the debunkers respond to that.

If one were to write an authentic history of New England one would not want to neglect such an important event as the celebrated "Speech of Miss Polly Baker," and the historian Charles W. Elliot in his 1857 book, *The New England History*, did not fail in that respect.[16] He included not only her speech but also all of the unhappy occurrences in her life, the information for which he credited to the book, *Eccentric Biography*. Impressed with her appearance in the *American Law Journal*, the distinguished biographer John Morley printed Polly's speech in the 1886 and 1905 editions of his book *Diderot and the Encyclopedists*,[17] so now Polly had just vaulted into the twentieth century.

Having gained fame in biography, history, and law, Polly was about to make her mark in a new area, the evolving field of sociology. For more than a generation, Arthur W. Calhoun's respected book, *A Social History of the American Family*, was a standard work used in colleges and the profession of sociology.[18] It was first published in 1917 and again in 1945. Volume 1 of the 1945 edition discusses how domestic troubles were treated by the courts in colonial New England. It states: "Discretion was not always mixed with the sentences. Witness the case of Polly Baker of Connecticut who was seduced and deserted and when her child was born was punished, various times whipped, fined, and imprisoned." Calhoun then quoted from Polly's speech and gave the results of the case.

With such demonstrated evidence of her immortality, more of Polly could be expected in this, the twenty-first, century. But with the recital over the centuries of Polly's tragic drama and ultimate triumph, there are some questions that deserve examination. Was Polly married to one of her judges, or to her first lover who had deserted her? How many children did she have? Was it five or fifteen? Was her story accurate as first reported in the London newspaper? Were the details of her biography as published in the *Edinburgh Magazine* authentic findings or fictitious elaborations? Was it even possible that the whole story and speech of Polly Baker was nothing but a fraud, a fake, a hoax?

The Truth Revealed

In 1818, the fog over the Polly Baker mystery suddenly lifted. In a letter Thomas Jefferson, former president of the United States, recalled an incident he had learned about when he was in Paris serving as ambassador to France.[19] The incident occurred in 1777, during the American Revolution. It took place in Benjamin Franklin's house near Paris. The principals involved were Benjamin Franklin and Silas Deane, who were American representatives to the French government, and the Abbé Raynal, philosopher and author of the best-selling book which included the speech of Polly Baker. Franklin and Deane were in the house talking about the Abbé's book when Raynal himself happened to enter. The following is a record of the conversation as reported by Jefferson:

> Deane, speaking to Raynal, said, "The Doctor and myself, Abbé, were just speaking of the errors of fact into which you have been led in your history." "Oh no, Sir," said the Abbé, "that is impossible. I took the greatest care not to insert a single fact for which I had not the most unquestionable authority." "Why," said Deane, "there is the story of Polly Baker, and the eloquent apology you have put into her mouth, when brought before a court of Massachusetts to suffer punishment under a law, which you cite, for having had a bastard. I know there never was such a law in Massachusetts."
>
> "Be assured," said the Abbé, "you're mistaken and that is a true story. I do not immediately recollect indeed the particular information on which I quote it; but I am certain that I had for it unquestionable authority."
>
> Dr. Franklin, who had for some time been shaking with restrained laughter, now entered the conversation: "I will tell you, Abbé, the origin of the story. When I was a printer and editor of a newspaper, we were sometimes slack of news, and to amuse our customers, I used to fill up our vacant columns with anecdotes, and fables, and fancies all of my own, and this of Polly Baker is a story of my making, on one of those occasions."
>
> The Abbé, without the least embarrassment, exclaimed with a laugh: "Oh, very well, Doctor, I had rather relate your stories than other men's truths." [What a wonderful example of what the French call "savoir faire."]

According to Jefferson, Franklin told him the story when they were both together in Paris in 1784 or 1785. Both John Adams and Voltaire, who were also in Paris during that period, further attested to the story as genuine. But was it created out of whole cloth, or was there a real Polly Baker? Max Hall, a young newspaperman, did extensive research into the story of Polly Baker, which he published in a book, *Benjamin Franklin and Polly Baker*, for which the account in this chapter is indebted. He searched for Polly Baker in the records of all the old courthouses of New England without success. The Puritans had decreed punishment of fines, jail, and whippings for crimes such as profanely swearing, absence from church on Sunday, and fornication, and Hall found many cases where women underwent these punishments. But he found no record of a Polly Baker or a Sarah Olitor.

The Real Polly Baker?

However, one case in particular resembled Polly Baker's. An unmarried woman named Eleanor Kellogg was convicted of having had a bastard child born in 1733 and was condemned by the court at Worcester, Massachusetts, to punishment by a fine or whipping. She paid the fine. In 1737, she was again charged with having a bastard child and had to be punished by severe whipping or a fine. She was charged yet again with having another bastard child in April 1740, and another in November of that year and, in addition, for "willingly, willfully, and unnecessarily absenting herself from public worship," for which she received a whipping, a fine of 20 shillings, and the cost of the prosecution.

Before a court of nine justices in 1745, she was further charged with the crime of fornication. Stating that this was the fifth crime she had committed, the court ordered that she be "severely and publicly whipped at the whipping post on the naked back between the hours of nine and twelve of the clock." The court also ordered that she pay fees and be committed until sentence be performed.

Less than a year and a half later, the speech of Polly Baker appeared in the London newspapers. It is likely that Franklin based his trial of Polly Baker on the case of Eleanor Kellogg, but even if it were not based on Eleanor Kellogg's unhappy story, many other cases provided him similar facts.[20]

Franklin's Other Persona

While neither Franklin nor any other man of that period could be called a women's liberationist, the Polly Baker story demonstrates Franklin's empathy for women regarding the injustices they had to endure during this period. Franklin had good friendships with women of all ages, making many friendships which lasted a lifetime. In his writing, he often adopted the persona of a woman. At 16, he invented Silence Dogood, whom he described as a widow with three young children, and he secretly wrote a series of letters in her name to his brother's newspaper.[21] Silence and Franklin's other female creations were not the retiring homebodies of the times, but, like today's women, were both outgoing and outspoken. For example, Silence defended her sex, insisting that they had no more faults than men, but she admitted that women were guilty of some follies.

She was critical of the women's clothing then in fashion in Boston, describing their hoop petticoats as "monstrous topsy-turvy mortar pieces, like engines of war, neither fit for the church, the hall, or the kitchen." Silence spoke up for women: for their education and for insurance for them in case they became widowed. As Silence, Franklin also showed compassion for spinsters who had to travel through life without a husband and children and to suffer financial hardship without a breadwinner, in addition to derision for being an old maid. For these poor unfortunates he proposed they receive a generous cash allotment on their thirtieth birthday, providing they had not received or refused any offer of marriage.

Franklin's interest in improving the condition of women was based on his underlying desire to improve the world he lived in. This desire prompted his inventions like the lightning rod and the stove, from which he refused to make money, and his desire to improve the lot of poor unfortunates who lacked the opportunity to succeed. Never forgetting his own low beginnings, he felt an affinity for the underdog. Even in his youth he had demonstrated this feeling in writing a piece opposing unearned titles of rank and honor that were common in England. He ridiculed these titles by applying them to biblical personalities like Noah and Abraham, saying, "We never read of Noah Esquire nor the Right Honorable Abraham, Viscount of Mesopotamia, Baron of Carran."[22]

Although himself a slaveholder who sold slaves and advertised runaway slaves in his newspaper when he was young, Franklin grew sensitive to the plight of these people and later worked for their freedom. Although at first he had regarded the Indians as savages and ridiculed their customs, later when he became better acquainted with them he came to respect their ways and insist that they be treated fairly by the white settlers. In 1771, Franklin made a tour of Ireland and Scotland and wrote:

> In those countries a small part of the society are landlords, great noblemen, and gentlemen, extremely opulent, living in the highest affluence and magnificence: the bulk of the people, tenants [are] extremely poor, living in the most sordid wretchedness, in dirty hovels of mud and straw, and clothed only in rags.[23]

It is easy to see why in 1776 Franklin sided with the rebellious American colonists against the British King and the exploiters.

The Hoaxer

Frequently in his writing, Franklin made his point indirectly by the use of a hoax, as he did with Polly. The French novelist Balzac declared, "The hoax is a work of Franklin, who invented the lightning rod, the hoax, and the republic." From 16, when he put on the mask of Silence Dogood, to the age of 84, when he concocted a speech against slavery that he attributed to Sidi Mehemet Ibrahim of Algiers, he assumed many literary disguises.[24] One such hoax was the "Edict by the King of Prussia." This was written during the 1770s, when America was suffering heavy taxation and other offenses by the British, which were intolerable to Americans. Franklin had just written an anonymous, satiric piece for an English newspaper which he titled "Rules by Which a Great Empire May Be Reduced to a Small One," and in which he enunciated the grievances of the Americans.

Now, with several English gentlemen, he was invited to the palatial country home of Lord Le Despenser. At breakfast one morning, one of the gentlemen came storming into the room holding a newspaper. "Here!" says he, "here's news for ye! Here's the King of Prussia claiming a right to this kingdom!" All of the men stared in astonishment. "Damn his impudence!" Declared one of the men. "Outrageous!" Declared another. The newspaper account told of an official document by which King Frederick of Prussia made demands of taxes, customs duties, trade restrictions, and limitations on manufactured goods in Great Britain. These demands were based upon the fact that the island of Britain was settled by Germans and, according to Frederick, strictly still belonged to the mother country. The demands were the same as those the British government had imposed on America, and Franklin had put the shoe on the other foot in his spurious article in the newspaper. Finally, the men caught on to the hoax, and all enjoyed a good laugh with Franklin.[25]

In another of Franklin's hoaxes, he gently chided the English for their ignorance of America. He arranged to have an anonymous letter placed in an English newspaper, which was in reply to an earlier report that the Canadians were making preparations for a cod and whale fishery on Lake Ontario. In his letter, Franklin stated,

> Ignorant people may object that the lakes are fresh water and that cod and whale are saltwater fish. But let them know, Sir, that cod, like other fish when attacked by their enemies, fly into any water where they think they can be the safest; that whales when they have a mind to eat cod, pursue them wherever they fly; and that the great leap of the whale in that chase up Niagara Falls is esteemed by all who have seen it as one of the finest spectacles in nature![26]

Some of Franklin's hoaxes were just for fun and to entertain friends. A close friend in France was a young scholar named Cabanis, who was a very serious fellow. Franklin told Cabanis a bizarre story about a curious bird he had seen in America that had two horned tubercles at the joint of its wings, like the horned screamer and horned lapwing. At the death of this curious bird, the two tubercles became the sprouts of two vegetable stalks, which grew at first by sucking the juice from its cadaver and subsequently attached themselves to the earth to live like plants and trees. Apparently, Franklin forgot to tell Cabanis that this was just a joke because many years later, after Franklin's death, Cabanis wrote that learned naturalists to whom he spoke about this fact "ignore it absolutely." "Therefore," Cabanis gravely commented, "in spite of the great veracity of Franklin, I cite it with a great deal of reserve, and I draw from it no conclusion."[27]

The Hoaxer Hoaxed

Surprisingly, Franklin, the great hoaxer, was himself fooled by a clever hoax. In 1782, while in France, Franklin received a notice from a friend that "a very ingenious gentleman, Mr. Kampl, Counselor to his Imperial Majesty's Finances for the Kingdom of Hungary," was coming to France to show off his mechanical inventions and improvements. Franklin was immediately interested, especially on learning that the gentleman had built a machine that played chess, a game Franklin loved. Kampl was a designer and engineer, and his machine was designed as a life-size figure of a Turk in traditional costume with large turban. The hands moved to indicate the places for the chessmen on the board, and the head also moved to make the Turk appear alive.

Kampl challenged anyone to come and play chess with his machine. The Turk sat on a chair in front of which was a table with the chessboard. The table contained wheels, levers, cylinders, and other moving parts, all publicly displayed before the game. The Turk's clothes were lifted over his head, and the body was seen to be similarly filled with wheels and levers and with a little door by his thigh, which also was opened for public viewing. After each move, wheels could be heard turning, and the Turk turned his head back and forth.[28]

The Turk appeared at a famous chess club in Paris and created a sensation playing the members. It is not known whether Franklin ever played the Turk, but he was greatly impressed, as he indicated in a letter he wrote to Count Mauritius von Brühl, a celebrated chess player in England, in which he said, "M. de Kempl, the ingenious author of the automaton that plays chess, will have the honor of putting this line into the hands of your Excellency; and I beg leave to recommend him to your protection, not merely on account of the wonderful machine, but as a genius capable of being serviceable to mankind by more useful inventions which he has not yet communicated."

Of course, there were many people who suspected that the Turk was a fake, but the spectators were taken in by the complicated machinery they were allowed to observe. The scam was very profitable and continued for many years. It eventually toured in America and was seen by Edgar Allan Poe in Richmond, Virginia. Poe commented it was impossible for the chess player to be a pure machine, performing without any immediate human agency. "The only question is the manner in which human agency is brought to bear." Finally, in 1834, the deception was revealed by a Frenchman who had been in the employ of the exhibitor. Poe was right. The trick of the operation was a skillful, chess-playing midget hidden in a secret compartment of the table.

Franklin was certainly spoofed by this hoax. Being mechanically adept, he was no doubt charmed by the intricate machinery in the Turk. In addition, as a scientist and inventor, he had great faith in the progress of science and invention. Had he lived another 200 years, his faith would have been vindicated, for he could have witnessed the glorious triumph of the IBM super computer, Big Blue, over the world's human chess champion.

$$\left(\,3\,\right)$$

Benjamin Franklin at the Dawn of the Space Age

"We think of nothing here at present but of flying." The famous American who said those words was not Orville Wright, Charles Lindbergh or Amelia Earhart. He was another famous American, Benjamin Franklin; the date was December 6, 1783, and the place was Paris, France.[1] This was the year eyes began looking upward in preparation for the day almost 200 years later when men would set foot on the moon and send out rockets to explore the planets and the vast expanses of space.

The sky-seeking vehicle in those days was the balloon, the first of which was constructed by the brothers Montgolfier and set aloft at Annonay, near Lyons, France, on June 5 of that eventful year, 1783.[2] That balloon was a linen globe 105 feet in circumference inflated with hot air from burning straw. Being lighter than the cold outside air, the hot air allowed the balloon to ascend. The flight lasted only ten minutes, but it signaled the beginning of man's journey into space. Our correspondent in Paris to report firsthand on these ballooning activities was a world-renowned scientist, who himself had looked upward to lure lightning from the skies and tame it. He was 77 years old and had been in Paris since 1776 in his capacity as United States ambassador to France. Franklin eagerly followed every detail of the sensational new experiments and gave accounts of them to fellow scientists abroad. He personally encouraged the participants and used his prestige and influence to aid them.

Figure 3.1 The Montgolfier balloon of 1783. The Montgolfier balloon carried the first two human beings into space on November 21, 1783 — it was the beginning of the "age of space." Benjamin Franklin was present, observing and describing this event. He had met that evening with Montgolfier and one of the two aerostats, as they then referred to the participants in the flight.

The second public demonstration of "flying" occurred on August 27 in Paris under the supervision of Jacques A. C. Charles, a disciple of Franklin, who is known to every freshman chemistry student through Charles' Law, which relates the volume of a gas to its temperature. Franklin so admired Charles' abilities as a scientist that he said, "Nature cannot say no to him." Charles' balloon, dubbed a Charlière, was filled with hydrogen, the lightest of gases, 14 times lighter than air, which had been isolated only 15 years earlier. The ascent, we are informed by correspondent Franklin, was witnessed by no fewer than 50,000 people:

> At 5 o'clock notice was given to the spectators by the firing of two cannon, that the cord was about to be cut and presently the globe was seen to rise.... There was some wind, but not very strong. A little rain had wet it so that it shone, and made an agreeable appearance. It diminished in apparent magnitude as it rose, till it entered the clouds when it seemed to me scarce bigger than an orange.
>
> The multitude separated, all well satisfied and much delighted with the success of the experiment, and amusing one another with discourses on the various uses it may possibly be applied to, among which many were very extravagant.[3]

Franklin described some of these curious ideas on flying:

> Among the pleasantries conversation produces on this subject, some suppose flying to be now invented, and that since men may be supported in the air, nothing is wanted but some light handy instruments to give and direct motion. Some think ... a running footman or a horse slung and suspended under such a globe so as to leave no more of weight pressing the earth with their feet, than perhaps 8 or 10 pounds, might with a fair wind run in a straight line across countries as fast as that wind, and over hedges, ditches, and even waters.[4]

Novel schemes for refrigeration and for money making were also postulated:

> It has been even fancied that in time people will keep such globes anchored in the air, to which by pulleys they may draw up game to be preserved in the cool and water to be frozen when ice is wanted. And that to get money, it will be contrived to give people an extensive view of the country, by running them up on an elbow chair a mile high for a guinea, etc., etc.

Franklin himself was more sober and realistic as to the significance of this new invention. "Possibly it may pave the way to some discoveries," he wrote, "of which at present we have no conception."

The Charlière remained in the air for three-quarters of an hour, then fell into a field 15 miles in the country. The peasants who saw it descend toward them were terrified.[5] At first they thought the moon had broken loose and was coming down to crush the earth. A farmer working in the fields was said to look up and see this terrible apparition rolling toward him. He scurried, pale and breathless, to the house to tell his wife, who ran out and frantically sprinkled the phantom with holy water to make it disappear. Then, according to one account, a small crowd appeared, gained courage from numbers, and for an hour approached by gradual steps, hoping meanwhile the monster would take flight. At length one bolder than the rest took his gun, stalked carefully to within shot, fired, witnessed the monster shrink, gave a shout of triumph, and the crowd rushed in with flails and pitchforks. One tore what he thought to be the skin and caused a poisonous stench; again all retired.

Here is another account reported in a French newspaper:

> Peasants seeing the apparition in the sky, were overwhelmed
> with fear and refused to look behind them. After the balloon
> had alighted, it continued to twist and turn, bouncing and bound-
> ing in all directions.... The peasants ran away with all possible
> speed. But in vain: a sudden gust of wind sent the monster rolling
> in their direction, and it rapidly overtook them.... They gathered
> up some stones and hurled them at the monster in a frenzy of
> fear. The creature, shaking and bounding, dodged the first blows.
> Finally, however, it received a mortal wound, and collapsed with
> a long sigh. The bravest ... approached the dying beast and with
> a trembling hand, plunged his knife into its breast. The knife slid
> in easily, allowing the foul air to escape. Still the globe retained
> enough air to inspire fear. The machine was fastened to the tail
> of a horse and dragged through the mud ... in a very disheveled
> condition.[6]

On September 19, the next balloon carried the first passengers aloft. One was four footed, the other two were two footed: a sheep, a duck, and a rooster. They rose to an altitude of 1,500 feet in an elaborately decorated balloon with rococo ornaments painted all over its surface. It was a command performance at Versailles with King Louis XVI and Queen Marie Antionette among the excited spectators. The flight lasted only 11 minutes but everyone was pleased with the show. The animals returned to the ground safely, except for the rooster, whose right wing was slightly injured. This, however, was attributed to a kick from the sheep, and since it was determined to have occurred after the balloon had landed, the rooster was denied the distinction of being the world's first aerial casualty.[7]

The king had generously offered to provide a criminal who had been condemned to death for the first manned flight, but Rosier, the king's historian, insisted that it was an honor and sought the place instead. Feeling that a historian was expendable Louis XVI finally granted the request. The balloon was a Montgolfière, that is, the hot-air type constructed by the Montgolfiers, employing sheaves of burning straw for heating the air and keeping the balloon inflated. After several trials when the balloon was tethered with an 84-foot rope, Rosier took a companion, the Marquis d'Arlandes, and on November 21 ascended in free flight in a wicker basket, referred to as a car, suspended on the underside of the balloon.

Each balloonist carried a bucket of water in case the fire got out of control. As the aeronauts rose over Paris, Franklin saw them brush against some trees and was worried that they would be thrown out or burned. (No such thing happened, but in a later flight Rosier tested a two-stage Montgolfière-Charlière and went crashing to his death when the hydrogen balloon caught fire and exploded. He was thus the first to fly and the first to die in lighter-than-air craft.) By the use of cords which were still attached, the air pilots righted themselves and soon were sailing over Paris reporting that they had a charming view of the city. By controlling the fire they were able to regulate their ascent, reaching a height of 500 feet and, after receiving the applause of the delighted crowds, they completed their 25-minute tour across the city and came gently to Earth. That evening the Marquis d'Arlandes and Montgolfier visited Franklin to give him a personal account of the voyage, and he signed the official report of their experiment. Franklin mused that, just a few months earlier, the idea of men riding through the air on a bag of smoke, like witches on broomsticks, would have appeared equally impossible and ridiculous.[8]

Not to be outdone, Jacques Charles ten days later had ready a new Charlière, beautiful in its red-and-white varnished silk and a "handsome triumphal car" hanging beneath it. He had designed an exhaust valve, which was placed at the top of the globe and was opened or shut with a rope by the men in the car. So well had Charles designed his balloon that with few modifications this type of gas-filled balloon is used to the present time, although the hot-air balloon is also used today. The actual construction of the balloon was credited to two brothers, Charles and M. N. Robert, and the latter accompanied Charles in the ascent.[9] The construction was financed by popular subscription, and Franklin, always generous toward projects he believed in, dug into his pocket to share in the cost. (There was an intense rivalry between Charles and the Montgolfiers. Franklin, having just concluded the treaty of peace between America and England, tried to make peace between the balloon makers by suggesting a sharing of the credit. He stated that the balloon should be considered a baby, with Montgolfier the father and Charles the wet nurse.)

This was the most heralded balloon flight to date. According to Franklin, the spectators were "infinite," notice of the event having been given for several days in the newspapers so that all Paris was out:

> Never was a philosophical experiment so magnificently attended. Some guns were fired to give notice that the departure of the machine was near. Between one and two o'clock all eyes were gratified with seeing it rise majestically from among the trees and ascend gradually over the buildings, a most beautiful spectacle.[10]

When the balloon was about 200 feet high, the brave adventurers waved a little white pennant to salute the spectators, who returned loud claps of applause. Franklin, seated in his carriage near the statue of Louis XVI, watched the balloon through his pocket telescope till "it appeared no bigger than a walnut." In his old age Franklin suffered from a bladder stone which brought him great pain when he was jarred by the motion of his horse carriage. As he watched the balloon floating in the air he thought how much more comfortable this conveyance would be for him but regretfully predicted it would not be perfected as a means of common transportation in his time.

A London magazine (*The Town and Country Magazine* or *Universal Repository of Knowledge, Instruction, and Entertainment*) took a more optimistic attitude: "We may expect in a short time to see [the balloons] as generally used for traveling as stagecoaches...." Franklin's estimates proved to be more accurate, since another century was to pass before a steerable airship would go aloft and return successfully to the same spot.

After ascending to 2,000 feet, the balloon landed in a small town 27 miles from Paris. Robert left the car but Charles decided to make a second ascent all by himself — the first solo free ascension. That was Charles' account. Another version has it that the airship, relieved of Robert's weight, shot up so rapidly that Charles was unable to exit and was carried upward to 9,000 feet, a record altitude. Charles suddenly found himself alone in an awesome, silent world where no one had ventured before. He had seen two sunsets in one day and had a sensation of exhilaration not unlike that recorded by our modern astronauts in their expeditions into space:

No living being, I reflected, has yet penetrated these solitudes; man's voice has never been heard here, and I struck the air with a few sounds as if to stir that tremendous silence all around me. The calm, the gathering darkness, that immensity in the midst of which I was floating, all this gripped my soul in the deepest way.[11]

We must remember that this reverie was composed after Charles was safely back home. His balloon had ascended into the rarefied atmosphere nearly two miles above the earth; it was December, and he was freezing cold. He observed that the temperature decreased so rapidly that in ten minutes he passed "from the warmth of spring to the cold of winter." Despite his ecstatic rhetoric we must assume that this experience chilled his ardor for adventure since this was his first and last flight in a balloon.

The popular fervor for ballooning following these successful, guided ascents was immediate and tremendous. People were convinced a marvelous new method for traveling had arrived. The following newspaper advertisement gives a suggestion of this attitude: "Wanted immediately — an agreeable companion in an air balloon which is to make the tour of Europe, descend at all the capital cities upon the continent, visiting the nunneries by alighting in their gardens without being compelled to gain regular admittance at their gates, and take up such young ladies as are inclined to go to Heaven before the time allotted them by their father confessors."

In commenting on the flight of Charles and Robert, Franklin noted that they made a trip "through the air to a place farther distant than Dover is from Calais." He was obviously anticipating the time someone would make an international voyage across the English Channel. That feat was actually accomplished one year later (1785) by an American surgeon from Boston, John Jeffries, and a French pioneer in aviation, Jean-Pierre Blanchard.

Jeffries, 41, was a Harvard graduate who had practiced medicine in Boston and done further medical studies in Scotland.[12] He was a key witness for the defense in the Boston massacre trial in 1770 and, as a loyalist, left Boston in 1771. During the Revolution he served as surgeon general in the British military fighting in America. Blanchard, 32, had made three balloon ascents in Paris the year before. In London in 1784 Jeffries paid Blanchard to take him up in his balloon to make scientific measurements of the atmosphere. Their flight from London to Kent lasted over an hour, and Jeffries was smitten. He was eager to accompany Blanchard on the channel crossing but Blanchard wanted to do it by himself and get all the credit. Blanchard finally agreed to the partnership with the understanding that Jeffries would not only pay all the expenses but would also jump out if it became necessary to lighten the load to stay aloft. Unbelievable as it may seem, Jeffries agreed to these conditions.[13]

The Jeffries-Blanchard balloon that crossed the English Channel was a bizarre affair with a built-in, rigid parachute, a rudder and oarlike wings with which the pilots hoped to propel and steer it. There was also a "moulinet," a hand-cranked fan, something like a propeller. Eighty pounds of ballast in bags of ten pounds each were put aboard. In addition, there were two small landing anchors, two cork life jackets, and a number of inflated bladders to keep the car afloat in case the balloon descended into the water. Blanchard wore a heavy cape over his clothes for protection against the cold, but Jeffries decorated himself with a colorful, leopard-skin hat; a coat; a red, green and cream-colored waistcoat; and purple-striped stockings.

Jeffries listed their weight on departure in addition to the ballast as follows: the balloon, 148 pounds; the net over the balloon, 57 pounds; the car and instruments, 72 pounds; Blanchard's books, 34 pounds; Blanchard and his clothes, 146 pounds; Jeffries, 128 pounds; sundries, 29 pounds. The balloon was a Charlière, hydrogen filled, which was to become a problem in their flight. The hydrogen balloon, being much lighter than air, rose rapidly, but as it reached higher altitudes, where the air pressure was less, the hydrogen expanded, and some had to be released through the gas valves to keep the balloon from exploding. The loss of hydrogen thereby reduced the lifting power of the balloon.

On January 7, 1785, the two adventurers were ready to take off from the cliffs of Dover for their trip to France. Each ceremoniously presented the other with his country's flag and then loosened the ropes to let the balloon rise. Finding the weight too great, Jeffries noted in his diary,

> We cast off one sack of ballast; still too heavy and on the very brink of the cliff cast our a second, then a third and fourth, and arose so as to clear the cliff, but being rather inclined to descend, we gradually emptied the fifth sack and then rose majestically.[14]

At 1:15 in the afternoon they left the cliff with thousands of people on the shore and in boats cheering them on. It was a cold, clear day, and they had an enchanting view of the countryside for a hundred miles around; they were able to count 37 English towns and villages. They passed over many sailing vessels, which they saluted, and received shouts and cheers in return. At 1:50, they found themselves descending rapidly and dumped another bag of ballast. Not rising, they emptied half another bag and began to rise again. They were now one-third of the way toward France. Ten minutes later they were once more rapidly descending. They cast out the remaining ballast without effect. They tossed out a parcel of Blanchard's books and felt themselves rising. They were then half way between the English and French coasts. By 2:30 they were dismayed to be descending again. They pitched overboard the rest of the books but without avail. They now had nothing left but the wings and apparatus. By 2:40 they were three-quarters of the way across and had a fine view of Calais and the French coast, but suddenly they began to descend again. They tossed over all the little things they could find —

Figure 3.2 John Jeffries, in his leopard-skin cap and finery, ready for his balloon trip across the English Channel.

apples, biscuits, and then one wing. Still going down, they dropped the other wing. Not rising, they proceeded to cut away the damask curtains around the car, with the gold cord tassels, and then stripped off all the silk lining and the decorative ornaments on the car.

The situation was evidently desperate, for the next item to be tossed out was their bottle of French brandy. Jeffries noted mournfully, "It was the only bottle we had taken with us." In its descent, he observed, "it cast out a stream like smoke, with a rushing noise, and when it struck the water, we heard and felt the shock very perceptibly in our car and balloon." Still descending and now approaching the sea 160 yards below, they began to strip. Blanchard discarded his heavy cape and overcoat. Jeffries said, "After which I cast away my coat." Then Blanchard slipped out of his jacket and long trousers. They were then putting on their cork life jackets to prepare for a splash down into the water. Blanchard may have been thinking of the clause in their contract, but suddenly they began to rise. It was now 2:50, and they were 4 miles from shore. Now rising very rapidly they reached France at exactly 3:00, and Jeffries noted, "Nothing can equal the beautiful appearance of the villages, fields, and roads under us, after having been so long over water." It had actually been less than two hours, but their experience must have made it seem much longer. Though "almost benumbed with cold" they congratulated each other.[15]

At that moment they found themselves hurtling at great speed toward some tall trees. This was a precarious situation since they had previously cast away their landing anchor and ropes in the channel to lighten the load. They would have to land in the forest using the tops of the trees to slow them down. They feared that the car would be forced into the trees so violently that it would be wrecked and they would be injured or killed. Jeffries considered himself a superior person; he was a physician, a surgeon, and an officer in the British army. He had successfully crossed the English Channel; he was not about to give up now. But what could he do? He said, "I felt the necessity of casting away something to alter our course...." But everything had already been cast away. In this moment of crisis, Jeffries' genius did not fail him. He recorded in his diary:

> Happily, from the recollection that we had drank [sic] much at breakfast; and not having had any evacuation; and from the severe cold, little or no perspiration had taken place, that probably an extra quantity had been secreted by the kidneys, which we might now avail ourselves of by discharging, I instantly proposed my idea to M. Blanchard, and the event fully justified my expectation; and taking down from the circle over our car two of the bladders for reservoirs, we were enabled to obtain, I verily believe, between five and six pounds of urine; which circumstance, however trivial or ludicrous it may seem, I have reason to believe, was of real utility to us.[16]

When the bladders were ditched their descent was slowed, so they were able to grab the branches of a tree and open the gas valves in order to sink slowly into the trees. Some farmers came along with ladders and rescued them from the trees, taking the voyagers to Calais for a heroes' welcome.

Going on to Paris, on January 14, Jeffries completed an important mission. He delivered a letter which he had carried with him from England — *the world's first airmail letter*. Its recipient was none other than the U.S. ambassador to France, the first American postmaster general, Benjamin Franklin. The letter was from Franklin's son in London to Franklin's grandson, who was with Franklin in Paris.[17] Although Jeffries was a Tory and had served with King George's forces against the American Revolution, all was forgiven in the name of science and adventure, and Jeffries reported how warmly he was received and treated by Franklin. Franklin used his personal influence with the Duke of Dorset, the English representative at the French court at Versailles, to obtain a pension for Jeffries from the English government in reward for his brave achievement. Dorset entertained Franklin and Jeffries and requested that William Pitt, the British prime minister, grant the pension.

Further evidence of Franklin's graciousness is found in Jeffries' diary:

> Evening, at nine, Mr. Franklin called on me, and carried me and introduced me to Madame Morrell, where I was most kindly received indeed, and met there the charming Mad. de Villars, friend to Mad. B., both of them being from Lyons.[18]

As a proven master in the art of disrobing, Jeffries' observations on the subject must be regarded with great interest:

> I cannot describe the lovely ease and elegance, yet delicate decency, with which Mad. Morrell and Mad. de Villars undressed themselves in my presence, and dressed again in lovely dishabille, previous to our going to the masqued ball at the opera, where I had the honor to attend them, and found them there as elsewhere most lovely and engaging.... I wish my charming countrywomen would catch and initiate their elegant ease of carriage and manners.[19]

Jeffries' visit in Paris lasted from January 7 to February 27, when he arrived back at Dover and the cliffs where he and Blanchard had taken off on their triumphal flight. Each day and night in Paris Jeffries wrote of being entertained and ceremoniously celebrated by the nobility and their ladies at their estates, at balls, at plays, and at the opera. Excerpts from Jeffries' diary entry of January 16 describe the heroes' reception by the king and queen at the royal palace in Versailles.[20]

> Went with Mr. Blanchard to Versailles at Court; presented to the Queen; heard the Duke de Polignac repeatedly speaking to the Queen of me, and as often caught her lovely eyes on me, and the King's while at dinner.... Evening, returned to the drawing room; saw two ladies presented; one the Princess Lamballe, most lovely, and the most brilliant and rich dress I have ever seen.... Evening at the grand ball, where I was received by universal and continuous

shouts and claps of applause, embraced and complimented by hundreds of the first ladies and gents in Paris. Presented with a garland crown by the prettiest mademoiselle of Paris, placed on my temples by a lovely fair one, Madam Baunoir.... The most particular favors and marks of attention through the whole evening from the lovely little vivacious Madame de Jalairac, who with lovely freedom and simplicity of heart told me she was eighteen, had married at fifteen, had an infant, etc., etc.; took affectionate leave of me and engaged me to come and see her.

Jeffries was in Franklin's company for six days of his Paris visit, at the Comédie Française on January 17, where he saw *Figaro* (written by Franklin's friend Beaumarchais and later to be turned into operas, the *Marriage of Figaro* by Mozart and the *Barber of Seville* by Rossini) on February 3 at a masked ball, and on January 22 and 31 and February 11 and 14 at the American ambassador's residence in Passy. There he said he had the pleasure of dining with Franklin and his guests: Lafayette and his wife, John and Abigail Adams with their daughter, and Commander John Paul Jones, among other notables. Jeffries was flattered by the compliments he received from Commander Jones, a hero in his own right, and gallantly returned them saying, "he deserved them much more than me."[21]

One visit was not in keeping with the rounds of entertainment and social frivolity that marked Jeffries' stay in prerevolution France. In company with a French physician he visited the Hotel de Dieu, a large hospital on both sides of the Seine river, connected by a bridge. According to Jeffries, it housed between five and six thousand patients with four rows of beds in many of the wards. "Patients of all descriptions, ages, sexes, and nations are admitted ... the female wards, some very low and dark, three, four, and five sick adults in the same bed, lying heads and points." Wards for all sick children, from two and three months to two and three years, struck him as novel. He commented favorably that warm and cold baths were frequent and conveniently placed. Jeffries also records visiting the gardens and arsenal of the royal prison of the Bastille, which he described as "a dreadful place."[22] This was just four years before the storming of the Bastille by the Paris mob made history by ushering in the French Revolution.

Blanchard was handsomely rewarded by the king, who also erected a monument at the site of the balloon landing in France. After his great adventure Jeffries retired from ballooning and returned to Boston in 1790, where he resumed his practice of medicine and died in 1819. Blanchard, on the other hand, continued on as an aeronaut. In 1785 he made news by dropping out of a balloon a dog fitted with an invention that he termed a parachute. On January 9, 1793, Blanchard made the first aerial ascent in America, in Philadelphia, with President George Washington in attendance. Blanchard died in 1809 after falling out of a balloon without his parachute. However, his wife carried on in his place, performing a balloon flight in celebration of the marriage of Napoleon and Marie-Louise of Austria. She was very popular, throwing lighted fireworks from the balloon, but unfortunately she too had an accident and was killed.[23]

There had been a report in the *Journal de Paris* of an earlier balloon ascension in America just 38 days following Rosier's historic venture, but this proved to be just a hoax. It had stated that David Rittenhouse and Francis Hopkinson, two of Franklin's Philadelphia friends, had engineered a flight by a carpenter in a contraption lifted by 47 small hydrogen balloons. The carpenter reportedly rose to a height of 97 feet, then, gripped with fear as he approached the Schuylkill River, punctured too many of the balloons, plummeted to Earth and sprained his wrist. This hoax has been attributed to a Colonel Thomas Forrest of Philadelphia, but another Philadelphian, Benjamin Franklin, was himself a master hoaxer. Claude-Anne Lopez, in her delightful book *Mon Cher Papa*, reveals a humorous hoax about balloons in his handwriting. Franklin wrote an anonymous letter to a Paris newspaper pretending to be a lady subscriber with a practical suggestion:

> Our chemists, it is said, are sparing no effort to discover a kind of air both lighter and less expensive than inflammable air, in order to fill our aerostatic machines (the name given to balloons by our learned Academy). But it is really singular that men as enlightened as those of our century should be forever searching in art for what nature offers everywhere and to everybody, and that an ignorant woman such as me should be the first to think of the solution. Therefore, I am not going to keep my invention a secret, nor shall I solicit any recompense from the government, or exclusive privilege.
>
> If you want to fill your balloons with an element ten times lighter than inflammable air, you can find a great quantity of it, and ready made, in the promises of lovers and of courtiers and in the sighs of our widowers; in the good resolutions taken during a storm at sea, or on land during an illness; and especially in the praise to be found in letters of recommendation.[24]

In a more serious vein Franklin wrote to the scientist Ingenhousz of a new, inexpensive source of inflammable air (hydrogen). A French chemist, M. de Morveau, Franklin reported, had made inflammable air from coal at only ⅟₂₅ of the cost from iron filings and sulfuric acid. Franklin's enthusiasm was justified, but it was 40 years until coal gas (containing 50 percent hydrogen and having 70 percent of the lifting power of hydrogen) became commercially available and was used to fill balloons.

Not all balloonists were treated so affectionately as Jeffries and Blanchard, particularly the unsuccessful ones. We are told by our on-the-spot reporter, Ben Franklin, about a resident of Bordeaux who had induced a number of people to invest in his balloon, but when he was unable to make it rise "the populace was so exasperated that they pulled down his house and had like to have killed him."[25] In London a Frenchman, de Moret, had planned an ascent from a Chelsea garden, but when he failed, the angered mob tore his fire balloon to bits. Shortly thereafter an Italian balloonist, Vincent Lunardi, was scheduled to ascend from the same place, but owing to the prior incident permission was prudently withdrawn. A month later he was allowed to take off from a different site. An Englishman named Biggin was to be his companion, but when the crowd of 20,000 appeared to become irritated waiting for the balloon to be inflated, Lunardi got panicky and hopped in when it was only half full; since it could then support only one man, Lunardi made the flight alone, to the surprise and pleasure of the crowd, which included British notables such as Edmund Burke, William Pitt, Charles Fox, Lord North and the Prince of Wales.[26]

Women were quick to try ballooning; the first was a Madame Thible, who went up in June of 1784 with a male aeronaut in the presence of the king of Sweden and his court. During the next year a good friend of Franklin, Madame Le Roy, wife of Franklin's scientific companion Jean Baptiste Le Roy, made a balloon flight accompanied by other ladies. Franklin, who had recently returned from France to America, was thrilled to receive the news and wrote to her:

> How courageous of you to go up so high in the air! And how kind
> of you, once you were so close to Heaven, not to want to leave us
> all and stay with the Angels! I kiss you tenderly.[27]

Franklin hoped that these new airships might convince sovereigns of the folly of wars since they would make it impracticable for them to guard their dominions. As he saw it, 5,000 balloons capable of taking two men each could not cost more than five ships of the line:

> And where is the prince who can so cover his country with troops
> for its defense, as that 10,000 men descending from the clouds
> might not in many places do an infinite amount of mischief, before
> a force could be brought together to repel them?[28]

In fact, it wasn't too many years later that balloons were first tested in warfare. In the French revolutionary wars a corps of French balloonists lifted a siege by Dutch and Austrian forces in Belgium. Hydrogen balloons with a crew of two men each rose to a height of 1,800 feet. The amazed Austrians, thinking that their movements were utterly exposed, became demoralized and promptly quit the scene. In a following battle near Liege the enemy immediately surrendered upon sight of the balloons.[29] Napoleon was so enthusiastic about balloons that he ordered another corps of *aerostiers* ready for his campaign in Egypt, but the balloon materials were destroyed in the naval battle of Aboukir Bay, and the corps was disbanded.[30]

Despite their early triumphs, balloons were of only limited use in warfare due to their vulnerability and lack of maneuverability. Nevertheless, balloons were used for observing the enemy in the U.S. Civil War, the Spanish American War, and every European war up to the First World War.[31] Barrage balloons were used in warfare in the First and Second World Wars. These were balloons that were anchored to the ground and connected to each other with steel cables to inhibit enemy aircraft from invading the airspace. They did yeoman service in the Allied invasion of Normandy in World War II when 120 barrage balloons protected critical landing beaches and supply bases. The balloons were hidden in the clouds above the site, and German airplanes were torn apart by the invisible steel cables when the planes ran into them while attempting to drop their bombs over the target.[32]

For sport, modern balloonists have far outdone Jeffries and Blanchard, with Bertrand Piccard of Switzerland and Brian Jones of England circling the Earth in their balloon in 20 days in March 1999. But balloons' greatest utility has been in science, where they made it possible to study the lower and upper atmospheres. For the gas-filled balloon, hydrogen has been replaced by the nonflammable helium, but the hot-air balloon is still widely used in popular recreational ballooning.

In a more general sense, however, the balloon's greatest accomplishment is that it made us look upward in anticipation of new inventions and daring new exploits—as Franklin said, "of which at present we have no conception." There were always cynics ready to deprecate such exploits and demand immediate practical applications. One such fellow was standing beside Franklin as the latter watched with awe and delight as the first balloon sailed over the Parisian rooftops. What good could a balloon be? the skeptic inquired. Franklin responded impatiently with his classic retort, "What good is a newborn baby?"

4

That Famous Kite

A cannonball and a bag of feathers, an apple, and a kite: What do they have in common? They are all objects of popular scientific folklore. The cannonball and feathers were supposedly dropped by Galileo from the Leaning Tower of Pisa to show that, regardless of their weight, they will drop to the ground at the same time. The apple, as every schoolchild has heard, dropped on Isaac Newton's head and awakened him to the realization that the force that made the apple fall also keeps the planets in their orbit. The kite was used by Benjamin Franklin to defy the force of gravity that made the cannonball, feathers, and apple fall. He used it to reach into the heavens in order to probe the sky where the bolts of lightning originated. Was the story of the kite just a folktale like Galileo's experiment and Newton's apple? We have only Franklin's word for its occurrence. No one, except his son, was there to see him do it, and his son never told us about it.

It was not until three months after this supposed occurrence that Franklin reported his adventure in a letter he wrote in October 1752 to Peter Collinson, his correspondent in England, and he also published it in his newspaper, *The Pennsylvania Gazette.* Later he related it to Joseph Priestley (the discoverer of oxygen), who included it in his book, *History and Present State of Electricity.*[1] In his report Franklin told how he made the kite and how someone might perform the experiment: using silk cloth instead of paper, to withstand the rain and wind; with a very sharp, pointed wire rising a foot or more from the top of the kite; and with a long tail, and a length of twine as in ordinary kites. At the bottom of the twine, near one's hand, a silk ribbon is attached, and where the twine and silk ribbon join, a key is fastened. After the kite is raised, and when a thunder gust appears, the person holding the string must be standing under a shelter so as not to get wet. Then:

> as soon as thunder clouds come over the kite, the pointed wire will draw the electric fire [electricity] from them, and the kite, with all the twine, will be electrified and the loose filaments will stand out every way, and will be attracted by an approaching finger. When the rain has wet the kite and twine, so that it can conduct electric fire freely, you will find it [sparks] stream out plentifully from the key on the approach of your knuckle. At this key the vial [capacitor] may be charged, and from electric fire thus obtained, spirits may be kindled and all other experiments be performed which are usually done by the help of a glass globe or tube, and thereby the sameness of the electric matter with that of lightning completely demonstrated.[2]

Franklin could certainly have performed this experiment; he was competent with kites. He told an acquaintance that as a boy he used a kite while swimming, to pull him across a lake. But why the secrecy? Because of this secrecy, people now might question whether he had actually done the experiment. In fact, a modern writer in a learned journal questions whether the story of the electrical kite was fabricated out of whole cloth. Another question: He had told Priestley that the kite experiment was performed in June; why then did he wait until October to report it? From his previous experiments with electricity he felt confident of his theory that storm clouds contained electricity, and he concluded that this experiment would work. It was a very dangerous experiment, as we today fully realize. Could he have taken the safe alternative of writing it up without actually doing it?

The reason for the secrecy, according to Priestley, was his great fear of ridicule and derision for so unusual and apparently silly an action if the experiment didn't work. Priestley reported that Franklin, "dreading the ridicule which too commonly attends unsuccessful experiments in science[,] communicated his intended experiment to nobody but his son, who assisted him in raising his kite." [3] Franklin performed the experiment in fields outside Philadelphia so he would not be seen doing it. He was a respected leader in his city and was very sensitive about his reputation; he did not want to become a laughingstock for what might have been considered a ridiculous performance if it were unsuccessful. "Imagine trying to pull lightning out of the sky and using a child's kite to do it," his fellow citizens could have howled at his expense.

But, if it was successful, why did he delay from June, when the experiment was done, to October to report it? Several possible reasons suggest themselves. First, he may have wanted to repeat the experiment before publicizing it. After all, it was an incredible experiment with amazing results, which would have been hard for people to believe. Second, he was an amateur in his scientific work; his experiments were just a diversion from his regular activities, and in August he wrote that affairs were pressing and "business sometimes obliges one to postpone philosophical amusements," which he called his scientific experiments. Finally, what was the hurry?

The best test of the authenticity of Franklin's kite experiment would be whether others could repeat it. Such an astounding experiment was sure to be attempted, and indeed it was. At least five others followed Franklin's lead, and all of them were successful in confirming Franklin's results. They included Jacques de Romas, a Frenchman who conducted his experiment in May 1753; John Lining, an American, who wrote about his work in January 1754; an Italian, A. W. Giovanni Beccaria, who in 1756 obtained electricity with his kite even in clear weather; Franklin's colleague Ebenezer Kinnersley in 1761; and the Dutch physicist Peter Van Musschenbroek, who had invented the vial (Leyden jar, condenser or capacitor) that Franklin and the others used to collect the electricity.[4]

Was Franklin First?

Americans pride themselves that Franklin, with his kite, was the first to demonstrate that lightning was electricity. Disappointing as it may be, he wasn't. A Frenchman named D'Alibard performed the experiment in May, 1752, one month preceding Franklin's feat. D'Alibard didn't use a kite but a long iron rod. Carl Van Doren, in his prize-winning biography of Franklin, records that event:

> In a garden in Marly, six leagues from Paris, he set up an iron rod, an inch through and forty feet long, pointed with brass. Having no cake of resin with which to insulate it from the ground, he used a stool which was merely a squared plank with three wine bottles for legs. At twenty minutes past two on the afternoon of 10 May 1752, there was a single clap of thunder followed by hail. D'Alibard was just then absent. A former dragoon named Coiffier, left to watch the experiment, heard the thunder and hurried to the rod with an

electric vial. Sparks came from the iron with a crackling sound. Coiffier sent a child for the prior of Marly, who had heard the thunder and was already on his way. Meeting the child in the road, he began to run. The villagers, believing that Coiffier had been killed, ran after the prior through the beating hail. Terrified, they stood back ten or a dozen paces from the rod, but in broad daylight they could see the sparks and hear the crackling while Raulet, the prior, drew off all the electric fire. He sat down and wrote a letter which Coiffier took to D'Alibard, who three days later made his report to the Acadamie Royale des Sciences.[5]

Thus the credit belongs to France, not to America? Yes and no. D'Alibard deserves the credit for being the first to satisfactorily complete the experiment, but it was actually Franklin's experiment, which he had detailed in a paper he had written three years earlier, titled "Opinions and Conjectures Concerning the Properties and Effects of the Electrical Matter, Arising from Experiments and Observations Made at Philadelphia, 1749" that publicized the experiment. The paper reads as follows:

> To determine the question, whether the clouds that contain lightning are electrified or not, I would propose an experiment to be tried where it may be done conveniently. On the top of some high tower or steeple, place a kind of sentry-box big enough to contain a man and an electrical stand. From the middle of the stand let an iron rod rise and pass bending out of the door, and then upright 20 or 30 feet, pointed very sharp at the end. If the electrical stand be kept clean and dry, a man standing on it when such clouds are passing low, might be electrified and afford sparks, the rod drawing fire to him from a cloud. If any danger to the man should be apprehended (though I think there would be none) let him stand on the floor of his box, and now and then bring near to the rod the loop of wire that has one end fastened to the leads, he holding it by a wax handle; so the sparks, if the rod is electrified, will strike from the rod to the wire, and not affect him.[6]

Franklin sent this paper to Collinson in England, who had it published in 1751, along with Franklin's other electrical experiments in a book, *Experiments and Observations on Electricity*.[7] D'Alibard translated the book into French and published it in 1752, creating a sensation in France. Some of the experiments in Franklin's book were performed in France for the king, Louis XV, which led D'Alibard to try performing Franklin's lightning experiment:

> The Philadelphian experiments ... having been universally admired
> in France, the King desired to see them performed.... His Majesty
> saw them with great satisfaction, and greatly applauded Messieurs
> Franklin and Collinson. These applauses of his Majesty have
> excited in Messieurs de Buffon, D'Alibard and de Lor, a desire of
> verifying the conjectures of Mr. Franklin, upon the analogy of
> thunder and electricity, they prepared themselves for making the
> experiment.[8]

As already noted, D'Alibard performed the experiment at Marly, and one week later de Lor, the king's naturalist, repeated the experiment at Paris. D'Alibard, in his report of the experiment to the French Academy, graciously gave credit to Franklin, saying, "In following the path that M. Franklin traces for us, I have obtained complete satisfaction." Franklin credited D'Alibard, saying that he "was the first of mankind to have the courage to attempt drawing lightning from the clouds" (a perfect example of that mutual cordiality the French call savoir faire).[9] The king was so pleased that he praised everyone concerned and requested that his compliments be conveyed to Franklin. For a king to take notice of a commoner, a tradesman, in a foreign country, let alone send him his praise, was, to say the least, most unusual. When this news reached Franklin through Collinson, he wrote to a friend:

> The Tatler [a magazine] tells us of a girl, who was observed to
> grow suddenly proud, and no one could guess the reason, till
> it came to be known that she had got on a new pair of garters.
> Lest you should be puzzled to guess the cause, when you observe
> anything of the kind in me, I think I will not hide my new garters
> under my petticoats, but take the freedom to show them to you, in
> a paragraph of our friend Collinson's letter, viz.—but I ought to
> mortify and not indulge this vanity; I will not transcribe the para-
> graph—yet I cannot forbear.[10]

The Franklin experiment, which was first performed at Marly, was soon repeated and verified in France, England, Germany, Italy, Holland, and Sweden. It was also run a year later in Russia, but with fatal consequences. The experimenter in St. Petersburg, George Wilhelm Richman, was not standing on the insulated stool when he received a direct strike by a bolt of lightning and was instantly killed. The experiment was actually much more dangerous than Franklin and the others had realized.[11]

Another question arises. If D'Alembert ran Franklin's experiment in May and proved that lightning was electricity, why did Franklin bother to perform his kite version at a later date? We must realize that the news had to travel from France, first to Collinson in England, and then by sailing ship across the ocean to Philadelphia, which could take as much as three months. And since his experiment had been run in Europe before Franklin got the news late in August or September, he was actually famous throughout Europe before he heard about it in America. Franklin had been intending to do the experiment himself months earlier, as he had written it up, using a high tower or church steeple to obtain sufficient height. He had planned to use the steeple of Christ Church, the highest point in Philadelphia, but the steeple had been taken down for repairs. After waiting months for it to be returned, he finally gave up and decided on the alternative of a kite.[12]

Experiments with Electricity

The idea of the famous experiment did not come to Franklin like a bolt out of the blue. It resulted from his years of experimental work in electricity. When Franklin started his experiments, electricity was just a novelty, a curiosity; it had no practical uses. The king of France had amused himself by having 200 monks hold hands as he delivered a heavy electric shock to see them all jump up together.[13] It was Franklin's work that started electricity on its way to becoming the necessity that it is for us today. Franklin first became acquainted with electricity when he saw a show of electrical oddities performed by a visitor from Scotland. He was so fascinated that he bought all of the visitor's equipment and spent the whole winter working with it. He was now retired from business and had the time to pursue what he called his philosophical amusements. He put on shows for the townspeople, using the electrical apparatus to make ladies' hair stand up on end, to make an artificial spider run up the wall, and to give a young couple a shock when their lips touched in kissing. He fitted out an unemployed minister, Ebenezer Kinnersley, with equipment to put on lecture demonstrations, with which he would tour the country and make a living.

Franklin was also doing serious experimenting, too. Many of the electrical terms we use today originated from Franklin's experiments, such as the "positive" and "negative" poles of a battery. The terms *battery, conductor, an-nature, charge, discharge, plus* and *minus*, when used in electricity, as well as the word *electrician* were coined by Franklin. In his work he gave us the single-fluid theory of electricity, which we now describe as a flow of electrons. He analyzed how the capacitor, Musschenbroek's

Leyden jar, works. Electronic equipment like radio, TVs, and computers contain many capacitors. He invented the first electric motor and powered it with a series of capacitors wired together, which he called a battery. He used the motor to turn a rotisserie, with which he roasted a turkey.[14] We owe our understanding of the conservation of charge and induced charge to his work. And the greatest invention of all, that which made him world famous, was the lightning rod.

The Lightning Rod

Before Franklin's invention, lightning was a mysterious, mystical, supernatural phenomenon. According to ancient Greeks, the Titan Prometheus drew fire (lightning) from heaven. To the ancient Romans lightning was Jove's thunderbolts, javelin-like weapons the god of the sky threw at his enemies. Many people in Franklin's time looked at the damage lightning and thunder as God's punishment for the sins they had committed. People often hid under their beds in fear and trepidation or, as our second president, John Adams, described it, "that panic terror and superstitious horror which was almost universal in violent storms of thunder and lightning." When a house was set on fire by lightning, firemen applied water to the neighboring houses but not to the one on fire, not daring to interfere with God's judgment.

The invention of the lightning rod came about as a result of Franklin's electrical experiments, namely his discovery of the "power of points." Franklin charged a cannon ball with electricity and found that a pointed iron rod six to eight inches away would draw off the charge as a spark, but a blunt rod would have to be much closer to produce the same effect. This experiment is similar to what occurs when we walk across a rug and reach for the doorknob; we get a shock as the electricity in the form of a spark leaves our finger and jumps to the metal knob. In his experiments Franklin produced sparks and noted their similarity to lightning. Others, like Isaac Newton, had also noted that similarity, but Franklin thought that if lightning really was electricity, his "power of points" might be useful in disarming it and preventing its damage. His thinking was as follows: Storm clouds are charged with electricity, and when they come close enough to a church steeple, a house, a tree, or other body attached to the ground they discharge their electricity in the form of lightning to that body and thereby to the earth. If he could put his pointed iron rod high on top of the house and connect it with wire to the ground, it would attract the lightning and carry it to the ground, where it would be discharged without doing any harm. It was with the same "power of points" that he would demonstrate that lightning was electricity. In 1749, three years before his kite experiment, he wrote to Collinson:

> The doctrine of points is very curious, and the effects of them truly wonderful; and from what I have observed in my experiments ... may not the knowledge of this power of points be of use to mankind, in preserving houses, churches, ships, etc. from the stroke of lightning, by directing us to fix on the highest parts of those edifices, upright rods of iron made sharp as a needle, and gilt to prevent rusting, and from the foot of those rods a wire down the outside of the building into the ground, or down round one of the shrouds of a ship, and down her side till it reaches the water? Would not these pointed rods probably draw the electrical fire silently out of a cloud before it came nigh enough to strike, and thereby secure us from that most sudden and terrible mischief.[15]

Franklin was so certain that his pointed rods would work that in 1751 he included in Kinnersley's lecture a demonstration to show that lightning is electrical and that houses could be protected with lightning rods. Franklin had faith that forces in nature must follow the same laws as his electrified bodies in the laboratory; therefore, he said, it appears that a pointed, grounded conductor "is a preservative against thunder [lightning]." But first it must be demonstrated that the clouds contained electricity. He listed ways that the sparks he generated in the laboratory were similar to lightning.[12] They were similar:

> 1. In giving light. 2. Color of the light. 3. Crooked direction. 4. Swift motion. 5. Being conducted by metals. 6. Crack or noise in exploding. 7. Subsisting in water or ice. 8. Rending bodies it passes through. 9. Melting metals. 10. Firing inflammable substances. 11. Sulphureus smell.... The electrical fluid is attracted by points. We don't know whether this property is in lightning. Let the experiment be made.[16]

The experiment was made. Franklin did it with his kite. Then he knew lightning was electricity, and the electricity came from the clouds. He went ahead and put up the first lightning rods in June or July of 1752 in Philadelphia. One was installed on the Pennsylvania State House, and the other was on the Academy, a school Franklin had started, which later became the University of Pennsylvania. In September he put a rod on his own house. Then he published in his famous *Poor Richard's Almanac* an article, "How to Secure Houses, etc. from Lightning," giving full directions on how to make and erect a lightning rod and attach it to the ground.[17] The *Almanac* was popular in all the American colonies, and soon lightning rods were appearing on houses and buildings all over the country.

In those days, buildings were more vulnerable to lightning damage than they are today because they didn't have the metal girders, wiring, and plumbing of modern houses, which can direct the lightning strike to the ground. Instead, the strike penetrated the building's wood and plaster, poor conductors, rupturing the building or setting it on fire. The wood, plaster, and brick are slightly conductive due to the moisture in them, but not conductive enough to easily transport the electricity to the ground. This moisture, however, is rapidly evaporated by the tremendous heat of the lightning, causing an explosion or fire. Franklin reported seeing lightning strike a tree, that then exploded, leaving it finely splintered like a broom. In August of 1752, he inspected two houses that had just been hit by lightning and noted that where there was metal in the houses, such as hinges, sash weights, iron rods, and so on nothing was damaged, but where the lightning "passed through plastering or wood work it rent and split them considerably." Kinnersley, in 1761 in Philadelphia, wrote to Franklin, who was then in London, that dwelling houses struck by lightning are seldom set on fire, but barns or storehouses containing large quantities of hay or hemp seldom, if ever, escape a conflagration, owing to their being more combustible than the wood of the houses.[18]

Franklin had the immense satisfaction in hearing Kinnersley's proof that his system for lightning protection really was working:

> We had four houses in this city, and a vessel at one of the wharfs, struck and damaged by lightning last summer. One of the houses was struck twice in the same storm. But I have the pleasure to inform you, that your method of preventing such terrible disasters, has ... given a very convincing proof of its great utility, and is now in higher repute with us than ever.[19]

Kinnersley also told of visiting William West, a merchant, whose family and neighbors at home had been stunned by a terrible explosion with a flash and crack at the same instant. Nobody was hurt and no damage was done. On inspecting their lightning rod on the roof, they observed that the tip of the rod and the thicker wire had been melted, and the thinner wire was "consumed in smoke," providing proof that lightning had struck the house, but the only damage was to the lightning rod. If this weren't reward enough, Franklin's own house was struck in 1787, when he was 81 years old, and his lightning conductor led Jove's thunderbolt safely to earth. He wrote:

> My own house was attacked by lightning, which occasioned the neighbors to run in to give assistance in case of its being on fire. But no damage was done, and my family was only found to be a good deal frightened with the violence of the explosion.... I found, upon examination, that the pointed termination of copper, which was originally nine inches long, and about one-third of an inch in diameter in its thickest part had been almost entirely melted; and that its connection with the rod of iron below was very slight.[20]

He then observed that this invention, in addition to the pleasure he had received from its having been useful to others, had proved to be of use as well to its himself. Franklin was wrong in his assumption that his rod would drain all the electricity out of a thundercloud and thus prevent a lightning strike. Actually the rod just captures a small part of the charge that is in the cloud and guides that to the ground. He became aware that his theory of depleting the cloud might not be correct, but he emphasized that he always allowed the alternative, that even if the strike were not prevented, it would be conducted harmlessly to the moist earth. If the theory was not correct, the practice could not be criticized. Franklin was used to his experiments disproving his most cherished theories and wrote to Collinson: "In going on with these experiments, how many pretty systems do we build, which we soon find ourselves obliged to destroy. If there is no other use discovered of electricity ... it may help to make a vain man humble."[21]

Points, Counterpoints

A curious controversy was generated on this matter of pointed rods. Benjamin Wilson, an English experimenter and Fellow of the Royal Society of London, believed that pointed conductors would unnecessarily attract lightning and promote "the very mischief we mean to prevent." Metal knobs on the rod would not attract the lightning, he insisted. He advocated blunt rods or rods ending in knobs, and he was so suspicious of the attractive power of the rod that in 1764 he advised that the rod should not extend above the building but should end below the roof. Others proposed that the attractive power of the rod could be reversed and the lightning stroke repelled by fitting the tip of the conductor with insulating glass balls. Such a contraption was installed on the steeple of Christ Church in Doncaster, England, but apparently was ineffective, for the steeple was struck by a lightning flash soon afterward and was demolished.[22] Another experimenter in France, the Abbé Nollet, objected to the use of lightning rods, saying, "I believe that they are more suitable to attract the fire of thunder to us than to preserve us from it." He used the death of Richmann in Russia as evidence for his position. However, Richmann had been killed using an ungrounded rod, not a grounded one, which Franklin had proposed for buildings.

The Abbé Nollet was a rival electrical experimenter of Franklin and had a great reputation in France. When Franklin's book on electricity was published, Nollet couldn't believe that anyone in primitive America could have done such work. He accused his enemies in Paris of having fabricated it to diminish his work. But even after D'Alibard's confirmation of Franklin's prediction in his book, Nollet bitterly attacked Franklin in his lectures and writings. In hearing of these attacks, Franklin wrote to his fellow American experimenter, Cadwallader Colden: "I see it is not without reluctance that the Europeans will allow that they can possibly receive any instruction from us Americans." Franklin always claimed to hate disputes and stated, "I concluded to let my papers shift for themselves, believing it was better to spend what time I could spare from public business in making experiments than in disputing about those already made." He counseled his friend Jan Ingenhousz, who was involved in a scientific dispute, to forget it and "Go on with your excellent experiments, produce facts, improve science, and do good to mankind. Reputation will follow.... You can always employ your time better than in polemics." Franklin was right: Ingenhousz is credited with being the first to explain photosynthesis. In Franklin's case, other scientists defended him, his fame soared and Nollet was discredited.[23]

In England, Wilson fervently promoted his advocacy of knobs rather than points, writing a pamphlet on the subject. Franklin was urged by friends to respond to it, but once again he demurred, saying, "I have an extreme aversion to altercation on philosophical points. I have never entered into any controversy in defense of my philosophical opinions; I leave them to take their chance in the world. If they are right truth and experience will support them; if wrong, they ought to be refuted and rejected. Disputes are apt to sour one's temper, and disturb one's quiet. I have no private interest in the reception of my inventions by the world, having never made, nor proposed to make, the least profit by any of them." True, he did not patent the lightning rod or any of his other inventions and made no attempt to profit from them. It was a matter of principle with him that as he had benefited from past inventions and discoveries, so the present and future generations should be able to benefit from his. There was a committee of the Royal Society to decide the matter of knobs versus points, and all members except Wilson favored Franklin's "points" as did the society as a whole. As a result, pointed rods were put on the British military gunpowder magazine at Purfleet. In 1772, it was hit by lightning and slightly damaged, dislodging just a few bricks.[24]

With the American Declaration of Independence in 1776, and Franklin on the side of the insurgents, King George III attempted to get the Royal Society to change its decision and to favor the knobs. The president of the society, Sir John Pringle, a friend of Franklin, refused, explaining that as much as he desired to execute the king's wishes, he could not reverse the laws and operations of nature. Pringle was promptly fired, and the rods on the Purfleet powder magazine were replaced with knobs. Franklin, then in America, responded, "The King's changing pointed conductors for blunt ones is, therefore, a matter of small importance to me. If I had a wish about it, it would be that he had rejected them altogether as ineffectual. For it is only since he thought himself and his family safe from the thunder of heaven, that he dared to use his own thunder in destroying his innocent subjects."

A friend of Franklin put the controversy in verse:

> While you, Great George, for knowledge hunt,
> And sharp conductors change for blunt,
> The nation's out of joint.
> Franklin a wiser course pursues
> And all your thunder useless views
> By keeping to the point.[25]

Erroneous Ideas

We now know that Franklin was wrong in requiring a pointed rod. His assumption that the laboratory results with sparks could be transferred to actual results with lightning was in error. Lightning bolts are so powerful that they do not require any advantage the points give but seek any direct pathway to the ground. Thus, a blunt rod does just as well as a pointed one, although rods are still being made with points.[26, 27]

For large buildings, Franklin said that two or more rods in different places might be necessary. Large buildings at Harvard University, with a number of lightning rods each, have been protected for over 100 years.

Franklin also prescribed for the rod to be connected to the ground with wire "no bigger than a goose quill," and that it be connected to the moist earth by an iron stake. If the earth were not moist it would be necessary to pound the stake deep into the ground, where the earth was moist, so there would be good electrical conduction. This advice was vociferously opposed by Reimarus of Hamburg, Germany, a contemporary of Franklin. He argued that since lightning striking a tree causes steam to be suddenly produced, and the resulting explosion split the trunk, a similar explosion could be produced if the iron stake was placed into wet soil. He therefore recommended that the stake be fixed in drier topsoil. This advice was widely followed in Germany, which led to thousands of faulty and dangerous installations lasting for over a century.[28]

There were many erroneous ideas prevalent in Franklin's century. One was that lightning striking the ground produces earthquakes. Franklin didn't subscribe to this notion. He believed that the lightning discharge was just the passage of electrical "fluid" from one cloud to another, from a cloud to the earth, or from the earth to a cloud. Thunder was an acoustic phenomenon, explained by the disturbance of the air by the lightning. Many people felt that delving in God's heaven and removing His lightning bolts was a presumption that would not go unpunished, as John Adams observed: "I have heard some persons of the highest rank among us say that they really thought the erection of iron points was an impious attempt to rob the Almighty of his thunder, to wrest the bolt of vengeance out of his hand." When an earthquake rocked Boston in 1755, the Reverend Thomas Prince, alarmed that the Almighty had showed his displeasure of the many lightning rods that had been erected in that city, delivered a sermon, stating:

> The more points of iron are erected around the earth, to draw the electrical substance out of the air; the more the earth must needs be charged with it. And therefore it seems worthy of consideration, whether any part of the earth being fuller of this terrible substance, may not be more exposed to more shocking earthquakes. In Boston are more erected than anywhere else in New England; and Boston seems to be more dreadfully shaken. 0! there is no getting out of the mighty Hand of God! If we think to avoid it in the air, we cannot in the earth: Yea, it may grow more fatal.[29]

Franklin, with his ever-optimistic disposition, took a more sanguine attitude toward God's intentions. He began his announcement of the lightning rod in his *Almanac*: "It has pleased God in his goodness to mankind, at length to discover to them the means of securing their habitations and other buildings from mischief by thunder and lightning." Differing from the then popular belief that lightning was a supernatural phenomenon, Franklin said, "Surely the thunder of heaven is no more supernatural than the rain, hail, or sunshine of heaven." If you erect a roof on your house to avoid rain, why not do the same kind of thing to avoid lightning?[30]

It so happens that churches were the buildings most vulnerable to lightning strikes. This was not because of any theological reason but because their steeples were the tallest structures in the area. A study in Munich in 1784 records that lightning had struck 386 church towers in a period of 33 years. The 340-foot-high bell tower of St. Mark cathedral in Venice was hit many times over the years. Severely damaged in a lightning strike in 1388, it was hit again, set on fire and destroyed in 1417, rebuilt and reduced to ashes by a hit in 1489, damaged again by hits in 1548, 1565, 1658, and destroyed again in 1745. It was rebuilt once more but hit again in 1761 and 1762. In 1766 a Franklin rod was installed, and there has been no lightning trouble since.

The same Munich study reported that in the 33-year period, 103 bell ringers in church bell towers had been killed. The church bells were rung when thunderstorms were imminent for either of two reasons—one superstitious, the other an attempt to be scientific: to drive away the evil spirits that brought the lightning, or, as Sir Francis Bacon had postulated, to disturb the air so as to interfere with the path of the lightning. The ritual for consecrating bells declared: "Whensoever this bell shall sound, it shall drive away the malign influences of the assailing spirits, the horror of their apparitions, the rush of whirlwinds, the stroke of lightning, the harm of thunder, the disasters of storms, and all the spirits of the tempest." Medieval church bells were cast with the inscription on them, "Fulgura Frango," meaning "I break up the lightning flashes." The bell ringers on tall, unprotected towers, pulling wet cords attached to metal bells were in absolutely the worst place to be in a lightning storm. Yet, such was their faith that no matter how many perished, there were plenty of others willing to take their place. It is reported that bell ringing in unprotected towers continued in some churches in Europe until early in the twentieth century and that many cases of churches without lightning protection in England and on the continent sustained damage as well. Such a case was the beautiful spire of Sir Christopher Wren's masterpiece, St. Martin-in-the-Fields in London, which was struck and damaged in 1842 and had to be rebuilt.[31]

But, by far, the most catastrophic effect of lightning on unprotected churches resulted from the superstitious faith that the safest place to store gunpowder was in the vaults of a church. Artillery, developed in the eighteenth century, required a vast quantity of gunpowder, and the church vaults seemed to be the ideal place to store it. Unfortunately, no one considered what might happen in case of a lightning strike, which as we have seen, was quite possible. In 1769, the church of St. Nazaire in Brescia, Italy, had 100 tons of gunpowder stored in its vaults, and when struck by lightning, the explosion blew away one-sixth of the city, killing 3,000 people. As late as 1856, the church of St. Jean on the island of Rhodes had its steeple struck by lightning. The explosion of the large store of gunpowder in its vaults resulted in the deaths of 4,000 people. Unprotected powder magazines in Tangiers in 1785, in Venice in 1808, in Luxembourg in 1815, and Navarino in 1829 were blown up by lightning strikes. In a fort in Sumatra 400 barrels of powder were blown up in 1782. They had been protected by lightning conductors, but these were removed by order of the Council of the East India Company because they had been advised that the rods attracted lightning and were a danger rather than a protection.

An unusual case of a building which remained free of lightning damage for 400 years without lightning rods occurred in the Middle East. The building was the famous, biblical Temple of Solomon. Accounts of the building describe it as having been covered inside and out with burnished plates of metal. The gilded dome was similarly covered and bristled with long, pointed spikes of iron to keep away thieves and birds. Iron cisterns below received rain from the roof through iron pipes. As a result, this structure was perfectly lightning proofed. Solomon had proved to be wiser than even he realized.[32]

Shocking Results

Franklin confessed that he had become obsessed with his experiments, his philosophical amusements, which he pursued despite what seemed to be a total lack of practical applications. He was a practical man and had faith that scientific discoveries would eventually have practical value. He conjectured, "The beneficial uses of this electrical fluid ... we are not yet well acquainted with, although such there are, and those very considerable." At another time, he said, "What signifies philosophy that does not apply to some use?" One of his avenues of investigation was the possible application of electric shock therapy for paralytic patients. People from different parts of Pennsylvania came to him hoping that the new medium of electricity might provide a cure for their ills. He gave them heavy shocks through the affected limbs, repeating the stroke three times a day. The patients at first reported warmth in the treated limbs and that night a prickling sensation in the flesh of the paralytic limbs. The limbs were also more capable of voluntary motion and seemed to receive strength. For instance, a man who could not lift his afflicted limb off his knee was able after one day to raise it four or five inches, the next day higher, and on the fifth day he was able, with a feeble, languid motion, to take off his hat.

These appearances put the patients in great spirits and gave them hope for a complete cure. But Franklin remarked, "I do not remember I ever saw any amendment after the fifth day; which the patients perceiving and finding the shocks pretty severe, they became discouraged, went home, and in a short time relapsed."[33] He allowed that the apparent beneficial results of the first few days might have arisen from the exercise of the journey and daily visits or from their raised spirits in the hope of success. Today, heavy shock treatment is sometimes given to mental patients in deep depression or with certain neurological disorders in an attempt to disrupt and reorder the nervous system. But generally, shock treatment has come into disrepute and is seldom used.

In another, hoped-for practical application, Franklin tried to kill a turkey with electricity. He thought that the jolt might rend the muscle fibers just as lightning did wood fibers, thereby making the meat tender. By mistake, he touched the wire himself and was knocked unconscious for several minutes. He wrote to a friend, "I meant to kill a turkey, but nearly killed a goose." He reported that he had not felt the shock but was sore from the effect. He did an experiment where he knocked down six men, all touching each other, with a single shock. When they got up they declared that they had not felt the stroke and wondered how they had come to fall. When he was treating a young woman for some problem of her feet, she bent down in placing her feet and unexpectedly contacted the electric generator. Said Franklin, "She dropped, but instantly got up again, complaining of nothing." He concluded, "Too great a charge might, indeed, kill a man, but I have not yet seen any hurt done by it. It would certainly ... be the easiest of all deaths."[34] Franklin didn't foresee it, but he had given rise to an American practice known as the "electric chair." This method of execution has recently come into disrepute as cruel and unusual punishment, but by Franklin's findings, it is no more so than other forms of capital punishment currently employed. The offense of electrocution is apparently greater to the observers rather than to the subject of the procedure.

The Lightning Detector

Nowadays we have radar, radio static detection, and orbiting weather observatories for detecting lightning, but Franklin made the first lightning detector. When Franklin put a lightning rod on his house, he was not satisfied with just affording protection for his home; he wanted to use the lightning as a source of electricity for his experiments. He put the rod on top of the chimney and connected it with a heavy wire to an iron pump in the ground. Then, where the wire passed a room, he cut it and connected each end to a little bell. The bells were about six inches apart in the room, and between the bells he suspended a little brass ball by a silk thread "to play between and strike the bells when clouds passed with electricity in them." He obtained sparks from the upper wire, which was connected to the rod, and used the electricity to charge his Leyden jars for experiments. One night, he was awakened by loud cracks in the staircase, and starting up and opening the door, he said, "I perceived that the brass ball, instead of vibrating as usual between the bells, was repelled and kept at a distance from both; while the fire passed, sometimes in very large quick cracks, from bell to bell, and sometimes in a continued, dense, white stream, seemingly as large as my finger, whereby the whole staircase was enlightened as with sunshine, so that one might see to pick up a pin."[35] The first electric light! But not a very dependable one.

When the rod obtained a charge from a passing cloud, the bell attached to the rod became charged negatively and attracted the brass ball. On touching the bell, the ball became charged negatively and, since like charges repel, was repelled, causing it to strike the other bell. It was attracted to the other bell, which had a positive charge since charges with unlike signs attract. Having touched the other bell, the ball accumulated its charge and was repelled, striking the first bell, and so on, back and forth. The first electric bell! Thus, when the bells rang, Franklin knew that lightning-bearing clouds were in the vicinity. In the case he described, the stroke was a very strong one, and the sparks from the lightning jumped the gap between the bells, producing the bright light and the loud, cracking sound. Years later, when Franklin was in England on a extended diplomatic mission, his wife wrote him that, in his absence, the ringing of the bells greatly worried and upset her. He replied, "If the ringing of the bells frightens you, tie a piece of wire from one bell to the other, and that will conduct the lightning without ringing or snapping, but silently."[36]

With this lightning detector, Franklin observed that the bells would sometimes ring when there was no lightning or thunder but only a dark cloud overhead. He used this apparatus to measure the polarity of the clouds, determining them to generally have a negative charge, but they were sometimes, though rarely, in a positive state, when he compared the charge on his detector with the known polarity of his friction generator. In 1950, B. F. J. Schonland, a pioneer in modern lightning research, com-

Figure 4.1 Portrait of Franklin showing the lightning detector attached to the rod he erected on his house in September 1752. This portrait, reproduced from an engraving, was painted by Mason Chamberlin in 1762. (The Burndy Library, Dibner Institute for the History of Science and Technology, Cambridge, Massachusetts.)

mented that it was a beautifully planned experiment, and Franklin "gave a definite answer to the question as to the sign of the charge on the base of a thunder cloud.... [It] remained the only direct and reliable information on this question for 170 years. Even today," Schonland said, "we would only substitute 'clouds' for 'bases of clouds.'"[37]

Whither the Lightning Stroke

Having observed induced charges in his experiments with the Leyden jar — that is, the effect a charged body has on another body separated by an insulating material such as air — Franklin concluded that the negative electricity in a storm cloud induces a positive charge on the earth, trees, or buildings directly beneath the cloud. When the cloud is low enough (Franklin called this the "striking distance"), the attraction of the unlike charges causes the electricity to overcome the insulating property of the air and be released in the form of lightning in order to establish an electrical equilibrium. Although we now know that electric current, a flow of negatively charged electrons, flows to the positively charged body, Franklin thought that the electricity flowed from the positively charged body, that is, the one with an excess of electrical "fluid," to the negative one; thus he stated "that for the most part in thunder strokes, 'tis the earth that strikes into the clouds, and not the clouds that strike into the earth."[38] However, he indicated that the effect of the strike would be nearly the same regardless of the direction of the strike.

Franklin's theory of the mechanism and direction of the lightning discharge remained unchallenged until the 1930s, when a camera invented by Sir Charles Boys, which could take one million pictures a second, allowed researchers to dissect the path of the lightning flash as it travels across the sky. Was Franklin right about the direction of the stroke? Those who answered "yes" were correct and those who answered "no" were also correct. What the Boys camera revealed was that the lightning strike is much more complex than what is seen by the eye alone. According to Martin Uman at the University of Florida, a leading investigator in lightning research, "The usual lightning flash between cloud and ground begins with a visually undetected downward-moving traveling spark, called the 'stepped leader.' Since the lightning flash begins with a downward-moving discharge, lightning moves from the cloud to the ground. The stepped leader descends in a zigzag direction from the cloud in consecutive steps of about 50 yards, each occurring in less than a millionth of a second." On the other hand, Uman notes, when the stepped leader gets near the ground, it is met by an upward-moving discharge from the ground. "The bright, visible channel, or so-called 'return stroke,' is formed from the ground up, and as one could say, therefore, the visible lightning moves from the ground to the cloud."[39]

Electricity in Clouds

As noted before, Franklin was correct in his determination that the thundercloud has a negative charge. But that subject, like the matter of the direction of the strike, is more complicated. We now know that thunderclouds have both negative and positive charges. It is suggested the charges are generated by the frictional effect of wind in the cloud on the drops of rain or particles of snow or hail. The heavier particles settle to the bottom of the cloud and have a negative charge, while the lighter particles accumulate higher up in the cloud and have a positive charge. These different charges result in lightning discharges inside the cloud which, in the United States, are five times as frequent as the cloud-to-ground discharges. There is also cloud-to-cloud lightning, but it is rare compared to the in-cloud occurrence.

How the clouds became electrified is a subject that Franklin pondered. He wrote to fellow American James Bowdoin about his hypothesis, which has some of the characteristics of modern thinking on the subject: "The friction of the particles of air ... in violent winds, among trees, and against the surface of the earth, might not, as so many glass globes [his electrical generator], pump up quantities of the electrical fluid, which the rising vapors might receive from the air, and retain in the clouds they form." But he was never satisfied with this explanation. He said, "I am still at a loss about the manner in which they [clouds] become charged with electricity; no hypothesis I have yet formed satisfying me." E. P. Krider of the University of Arizona, an authority in this field, comments, "Today, after almost 250 years of research, this fascinating question remains unanswered.[40]

Thunder and More

The cause of thunder was a mystery until Franklin's time. The ancients thought it resulted from clouds banging against each other. In discussing his electrical experiments, Franklin speculated that if two gun barrels that are electrified "will strike at two inches distance, and make a loud snap;

to what great a distance may 10,000 acres of electrified cloud strike and give its fire, and how loud must be that crack!" Franklin was again on target: Thunder was just the sound produced by lightning; without lightning there would be no thunder. We may not see the lightning flash, but if we hear thunder, it has to be preceded by lightning. It is caused by the explosive expansion of air resulting from the tremendous heat of the lightning's return strike. The temperature can be as high as 50,000°F in a narrow channel one-half to two inches wide.[41] Since the duration of the strike is only about twenty millionths of a second, the air surrounding the channel is heated so rapidly that it expands with explosive force, producing the sound of thunder. When the strike is close, we hear it as a crack or clap, and when it is far off we hear it as a rumble, caused by the rapidly expanding air compressing the surrounding air and so on, producing shock waves in all directions. Because light travels at 186,000 miles per second and sound travels only about one-fifth of a mile per second, we see lightning well before we hear the sound, depending on how far away the strike occurs. When the strike is very close, the sight and sound are almost simultaneous. There may be echoes as the sound waves bounce off objects, causing further rumblings.

Franklin's fertile imagination leaped from his small-scale laboratory observations to speculation about meteorological and electrical processes on a global scale, just as it had leaped from the snap of the laboratory spark to the tremendous crash of the lightning. Now, he was curious about the spectacular meteorological display called the aurora borealis. He associated it with an electrical phenomenon like lightning. He questioned whether there might be a "region of [electrical] fire" at high altitudes that is prevented by the atmosphere from joining the Earth. He supposed that electricity was most abundant where the air density is low and that some of it would attach to high clouds. Once electrified, the high clouds might, by attraction to the Earth, discharge that "ethereal fire." He wondered whether "the aurora borealis is currents of this fluid in its own region above our atmosphere, becoming, from their motion, visible."

As we learn more about these esoteric geophysical phenomena, we find them to be more complex. Franklin's guess that there is a "region of [electrical] fire" at high altitudes has been confirmed by the discovery of the ionosphere and magnetosphere and that the auroral lights are indeed electrical, produced by energetic electrons colliding with the upper atmosphere. These electrons are accelerated and focused by complex interactions between the solar wind, its magnetic field, and the Earth's atmosphere. But we have much more to learn, as Krider tells us, about what electric currents flow in these regions, the global electric circuit, and the auroral phenomena.[42]

With an explanation for lightning and for thunder, it would be expected that Franklin would not be without an explanation for the resultant rain that comes with the storm. He supposed that a discharge of cloud electricity increased the coalescence of the drops in the cloud and that "the concussion, or jerk, given to the air, contributes also to shake down the water ... hence, the sudden fall of rain immediately after flashes of lightning." Today we know, says Krider, that electrical fields do increase the probability of coalescence during drop collisions. Yet, there is still the question of whether rain is caused by lightning or vice versa.

An explanation for the "power of points," which Franklin had discovered in the laboratory, gave him a lot of trouble. He wrote:

> These explanations of the power and operation of points, when they first occurred to me, and while first floated in my mind, appeared perfectly satisfactory: but now I have wrote them, and considered them more closely in black and white, I must own, I have some doubts about them. Yet as I have at present nothing better to offer in their stead, I do not cross them out: for even a bad solution read, and its faults discovered, has often given rise to a good one in the mind of an ingenious reader.
>
> Nor is it of much importance to us to know the manner in which nature executes her laws; 'tis enough, if we know the laws themselves. 'Tis of real use to know, that china left in the air unsupported, will fall and break; but how it comes to fall, and why it breaks, are matters of speculation. 'Tis a pleasure indeed to know them, but we can preserve our china without it. Thus in the present case, to know this power of points may possibly be of some use to mankind, tho' we should never be able to explain it.[43]

The "power of points" has been amply demonstrated and confirmed, and we now have an explanation for it. We now explain, according to D. R. Herschbach of Harvard, that pointed conductors are very effective at drawing off the electrical charge because the "electrical field" is higher at a pointed conductor than at a rounded one, so some of the air is ionized and conducts better.[44] Krider reports that pointed rods are still being used today, insulated from the ground, or in series with sensitive current meters, by research investigators to detect electrified clouds and lightning.

The value of 24,000 times for the expansion of liquid water to the vapor state that Franklin used is too high. At room temperature, the vapor is only about 1,300 times the volume of the liquid. But, where it is considered that the temperature of the lightning can be as high as 50,000°F, four times hotter than the surface of the sun, the vapor at that temperature is about 100,000 times the volume of the liquid. Thus, Franklin's explanation of the explosive force of lightning in disrupting moisture-containing substances is even more reasonable.

Lightning and Its Effects

We still adhere to Franklin's warning about not standing under a tree during a lightning storm, but seek an open field or shelter in a building. We now advise, as Franklin would agree, that a person in an open field should crouch as close to the ground as possible so as not to be a human lightning rod. A person in a boat or swimming during a thunderstorm should get to land and shelter as soon as possible. If a person is near a tree or other object struck by lightning, the person's body may act like a lightning rod and receive an induced charge causing the lightning to hop onto the person in its path to the ground. A car is considered a safe refuge because of its metal shell, whereas a bicycle is not safe. In the home during a thunderstorm, Franklin advised persons to avoid sitting near the chimney or any metal object. Today, we advise avoiding baths, touching plumbing, or electrical apparatus like heaters, toasters, and telephones. In houses without lightning protection, Franklin suggested that persons apprehensive of danger might sit in a chair with their feet up on another chair. "It is still safer," he said, "to bring two or three mattresses or beds into the middle of the room, and folding them up double, place the chair upon them." For the safest refuge in any room, he recommended a hammock suspended by silk cords, equally distant from walls and ceilings. A question Franklin didn't have to answer is are we safe in an airplane flying through a thunderstorm? Airplanes flying through the clouds are hit by lightning, but it usually follows the plane's metal skin back into the air, doing little or no damage.[45]

Lightning is most common during thunderstorms, but it can accompany snowstorms, sandstorms, tornadoes, erupting volcanoes, even nuclear explosions—whenever there is an electrical disturbance of the atmosphere. Roughly 2,000 thunderstorms are in progress in the world at any one time, with about 30 to 100 flashes to the ground every second, 40 million a year in the United States. They are most numerous in Uganda and Java and, in the United States, in central Florida. A 50-mile-wide band across Florida from Tampa on the Gulf of Mexico to Daytona Beach on the Atlantic Ocean is known at "Lightning Alley." Northeastern United States is also susceptible to severe strikes. Uganda has a reported 242 days a year when thunder is heard, Java 223, Florida 90. The least amount of thunder and lightning in the United States occurs in Alaska and Hawaii and on the coasts of northern California, Oregon, and Washington. Above the Arctic Circle and at the poles there is little or no lightning. About two-thirds of the forest fires, ten thousand a year in the United States, are started by lightning.[46, 47, 48, 49]

There are 100–400 people killed by lightning in the United States each year, twice as many as by tornadoes, and five times as many as by hurricane, and many more are injured. About 70 percent of all lightning injuries occur in the afternoon. A direct lightning strike is lethal, but most people who are hit recover because they are not struck directly but receive the electrical shock from being close to a strike. The electricity in their bodies may paralyze the muscles so that they cannot move or speak. It may stop their heart and their breathing so that they appear dead. They are frequently revived if quickly given cardiopulmonary resuscitation.

Figure 4.2 The portable lightning rod of Barbeu-Dubourg, engraving from *Les Merveilles de la Science*. A novel application of Franklin's invention by one of his contemporaries. Not recommended.

Fred H. Heath of Gainesville, Florida, was paralyzed but conscious after he was hit and reported hearing observers calling him dead. He recovered on his own, only to be stricken again several years later with no great injury, and lived to a ripe old age.[50]

Contrary to the popular saying, lightning does strike twice or more often in the same place. The Guinness world record for the person hit most often is Roy C. Sullivan, a park ranger in Shenandoah National Park, Virginia, who stopped seven lightning bolts in his career and lived to tell about it. The Empire State Building, for many years the tallest structure in New York City, was struck as many as 48 times in one year and, during one thunderstorm, eight times in 24 minutes.[51, 52, 53]

The overall damage caused by lightning is great. The National Lightning Safety Institute estimates that the damage caused by lightning exceeds two billion dollars a year in the United States. It states that this figure is low because it does not include losses due to personal injury, business interruption, and essential services, which may far exceed the direct losses due to building and contents. Nor does it include the losses in buildings and timber in forest fires caused by lightning.[54] A study by the Lightning Protection Institute states that over 30 percent of church fires, more than 18 percent of lumberyard fires, and significant losses to 18,000 houses and 12,000 other buildings in the United States annually can be attributed to lightning strikes.[55, 56] The Industrial Risk Insurers, who insure only major industries, report that lightning ranks among their five topmost damage claims worldwide, with fire being the greatest, and that the average damage per claim from 1993 to 1997 due only to lightning was $44,000, whereas when lightning also caused fire damage it was $195,000.[57] Yet lightning strikes are infrequent, as Franklin clearly pointed out. In a letter to Kinnersley, Franklin, writing from London, notes that the feeling of security in having a lightning rod may even exceed the actual protection afforded:

> It is true the mischiefs done by lightning are not so frequent here as with us, and those who calculate chances may perhaps find that not one death (or the destruction of one house) in a hundred thousand happens from that cause, and that therefore it is scarce worthwhile to be at any expense to guard against it. But in all countries there are particular situations of buildings more exposed than others to such accidents, and there are minds so strongly impressed with the apprehension of them, as to be very unhappy every time a little thunder is within their hearing; it may therefore be well to render this little piece of new knowledge as general and as well understood as possible, since to make us safe is not all its advantage, it is some to make us easy. And as the stroke it secures us from might have chanced perhaps but once in our lives, while it may relieve us a hundred times from those painful apprehensions, the latter may possibly on the whole contribute more to the happiness of mankind than the former.[58]

Since houses are seldom hit by lightning and are usually covered by insurance, few homes nowadays are equipped with Franklin's invention. Uman recommends that all houses be fitted with lightning rods. He has them on his own house, his barn, and his two prized oak trees. Lightning protection, however, finds it greatest utilization in industry. Storage tanks that contain petroleum and other flammable liquids are especially vulnerable, having been set on fire by lightning, causing loss of lives and millions of barrels of oil. They are currently protected by rods or a system of wires suspended by tall, grounded metal towers surrounding the tanks. Telephone lines and high-voltage power lines also employ a similar system because lightning can cause power surges that will burn out equipment connected to these lines.[59] Computers and other expensive electronic devices are very sensitive and must be protected by shielding, surge arrestors, and proper grounding since they can be destroyed by even a minor strike.

Fame

Franklin's book on electricity and his lightning investigations brought him great fame. Collinson wrote to him in September 1752, that "All Europe is in agitation on verifying [your] electrical experiments on points—all commend the thought of the inventor." The Royal Society of London awarded him the Copley Gold Medal, their highest award, never before given to a nonresident of the British Isles. They followed by electing him to membership in their distinguished organization. Harvard awarded him the honorary Master of Arts degree, their first, which was followed in kind by Yale and William and Mary. In Italy his fame was broadcast by the Abbé Giovanni Beccaria, a distinguished professor of physics and an electrical experimenter. The German philosopher Emmanuel Kant called him "the Modern Prometheus." There were translations of Franklin's electrical book into French, German, and Italian, as well as the ten English editions. Honors continued, including a doctoral degree from St. Andrews University in Scotland and one from Oxford University in England. He served on many of the important committees of the Royal Society during his stay in England and was elected to many of the other leading scientific, medical, and academic societies in England and France. In France during the American Revolution, where his fame was the greatest, an epigram was created for Franklin: "He snatched the lightning from the sky and the scepter from tyrants." The French also gave America a warship that they named in Franklin's honor, *Le Bonhomme Richard*, for his *Poor Richard's Almanac*.

Commenting on Franklin's invention of the lightning rod, Joseph Priestley called it "the greatest, perhaps, that has been made in the whole compass of philosophy since the time of Sir Isaac Newton." Two centuries later, Schonland said, "Franklin's invention, in the greatness of its

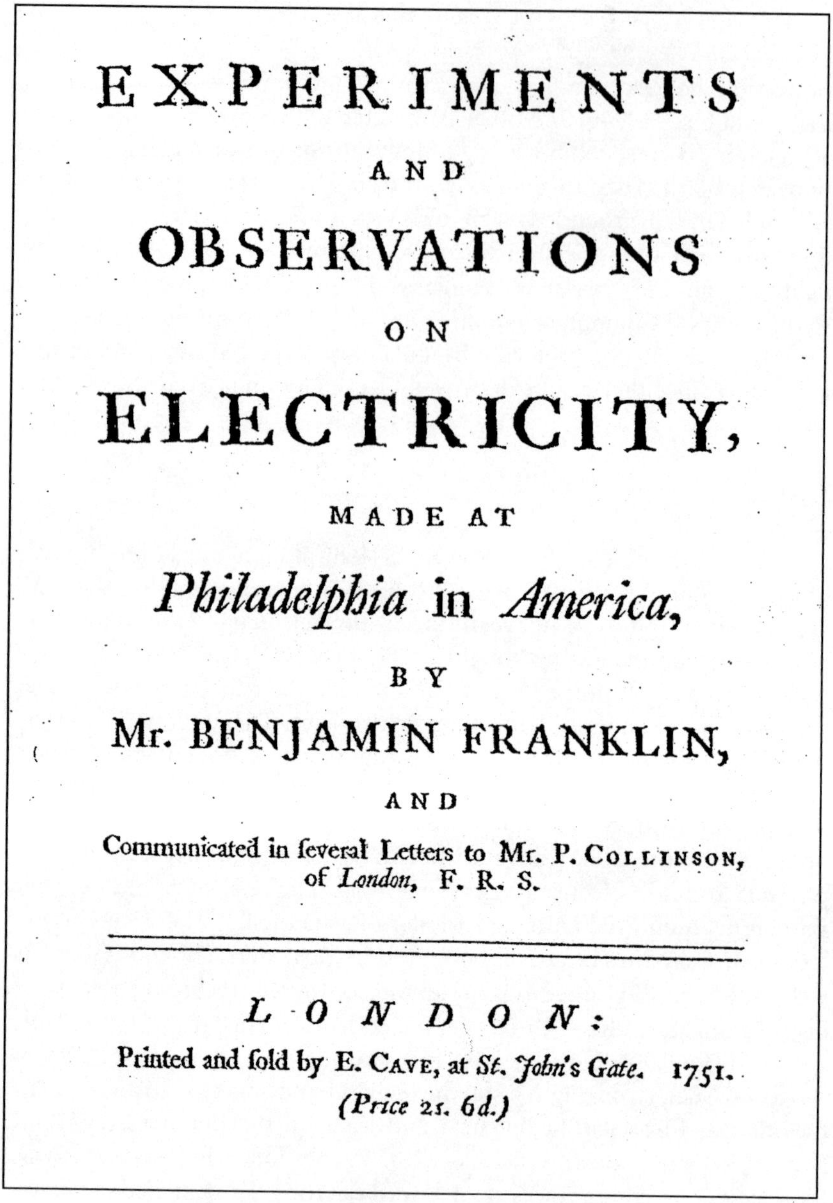

EXPERIMENTS

AND

OBSERVATIONS

ON

ELECTRICITY,

MADE AT

Philadelphia in *America,*

BY

Mr. BENJAMIN FRANKLIN,

AND

Communicated in feveral Letters to Mr. P. COLLINSON,
of *London,* F. R. S.

L O N D O N :

Printed and fold by E. CAVE, at *St. John's Gate.* 1751.
(Price 2s. 6d.)

Figure 4.3 Franklin's book on electricity.

conception and the considerable economic value of its application, was rightly considered outstanding. He had snatched the scepter not merely from George III but from Jove himself." It is remarkable, when we consider important inventions—the automobile, moving pictures, radio, computers— and how much they have changed with improvement over the years, that even today most lightning protection codes recommend Franklin rods for protecting structures, and their specifications and installation are almost the same as in his original instructions. But all the work that led up to that invention was what we call basic research, namely, an exploration of scientific principles, not directed toward any practical application. Our experience over the years has shown that basic research leads eventually to practical rewards, as in Franklin's case. Sir Francis Bacon in the early seventeenth century predicted that basic research would pay off, and Franklin's invention was the first example of that principle.

In the area of basic research, Franklin may not have had all the answers, but he asked the right questions. For Franklin's initial work, Krider says, "the broad field known as atmospheric electricity views Franklin as its founding father." Now, the difference is that instead of kites, the present investigators employ rockets and gas-filled balloons to catch the lightning.

We must credit Franklin's work for stimulating others to explore this very exciting field of electricity. Luigi Galvani, in 1791, pioneered the field of electrophysiology when he used a system like Franklin's lightning rod on his roof to see electricity make frogs' legs twitch. Galvani's physicist nephew, writing about the progress in electricity at that time, listed major contributors and then added, "and of him, who is worth them all, Franklin."[60] Allesandro Volta, who visited with Franklin in Paris, followed up on Galvani's experiments and produced the first electrochemical battery. In more modern times, Nobel-prize-winning physicists like J. J. Thomson, who discovered the electron, and R. A. Millikan, who measured its charge, indicated their great admiration of Franklin.

Significance

Franklin's fame helped produce great effects outside of science, too. When the newly declared republic of the United States needed help from foreign countries in its fight for freedom, it called on the only American known and respected abroad, Franklin. He became the American ambassador in Paris, where he used his great prestige and influence to bring France into the Revolutionary War as an American ally. It is recognized by historians that without Franklin's diplomatic effort America could not have won its war for independence, and there would have been no United States of America. To fully appreciate how Franklin was regarded in France at that time, and the basis for that unusual regard, we must turn to his fellow American in France, John Adams:

Figure 4.4 Franklin's kite experiment by Romas, a Frenchman, one of the many experimenters in different countries who repeated this experiment.

Nothing, perhaps, that ever occurred upon this earth was so well calculated to give any man an extensive and universal celebrity as the discovery of the efficacy of iron points and the invention of lightning-rods. The idea was one of the most sublime that ever entered a human imagination, that a mortal should disarm the clouds of heaven, and almost "snatch from his hand the sceptre and the rod." His Paratonneres [lightning rods] erected their heads in all parts of the world, on temples and palaces no less than on cottages of peasants and the habitations of ordinary citizens. These visible objects reminded all men of the name and character of their inventor.... His reputation was more universal than that of Leibnitz or Newton, Frederick [the Great] or Voltaire, and his character more beloved and esteemed than any or all of them.

Newton had astonished perhaps forty or fifty men in Europe; for not more than that number, probably, at any one time had read him and understood him by his discoveries and demonstrations.... But the fame was confined to men of letters. The common people knew little and cared nothing about such a recluse philosopher. Leibnitz's name was more confined still. Frederick was hated by more than half of Europe.... Voltaire, whose name was more universal than any of those before mentioned, was considered as a vain, profligate wit, and not much esteemed or beloved by anybody, though admired by all who knew his works. But Franklin's fame was universal. His name was familiar to government and people, to kings, courtiers, nobility, clergy, and philosophers, as well as plebeians, to such a degree that there was scarcely a peasant or a citizen, a valet de chambre, coachman or footman, a lady's chambermaid or a scullion in a kitchen, who was not familiar with it, and who did not consider him as a friend to human kind.[61]

Why, as Adams observed, were people so moved by Franklin's lightning experiments as compared to Newton's great contributions to our understanding of the world we live in? Newton looked into the heavens and explained why the planets revolve in their orbits around the sun. But what did he do about it? Franklin not only explained what lightning was, but he also did something about it! He captured the lightning out of the sky and guided it safely to earth. This was something all people could understand and appreciate. At a time in history when witches were burned and a minister could object to lightning rods as interference with God's works, the greatest, lasting effect of Franklin's daring experiment was upon people's thinking. They would no longer, as Franklin observed, look upon illness as ordered punishment from on high which they would have to endure but could now begin to look into the microscope for natural causes and to the laboratory for cures, as Franklin had studied lightning and then rid it of its terror. Thanks to Franklin and his successors, the world of modern science would replace the old world of superstition.

5

That Famous Stove

Mark Twain said about the weather, "Everyone talks about it but no-body does anything about it." Regarding Benjamin Franklin's stove, every-body has heard about it, but hardly anybody knows anything about it.

It is difficult for us in the comfort of our air-conditioned homes to realize that in Colonial America most houses had only a very inefficient fireplace to supply heat in the coldest winter weather. Schools, churches, and public meeting places usually had no heat at all. You put on your heavy clothes and stuck it out. The German and Dutch settlers had stoves for heating which they had brought from the old country, but the American colonists of British ancestry relied on the traditional fireplace. This might be explained by the fact that although Britain is known for rainy and foggy weather, it doesn't have the frigid weather of northern Europe because of the proximity of the Gulf Stream, which swings by the British Isles. As a result, the British were content to rely on their fireplaces, which gave them so much visual pleasure if little else. The family sat together in front of the fireplace, and all cooking was done over its fire.

Even though the winters of northern America were more like those of northern Europe than those of jolly old England, the fireplace tradition was retained by the British colonists on this side of the water. The young Franklin was not yet ready to upset tradition, but he didn't think it made sense to freeze when it was possible to be warm. The fireplace simply didn't warm the room. Even with a roaring fire in the fireplace, water in a glass a few feet away froze solid on a cold night. A man who stood in front of

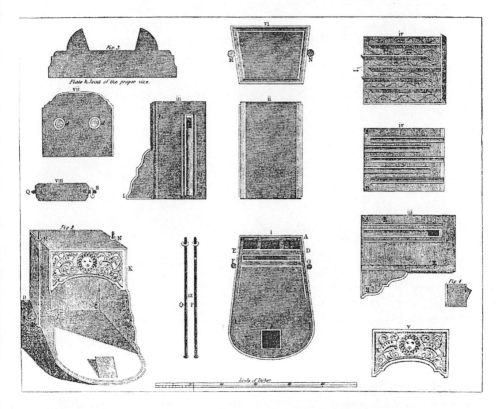

Figure 5.1 The Pennsylvanian fireplace.

the fire for warmth, as Franklin put it, "is scorched before, while he's froze behind." Some fireplaces were built the width of the room so that people could sit inside them on each side of the fire.

The Pennsylvanian Fireplace

To warm the whole room Franklin invented what he called the Pennsylvanian fireplace. It was actually a fireplace modified with a stove. The stove sat on the hearth but projected forward into the room so that it radiated heat into the room. Part of the front of the stove was cut away so that one could see the fire and tend to it (Figure 5.1). There are still so-called Franklin fireplaces being manufactured and sold today, but all wood-burning stoves have been incorrectly called Franklin stoves.

Franklin invented his Pennsylvanian fireplace in 1739 and wrote that

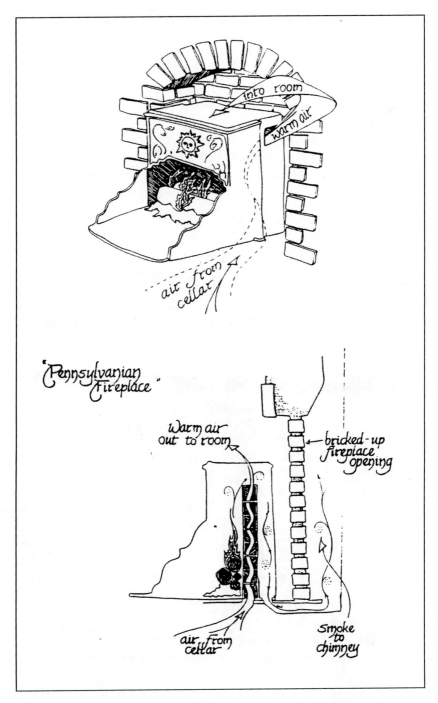

Figure 5.2 The air box on the Pennsylvanian fireplace. From *Wood Heat* by John Vivian. Rodale Press, Emmaus, PA. (By permission of John Vivian.)

he and his family and friends had enjoyed its warmth for three winters when, in 1742, he announced it was being manufactured and was available for public sale. The governor of Pennsylvania, Franklin tells us, was so pleased with construction of the stove, "that he offered to give me a patent for the sole vending of them for a term of years." But Franklin declined the offer based upon his principle: "That as we enjoy great advantages from the inventions of others, we should be glad of an opportunity to serve others by an invention of ours." He followed this principle throughout his life and never patented or made money from his subsequent inventions.

The problem with the common fireplaces was that when they were operated with the flue wide open most of the air heated by the fire went directly up the chimney, only to be replaced in the room by cold, outside air. The fireplace could actually produce a heat loss in the room if the outside air coming in to replace the air going up the chimney was cold enough to outbalance the heat radiated into the room by the fire. When the flue was closed to prevent the heated air from going up the chimney, the smoke backed up into the room, giving the occupants the unenviable choice of choking pollution or unbearable cold. Franklin wrote: "In common chimneys, the strongest heat from the fire ... goes directly up the chimney and is lost...." But in his stove, "the upright heat strikes and heats the top plate, which warms the air above it, and that comes into the room. The heat likewise, which the fire communicates to the sides, back, bottom, and air box, is all brought into the room." With his invention, Franklin employed devices to deal with both the problems of

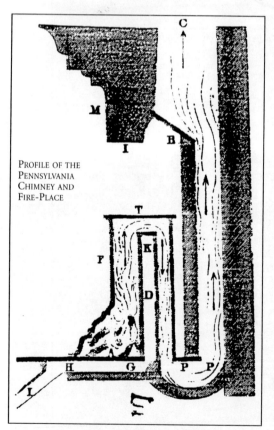

PROFILE OF THE
PENNSYLVANIA
CHIMNEY AND
FIRE-PLACE

Figure 5.3 The air siphon on the Pennsylvanian fireplace.

lost heat and smoke. One device was the air box (Figure 5.2). This was built into the stove and served to heat the air that replaced the air lost up the chimney. Air was drawn from the cellar or the room, which was warmer than outside air, into a duct at the bottom of a vertical series of baffles, where it was heated and expelled into the room from the sides at the top of the stove. The air box was heated by the fire but was separated from it; therefore, this air carried no smoke into the room.

The second device, the air siphon, which Franklin called an aerial siphon or siphon reversed, was another air passage in the stove whereby heated air and smoke from the fire were carried downward before it continued its passage upward in the chimney (Figure 5.3). Franklin understood that smoke was incompletely combusted fuel and that heat was lost if the smoke was allowed to escape unburned. The downward passage through the hot metal allowed more time for the smoke to be consumed, thereby adding more heat to the room. Since hot air rises, it is not natural for the air from the fire to move downward, but it did so because of the air siphon. In a water siphon, Franklin explained, water is lifted up unnaturally because the up-leg is pulled along by a longer down-leg. In Franklin's air siphon, the air was pulled down in the stove by the longer up-leg of rising air in the chimney.

According to the editors of the authoritative Franklin papers, the Pennsylvanian fireplace was efficient for several reasons: It reduced to a minimum the dissipation of heat up the chimney flue; it transmitted heat by radiation and by direct conduction; it also employed the principle of convection — the creation of a current of air which was heated and circulated into the room.[1]

The Pamphlet as Literature

Franklin not only invented his new fireplace, but he also arranged for its manufacture and sales, and he advertised it in his newspaper. He made no attempt to make money from it but gave dealerships to his brothers and friends. Not satisfied with what he had already done to launch this enterprise, he published a detailed pamphlet telling all about it: why it was necessary; how it worked; what its advantages were; and directions for its installation and operation, with labeled drawings of all its parts. There was even a section answering questions people might ask about it. It was written in a simple style to appeal to the ordinary citizen but contained notations and information one might find in a scientific treatise. One of Franklin's biographers was so impressed with this work that he said he was "inclined to lay down the principle that the test of literary genius is the ability to be fascinating about stoves."[2]

One of Franklin's scientific friends, Cadwallader Colden of New York, sent a copy of the pamphlet to a scientist in Holland, Johann Gronovius of Leyden, who wrote, "That invention hath found a great applause in this part of the world." Gronovius translated the pamphlet into Dutch, after which it was translated into French, German, and Italian. The pamphlet was titled "An Account of the New-Invented Fire Places."[3] Franklin begins: "In these northern colonies the inhabitants keep fires to sit by, generally seven months of the year … and in some winters near eight months. Wood, our common fuel* which within these 100 years might be had at every man's door, makes a considerable article in the expense of families." Elsewhere he had written that poor people, who can't afford to buy wood, were forced to go to bed early at night and to stay in bed late in the morning to avoid the cold, thereby not being able to do the spinning, sewing, and other chores that were done in the home. His new invention, he wrote, would produce more heat and use less wood and now had been experienced for three winters by a great number of families in Pennsylvania. He invited the reader to compare his system with that commonly in use.

In order to do that, however, they had to understand the properties of air and fire, so he begins with a lesson. "The same quantity of air takes up more space when warm than when cold." He then suggests several easy experiments to demonstrate this fact. One experiment uses a bladder half filled with air and the neck tied tight. When it is put near the fire, the air heats and expands, and the bladder is blown up. When cooled, it returns to its former sunken shape. The second basic lesson is that heated air is lighter than it was before and will rise, just as oil, which is lighter, rises to the top of the water. The air heated in the fireplace expands and becomes lighter, causing it to rise in the chimney and come out at the top. When this happens, that air is replaced by fresh air from the door or windows. If they are shut, strong drafts will issue from every crevice. If enough air is not replaced, the flow up the chimney will flag, and smoke will come into the room.

Having discussed some principles of fire and heat, the author lists the types of fireplaces and stoves available at that time and mentions their good and bad points. Regarding the Dutch and German stoves, they effectively and efficiently warm the room, but, since there is little change of air, the odor of human bodies and any smoke remains in the room for

---

*Coal had not yet been discovered in America, and oil and natural gas were unknown everywhere.

long periods. (It should be noted that most of the people worked hard in the fields, and running water and bathtubs did not come into most American homes for a century or two. Incidentally, later in life Franklin had a bathtub built for himself with a built-in bookstand so he could soak and read at the same time.) The Dutch and German stoves had another drawback; they were enclosed stoves, which lacked popularity among the English Americans "who love the sight of the fire."

Of the large fireplaces, Franklin says, "'tis impossible to warm a room with such a fireplace." He continues, "I suppose our ancestors never thought of warming rooms to sit in; all they proposed was to have a place to make a fire in, by which they might warm themselves when cold." The newer fireplaces with jambs, narrow hearth, and low arch or breast Franklin found an improvement. While they kept rooms generally free of smoke and, with a smaller flue opening, allowed the door to be shut when the fire was burning, "yet still requiring a considerable quantity of air, it rushes in at every crevice so strongly as to make a continual whistling or howling; and 'tis very uncomfortable as well as dangerous to sit against any such crevice." He attributed colds, rheums, defluctions, fevers, and pleurisies to such causes and quoted from a Spanish proverb: "If the wind blows on you through a hole, make your will and take care of your soul."

To support such somber attributions, Franklin utilizes a footnote in fine print, which goes on for two pages, quoting the works of a learned British physician, of an Italian physician written in Latin, of the great Dutch physician Boerhaave, and a Chinese treatise titled "The Art of Procuring Health and Long Life." In this footnote Franklin shows off his scholarship to impress readers that he is not just a tinkerer but a serious scientist who has thoroughly investigated his subject.

The present fireplaces, Franklin concludes, are unsatisfactory because at least five-sixths of the heat goes up the chimney and contributes nothing to warming the room. Now, coming to the basis of his own invention, he credits it to a Frenchman, Nicolas Gauger, described by him in his book *Mechanics of Fire*, which appeared in English translation in 1715. Gauger's design had the air box and the iron plates and jambs which Franklin incorporated in his own design. Franklin praised this invention, for it warmed all parts of the room as a result of the air box with its heated cavities. In addition, cold air was prevented from rushing through the crevices because the flue was sufficiently supplied by the air from the air box. Nevertheless Franklin noted deficiencies: The cost was great due to the intricacy of the design; there was difficulty in the installation; and much of the heat still went up the chimney as in the older fireplaces.

To avoid these problems he contrived his Pennsylvanian fireplace, which he describes in great detail, giving drawings of the different parts. He seems to have thought of everything. Consider the following paragraph:

> In rooms where much smoking of tobacco is used, 'tis also convenient to have a small hole about five or six inches square, cut near the ceiling through into the funnel: This hole must have a shutter, by which it may be clos'd or open'd at pleasure. When open, there will be a strong draught of air through it into the chimney, which will presently carry off a cloud of smoke, and keep the room clear: If the room be too hot likewise, it will carry off as much of the warm air as you please, and then you may stop it entirely, or in part, as you think fit. By this means it is that the tobacco-smoke does not descend among the heads of the company near the fire, as it must do before it can get into common chimneys.

Under the title "The Manner of Using This Fireplace," our inventor tells such things as how to start a fire in the morning, which kind of wood is preferable, and how to make adjustments to keep the room warm overnight. He then proceeds to discuss "The Advantages of This Fireplace," fourteen of them. The first is that the whole room is equally warmed. People do not need to crowd so close to the fire but may sit near the window and have the benefit of light for reading, writing, needlework, and so on. Another is that the supply of warm air is thought to reduce the incidence of contagious diseases: In the winters of 1730 and 1736, when the smallpox spread in Pennsylvania, it was observed that, with their room-warming stoves, very few of the Germans' children died in proportion to the English. Yet another advantage is the saving in wood: Some people who have used these fireplaces say they have saved five-sixths, others three-fourths, others much less. "My common room," Franklin says, "is made twice as warm as it used to be, with a quarter of the wood I formerly consumed there."

Next, he answers in advance objections that might arise. "We frequently hear it said … stoves have an unpleasant smell, stoves are unwholesome, and warm rooms make people tender and apt to catch cold." At some length he dispels each of these contentions. There is no offensive smell from iron stoves. Iron, hot or cold, is one of the sweetest of metals and never offends the nicest lady. "Iron is always sweet, and every way taken is wholesome and friendly to the human body — except in weapons." If iron stoves do smell, it is caused by candle wax, greasy hands, or that "filthy unmannerly custom of spitting on the stove to tell how hot it is."

Regarding the assertion that warm rooms make people tender and apt to catch cold, this is a great mistake among the English, he says. "We find we can leap out of the warmest bed naked in the coldest morning without any danger." The reason is that the pores all close at once, the cold is shut out, and the heat within is augmented, and soon we feel the glowing of the flesh and skin. The body is hardened as it were to plunge into a cold bath. The Swedes, Danes, and Russians are said to live in rooms as hot as ovens, yet their soldiers bear the fatigue of a winter campaign in so severe a climate, march whole days to the neck in snow, and at night entrench in ice.

In a triumphant parting shot, Franklin proceeds with the following statement:

> We leave it to the *Political Arithmetician* to compute, how much
> money will be sav'd to a country, by its spending two thirds less
> of fuel; how much labour sav'd in cutting and carriage of it;
> how much more land may be clear'd for cultivation; how great
> the profit by the additional quantity of work done, in those
> trades particularly that do not exercise the body so much, but
> that the workfolks are oblig'd to run frequently to the fire to
> warm themselves: And to physicians to say, how much healthier
> thick-built towns and cities will be, now half suffocated with
> sulphury smoke, when so much less of that smoke shall be
> made, and the air breath'd by the inhabitants be consequently
> so much purer.

There are a few more pages in this dissertation, but they would be of interest only to a specialist. They are Franklin's "Directions to the Bricklayer" who will be installing this equipment.

The Pennsylvanian fireplace had a cheerful front — an embossed image of the sun with a face and rays extended from it, plus the Latin inscription "Alter Idem" (another like me), suggesting that the stove was serving like the sun, with heat and light (Figure 5.4). Franklin con-

Figure 5.4 "Another Sun," the face on the Pennsylvanian fireplace.

cludes his opus in true literary fashion with a poem of his own composition, which suggests that his "sun" is even more dependable than the real thing:

> Another Sun!—'tis true; — but not THE SAME.
> Alike, I own, in warmth and genial flame:
> But, more obliging than his elder brother,
> *This* will not scorch in summer, like *the other*;
> Nor, when sharp Boreas chills our shiv'ring limbs,
> Will *this Sun* leave us for more southern climes;
> Or, in long winter nights, forsake us here,
> To cheer new friends in t'other hemisphere:
> But, faithful still to us, this *new Sun's* fire,
> Warms when we please, and just as we desire.

Short History of the Pennsylvanian Fireplace

A correspondent to a newspaper, the *Boston Evening Post*, of September 8, 1746, stated in regard to Franklin's stoves: "The advantages of them, both as in health and comfort, as well as the expense, are so well represented, and all the objections to them answered by the inventor in a little pamphlet wrote on purpose, so I can't add anything, but in testimony as a disinterested person to the truth of the facts." This writer reported that 1 to 1½ cords of good firewood would suffice all winter for an ordinary family in a sitting room, thereby producing a great saving in cost over the ordinary fireplace. He went on to propose that all who had experienced the comfort provided by this invention, like himself, would agree "that the inventor merits a statue from his countrymen." It is possible that the unidentified, "disinterested" correspondent may have been Franklin himself. He often wrote letters surreptitiously to newspapers under assumed names. A clue here is the suggestion that the inventor merits a statue, which is the proposal Franklin used in his Polly Baker hoax, where Polly states that "instead of a whipping, to have a statue erected in my memory."

Despite this testimonial and having perused Franklin's document and considered the glowing accounts of Franklin's stove in the history books, it will be startling, even shocking, to discover that Franklin's wonderful gift to the human race was a commercial flop, a bust, a dismal failure. It just didn't sell. Samuel Y. Edgerton of Williams College, who has made an exhaustive study of this subject[4,5], found that Peter Franklin, Benjamin's brother in Newport, Rhode Island, ordered eleven stoves for sale in 1744, but his ledger showed that twenty years later only two had been sold. In 1765, when Franklin wrote from London to Hugh Roberts, a merchant in Philadelphia[6] requesting two of his stoves, Roberts replied that they were much out of use and he could not find a secondhand one.[7] The parts had been used to make other stoves. Searching for Franklin's stove, Edgerton could find only one lone survivor — in a museum.

There is evidence that the stove may also have been produced in Britain. J. Bennett Nolan, author of the book *Benjamin Franklin in Scotland and Ireland*, notes that he saw a prospectus of an advertisement for ranges to be produced by the Carron Iron Works in Fallkirk, Scotland, which read, "made upon the model of Dr. Franklyn's Philadelphia stove." Franklin visited the Carron Iron Works in 1759 and probably advised the owners on the manufacture of his stove. There is no information, however, on whether the stove was produced or how many were sold since the company is no longer in existence.

What was the explanation for this useful invention failing to achieve commercial success? Could the whole account have been a fraud, or perhaps one of Franklin's famous hoaxes? Not likely. Franklin had put too much of himself and his reputation in this effort. He wrote about it to his most respected friends. There is no record of the facts so we must speculate on the reasons for its failure after such a great promotion. For one thing, the idea of heating the room was new and didn't really catch on till the latter part of the eighteenth century. The Americans were accustomed to their open fireplaces, which produced a feeling of warmth through radiation but did not heat the air. That was regarded as unhealthy.[8] Further, the stove was complex and therefore expensive. The lone survivor had been simplified, eliminating the air box and the air siphon. Stoves that followed Franklin's Pennsylvanian fireplace also lacked these features. The problem, it appears, was not only cost but also difficulty of operation. A number of factors could explain why the stove might not function well.

In the operation of a downdraft, air-siphon stove, the air heated by the fire had to be drawn down through the short leg of the siphon by a strong updraft in the longer leg, the chimney. To produce a strong updraft, the chimney must be hot for the air to expand and rise. Without the updraft, the smoke will not be carried through the down leg and will back up into the room. Many years later, when describing the operation of another downdraft stove he invented, Franklin admitted that there were problems in operating the stove, especially when the chimney was cold. Since Franklin was satisfied with his own stove's performance, it may be possible that the flue of his fireplace was connected to the kitchen flue or was close to it, since Franklin stated that kitchen fires were pretty constantly burning, and that would have kept the chimney hot.[9]

The height of the chimney, as Franklin noted,[10] could also affect the draft and the operation of the stove. A tall chimney increased the updraft, while in a short chimney the air siphon would not function as well. Chimneys up on Beacon Hill should draw well, Franklin wrote to a friend in Boston.[10] He also pointed out that the draw would be better if the north side of the chimney were protected from the north wind by the house, and the other three sides were exposed to the sun part of the day, helping to keep the chimney warm. For this reason he preferred the chimney to be on the south side of the house. He even suggested that the chimney should be painted black to better absorb the sun's rays. This recommendation was based on an experiment he had performed using small swatches of cloth, white, black, and varying shades of gray, which he placed on a bank of snow on a sunny day.[11] After several hours, the white swatch was still resting on top of the snow, but the others had sunk to different depths into the snow, the darker ones more deeply and the black swatch the deepest.

No doubt Franklin was sincere when he claimed that he and his family and others had used the stove successfully. Perhaps they had kept the fire going permanently during the cold weather and the chimney had retained its heat. Franklin did discuss keeping the hot embers overnight by reducing the opening to the flue, and this may have worked for him.[12] Unfortunately, he did not discuss these draft problems in his pamphlet, and we may assume that people who used the stove found it unsatisfactory in operation, accounting for the lack of sales. Franklin had designed and tested a simple apparatus that would have substituted for both the expensive air box and the troublesome air siphon. He tells about it in a paper published many years later: "Smoke is a very tractable thing.... I made it descend in my Pennsylvania stove. I formerly had a more simple construction, in which the

Figure 5.5 Another Franklin fireplace.

same effect was produced but visible to the eye."[13] Two hinged iron plates—A-B and C-D (Figure 5.5)—were fixed between the fire (E) and the opening of the chimney, leaving a space of about three inches. The heat of the fire got the upper plate very hot, "and its heat rose and spread with the rarified air into the room." Presumably it also helped to combust the smoke when the latter contacted the hot metal.

Chimneys, Fresh Air, and Ventilation

In his scientific investigations Franklin was always on the lookout for practical applications that could benefit people. The lightning rod was a spin-off from his electrical experiments. In his fireplace experiments he had observed that during the summer, when there was no fire in the fireplace, the draft in the chimney changed from upward to downward once each day.[14] This, he explained, occurred during the morning and afternoon hours when the chimney, having been cooled overnight, was colder than the outside air, and the outside air was cooled on entering the chimney and contracted, pulling air downward into the house. The draft was in the opposite direction during the night as a result of the chimney being warmed during the day. He stood in front of the fireplace day and night, candle in hand, observing the direction of the flame and the smoke caught in the draft. He recalled the expression "As useless as a chimney in summer" and wondered whether this daily shift in the draft during the summer might be put to some use.

One thought that occurred to him was to use this draft to help preserve food.[14] The food would be placed in the fireplace and covered with wet cloths. As the air from the up or down draft passed over the cloths, it would accelerate the evaporation of water, cooling the food, just as we are cooled by the draft from a fan. Since there were no refrigerators in those days, he thought this process might help to keep the food from spoiling for a few days longer. His idea was a good one, for our refrigerators today operate by evaporative cooling, and a similar system of cooling by water evaporation has been used effectively in the arid, southwestern United States for air conditioning homes and cars. Unfortunately, it wasn't practical for Philadelphia, where the humidity was too high. Another random thought he had on a possible application was to use the draft to deliver a small amount of mechanical power.

Benjamin Franklin, who was a fresh-air fanatic at a time when the popular opinion was that fresh air, particularly night air, was harmful, indicated that the chimney was very useful for bringing fresh air into the house. On an occasion when Franklin and John Adams, on a government mission during the Revolution, slept in the same room at an inn, Franklin insisted on opening the window wide. Adams, reflecting the prevailing attitude, vehemently protested, afraid he would become deathly ill. Adams confided in his diary, "I who was an invalid and afraid of the night air, shut it close."[15] (This invalid lived to be 91 years old, longer than any of the other founding fathers.)

Franklin was later confirmed in his opinion when he became friends with Sir John Pringle, physician to the English royal family. Pringle believed that disease could be spread through room air and insisted that nurses in hospital wards open windows for the intake of fresh air.[16] Franklin noted that doctors were beginning to come around to Pringle's opinion that respired air might be harmful for sick people, but regarding fresh, cool air, he stated, "It is hoped that in another century or two we may all find out that it is not bad even for people in health." When the government of England asked Franklin to make plans for the ventilation of the House of Commons, he provided vents for the intake of air by each member's seat so "that the personal atmosphere surrounding the members might be carried off."[17] No doubt this provision would make this building a more pleasant workplace. Another of Franklin's proposals was that tall chimneys should be constructed beside coal mines to bring fresh air through the mine shafts to miners deep in the ground.[18]

Smoky Chimneys and Smoky Houses

Franklin loved science, but his sense of duty kept him occupied for most of his life in government service. Speaking of the great scientist Sir Isaac Newton, Franklin said, "Had Newton been the pilot of a single common ship, the finest of his discoveries would scarce have excused or atoned for his abandoning the helm one hour in time of danger; how much less if she carried the fate of the Commonwealth."[19] But in 1785, after the war and after his long government service in France, he had the leisure on the long, shipboard voyage home to write down some of his ideas on scientific matters. During this trip he wrote a long letter to Jan Ingenhousz, physician to the queen of Austria, on the causes and cure of smoky chimneys.[21] Many chimneys resulted in smoke coming into the house, which, in Franklin's words, produced "damaged furniture, sore eyes, and skins almost smoked to bacon." This was a common problem in those days. Shakespeare had put a smoky house in the category of tedious things, along with a tired horse and a railing wife.[21] Lord Kames, president of the Royal

Society, wrote to Franklin that he had bought a house which he said would be the most complete in Edinburgh except that the chimney smoked.[22] He applied to Franklin as "a universal smoke doctor" to remedy it. Franklin told of a case he knew where the owner of a house despaired and was ready to sell it because of a smoky chimney and another case in which the owner went to great expense to overcome the problem, when the chimney was actually not at fault.[23]

He began by relating the history of chimneys, which he had read in a book written during the reign of Queen Elizabeth, when chimneys were hailed as a wonderful, new invention. In medieval times houses had just a hole in the roof for smoke to escape.[24] Smoke, Franklin explained, was heavier than air and was removed only by being carried away by a current of rising air. He described a simple experiment to show that smoke was heavier than air: If smoke and air from a pipe are blown through a straw into a vessel of water, the air bubbles will rise to the top, where the air will leave the water, but the heavier smoke will remain in the water.[25]

Franklin listed and discussed nine causes of smoky chimneys and proposed cures for each.[20] One of the causes was an air-tight room. When the air in the room is heated and rises in the chimney, it must be physically replaced by more air or it will not ascend and will back up, carrying smoke into the room. If it is replaced directly by cold, outside air, the draft will chill the people in the room. To remedy this problem, Franklin suggested utilizing the pocket of warm air that has risen to the ceiling and is trapped there. This air could be replaced with outside air entering through a louvered contraption at the top of the window. This device was called a "was is das" ("what is that?").[26] Since the words are German, Franklin concluded it was a German invention and that it earned its name from the curiosity of those who first viewed it. The outside air would be mixed with and warmed by the warm ceiling air and then circulated in the room before being swept up the chimney.

Another in the list of causes of smoky chimneys is that their openings in the room were too large, causing too much air to flow up the chimney, to be replaced by cold, outside air. This Franklin blames on architects whose ideas of proportion in the opening of a chimney were related to symmetry and beauty, respecting the dimensions of the room, while he asserts, its proportion with respect to its function and utility depends on quite other principles. Further, he adds, "In time, perhaps, that which is fittest in the nature of things may come to be thought handsomest. But at present, when men and women in different countries show themselves dissatisfied with the forms God has given to their heads, waists, and feet, and pretend to shape them more perfectly, it is hardly to be expected that they will be content always with the best form of chimney."[27] "Design with nature" and "form follows function" were the battle cries of architects and designers of the twentieth century, so it is a surprise to hear this outburst from a man of the eighteenth century, but this is typical of Franklin. Just coming from France, he may have been thinking of the extravagant dress of pre-revolution French society, such as the preposterous headdresses of the women, like one with a two-foot-long replica of a fully rigged sailing ship (Figure 5.6), or the "chapeau bras" for the men, which were hats not meant to be worn, just to be held in the arm, as part of the costume. These excesses rankled the Puritan in him, which still lingered from his child-hood. Even as a boy of sixteen, he had rebelled against women's fashions of early Boston, when he wrote ridiculing the hoop petticoats, which he described as "monstrous topsy-turvy mortar pieces."[28]

Some other causes of smoky chimneys were higher buildings nearby, causing wind to blow over them and, like water over a dam, flow down-ward into the chimney; or when there are two fireplaces and two chim-neys in one room, one overpowers the other in drawing the air, causing the air in the other to descend with the smoke; or too large openings at the top; or the effect of strong winds. Franklin discussed at length each of the nine causes, giving suggested remedies for each that are still appro-priate. But there was one chimney that this "universal smoke doctor" had to admit stumped him.[29] It was in a friend's country house near London. His best room had a chimney in which he could never have a fire because all the smoke came out into the room. "I flattered myself," said Franklin, "I could easily find the cause and prescribe the cure." He carefully and methodically checked all of his nine causes, and it was not any of them. He eventually gave up: "In fact, after every other examination I could think of, I was obliged to own the insufficiency of my skill. But my friend, who made no pretension of such kind of knowledge, afterwards discov-ered the cause himself." He got up on a ladder and looking down the chim-ney saw it filled with twigs and straw, cemented by earth, and lined with feathers. The house had been empty for a few years, and large birds had found the chimney an excellent place to make their nest.

A Stove in the Shape of an Urn

Of all Franklin's inventions, stoves for house heating occupied more of his attention and interest over his lifetime than any other. His inven-tion of bifocal eye glasses is used by more people today than any of his other inventions, yet he gave it the least attention. He merely mentioned

Figure 5.6 Paris fashions. From *Mon Cher Papa: Franklin and the Ladies of Paris* by Claude-Anne Lopez. Yale University Press.

that he got tired of having to change glasses for long distance and close-up viewing and ordered the glass cutter to cut the lenses of each pair in half and fit half of each type with the other in one frame. He then dismissed the subject with the following, typically Franklin comment:

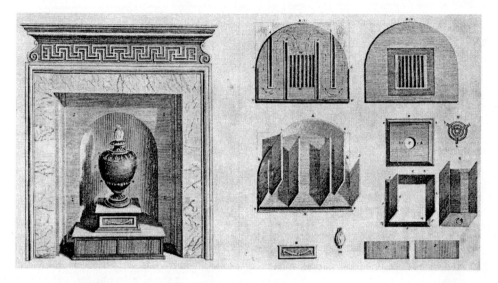

Figure 5.7 The Vase Stove.

This I find more particularly convenient since my being in France, the glasses that serve me best at table to see what I eat not being the best to see the faces of those on the other side of the table who speak to me; and when one's ears are not well accustomed to the sounds of a language, a sight of the movements in the features of him that speaks helps to explain; so that I understand French better by the help of my spectacles.[30]

He had little to say as well about his greatest invention, the lightning rod. But he was working on and writing about stoves, chimneys, and ventilation from 1739 to 1785, a few years before his death. In 1758 he was busy experimenting in his London apartment. He described "an easy, simple contrivance ... for keeping rooms warmer in cold weather ... with less fire." The opening of the chimney was narrowed by brickwork faced with marble slabs and the breast brought down to within three feet of the hearth. A grooved iron frame was placed in the chimney opening with an iron plate that slid horizontally so as to shut off the chimney when thrust all the way in. (We now call it a damper.) This plate was drawn out, leaving about two inches open at the back for the smoke to pass. This reduced the amount of hot air lost to the chimney and returned heated air to the room. In addition, the plate was hinged so it could come down and close off part of the opening to the fire to intensify the draft and the blaze. Another feature he mentioned was plates of polished brass lining the fireplace jambs (sides). "They throw a vast deal of heat into the room by reflection." He considered this his most successful "warming machine" to date, saying, "after more than twenty years experience of my own contrivances and those of others ... I am of opinion that this ... is by far the best for common use.... Since I first used this in my lodgings here, many hundreds have been set up ... in and about this city."[31]

In 1785 Franklin published a paper with descriptions of stoves he had invented in 1771 and had used in England and later when he resided in France.[32] One of these was in the shape of a vase or urn (Figure 5.7). It was his masterpiece, combining function and beauty. He had seen large stoves of this shape, beautifully decorated, in London, which were used to heat large rooms like banquet halls. He adopted the shape in his smaller version but incorporated his air siphon for efficiency through its consumption of the smoke. This stove used coal, which was readily available in England and which produced more heat in the same space than wood. A modification of the design, however, would allow it to use wood. The air entered the top of the vase and was pulled down by the chimney draft through a bed of hot coals, then down through the hot iron base, fitted with baffles, and finally up the chimney. The vase, the box, and the base all radiated heat into the room. The rounded curvature of the fireplace also reflected heat into the room. When the smoke was burned in this stove, Franklin claimed, you got not only greater warmth, but also no soot for chimney sweeps to have to remove. In fact, Franklin remarked, "The effect of this machine, well managed, is to burn not only the coals, so that while the fire is burning, if you go out and observe the top of your chimney you will see no smoke issuing, nor anything but clean, warm air." He found it functioned even beyond his expectations. Being an enclosed stove, it had a much greater efficiency than an open fireplace or a fireplace stove.

But this stove was not for everyone. Note Franklin's qualification: "well managed." Unfortunately the down-leg of the air siphon in this stove gave trouble, and Franklin admitted, "Being somewhat complex, it requires ... a variety of attention. Good for a studious man ... [who] has a pleasure in managing his own fire.... It is by no means fit for common use in families." To operate properly this stove needed a strong updraft, which required that the chimney be hot. For starting the fire when the chimney was cold, Franklin recommended the following: "Let the first fire be made after eight in the evening or before eight in the morning, for those times and between those hours all night, there is usually a draft up the chimney." During the other twelve hours, however, "There is often, in a cold chimney, a draft downwards, when, if you attempt to kindle a fire, the smoke will come into the room." Franklin gives directions for starting a fire in this stove during the daytime hours, but it is more troublesome to do so. When operating properly with a warm chimney, however, this stove was probably as efficient as modern stoves today. What Franklin needed to make his downdraft stoves function satisfactorily was an insulated chimney flue, as presently manufactured, to make the chimney easy to warm and to retain its heat.

This unusually shaped stove with its inverted air flow was the subject of comic ribbing by British loyalists in the following poem:

> Inscription on a Curious Stove in the Form of an Urn, Contrived in Such a Manner as to Make the Flame Descend Instead of Rising From the Fire, Invented by Dr. Franklin.
>
> Like a Newton sublimely he soared
>   To a summit before unattained,
>
> With a spark which he caught from the skies
>   He displayed an unparalleled wonder,
> And we saw with delight and surprise
>   That his rod could secure us from thunder.
>
> Oh! had he been wise to pursue
>   The track for his talents designed,
> What a tribute of praise had been due
>   To the teacher and friend of mankind.
>
> But to covet political fame
>   Was in him a degrading ambition,
> The spark that from Lucifer came
>   And kindled the blaze of sedition.
>
> Let candor then write on his urn,
>   Here lies the renowned inventor
> Whose fame to the skies ought to burn
>   But inverted descends to the centre.[33]

After Franklin's death, the famous portrait painter Charles Wilson Peale made a large version of this vase stove which he called the "Smoke Eater" and used it for heating his museum. Like Franklin, he invited visitors to view the exhaust to show that there was no smoke.[34]

Peale and others who took ideas from Franklin failed to give him credit. Edgerton reports that in the next fifty years Franklin's followers made significant practical improvements on his initial ideas, but "Too often in their eagerness to capitalize on these modifications, they conveniently forgot to cite his pioneering efforts."[35] Franklin, on the other hand, was generous in giving credit. The air box and other aspects of his Penn-

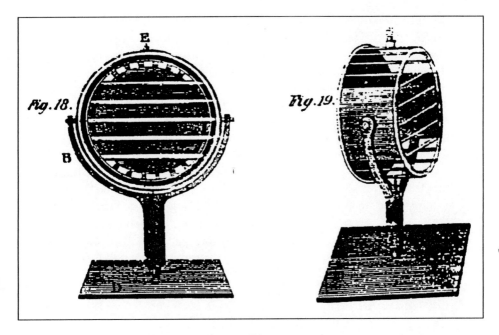

Figure 5.8 The revolving grate stove.

sylvanian fireplace he credited in his pamphlet to the Frenchman Gauger and called his work ingenious. The air siphon came from another Frenchman, a seventeenth-century investigator whose name he couldn't remember, but whom he learned about in a German book, *Vulcanus Famulans*, by John George Leutmann, published in 1723. In his autobiography, Franklin mentions his invention of the Pennsylvanian fireplace.[36] He says, "The use of these fireplaces in very many houses ... has been and is a great saving of wood to the inhabitants." He is obviously talking about the stoves that copied his, for he knows that his stove did not continue to be made. He adds, "An ironmonger in London, however, after assuming a great deal of my pamphlet and working it up into his own, and making small changes ... got a patent for it there, and made as I was told a little fortune by it." He considered these imitations as inferior since they lacked an air box for warming the air (Figure 5.2), which he says is a major feature of his stove.

Franklin's least known and most unique stove is his revolving grate stove (Figure 5.8), which he used in the fireplace of his Paris lodging.[37] It is a smoke-consuming stove, but unlike his other stoves, it is small and portable. It is an updraft stove which doesn't have the problems of the downdraft variety. It is able to consume the smoke because the hot coals are at the top of the fire. New coals are added at the top of the grate, then the grate is rotated 180 degrees on its stand, so the new coals are at the bottom and the hot coals at the top. The volatiles and carbon particles of the smoke coming from the new coal, when it becomes hot, has to pass up through the hot, glowing coals, where they are burned to smoke-free gases. This stove is round in shape resembling, Franklin said, "The great giver of warmth to our system," the sun. While this stove does not consume the smoke as completely as the vase, it has certain advantages. It can be easily turned to direct its heat in any direction, and when in a horizontal position, water in a tea kettle can be boiled on it. Like his Pennsylvanian fireplace it gives a view of the fire. Franklin thought it would be "fitter for common use" than his vase stove. Neither this ingenious contrivance nor the beautiful vase stove was ever produced and marketed, but they aroused interest and stimulated many others to try their hand in solving the important heating problems.

On Heat and Fire

It is clear from his design of the stoves and his writings that Franklin had a practical if not a basic understanding of the nature of heat. He thought that heat was like light, but he said that the nature of light left him in the dark. He designed his stoves to take advantage of the conduction, radiation, reflection, and convection of heat. In explaining conduction, he pointed out that in a cold room a metal surface would feel colder than a wood surface although both were at the same temperature — because the metal is a better conductor of heat than the wood and conducts the heat away from the body faster. Alternately, when both metal and wood are heated, the metal seems hotter since it conducts its heat to the body more readily. He explained insulation as poor conduction of heat; thus wool and fur on animals helps them to retain their body heat.[38] He also stated that the body's heat is produced from the food we eat, by digestion and fermentation, just as wood produces heat in a fire. "Fire," he said, "penetrates bodies and separates its parts." He observed the volatiles flashing, giving off a bright light, while the coals remaining burned slowly. At a time before his friend Priestley would discover that air contained oxygen and his friend Lavoisier would demonstrate the function of oxygen in combustion, Franklin was frankly puzzled by the action of air in a fire. He noted that as the air was increased, the fire burned hotter and more fiercely, but he could not fathom why even more air caused the fire to be extinguished, as when he blew out a candle.[39] He did not figure out that too much cold air cools the fire below the ignition point of the fuel, causing the flame to be extinguished.

Franklin's Stoves to Modern Stoves

During his lifetime Franklin designed, built, and operated five different stoves. Although his stoves were not successful in themselves, they gave rise to a host of followers which exist even to this day. The patent records are filled with innovations based upon the features of Franklin's stoves. He demonstrated that it was no longer necessary to suffer the discomfort of a cold house, which invited others to seek to make improved stoves and capitalize on them. Among Franklin's basic contributions were increased conduction and radiation by making his Pennsylvanian fireplace of iron and by projecting it into the room. Convection and circulation were facilitated by the air box and the space between the rear of his stove and the fireplace wall. By controlling the draft with an adjustable damper, he was able to reduce the hot air going up the chimney, thereby improving the efficiency and adding to the comfort by reducing the cold intake air. He luted the seams of his stoves to prevent stray drafts, which would lower efficiency. All stoves today are made airtight for the same reason.

The air siphon is no longer used in modern house stoves; instead they use one or more horizontal baffles to effect longer contact of the air with the hot stove for greater combustion of the smoke without the downdraft (Figure 5.9). Some central heating furnaces, however, do use the downdraft principle to force

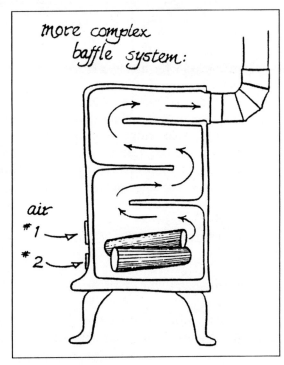

Figure 5.9 Baffled modern stove. From *Wood Heat* by John Vivian. Rodale Press. Emmaus, PA. (By permission of John Vivian.)

fuel gases produced by the fire into the coals or the flame so the fuel will burn as completely and as economically as possible. A successful, modern wood stove for home use also uses the downdraft, as in Franklin's vase stove.[40] Modern stoves don't have Franklin's air box, but they use other heat exchangers with names like Heat-O-Later, Thrift Changer, and Magic Heat to transfer heat from the fire to the room air.[41] One simple heat exchanger for fireplaces is made of hollow metal tub-

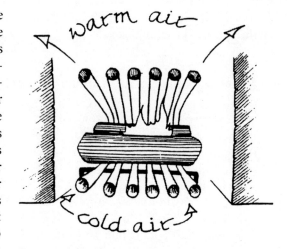

Figure 5.10 Hollow tubing grate. From *Wood Heat* by John Vivian. Rodale Press. Emmaus, PA. (By permission of John Vivian.)

ing to form a grate (Figure 5.10).[42] When there is a fire in the fireplace, room air enters the opening of the tube at the floor level, is heated and expanded by the fire, and is expelled at the top end of the grate into the room. The tubular grate was invented in 1791 and is still available for sale.[43] A recent development in stoves that Franklin would envy is the use of a catalyst, like the antipollution equipment required on automobile exhaust systems, to efficiently convert the smoke into heat at a lower temperature. According to a stove manufacturer, older stoves produced 40–80 grams of smoke per hour, whereas the new stoves produce only 2–5 grams.[44] While Franklin's fireplace stoves may have increased the efficiency of the fireplace from ten to about twenty or even thirty percent, modern closed stoves claim efficiencies of almost eighty percent, with the use of the catalyst, automatic dampers, heat exchangers, thermostats, and blower fans.[45]

Wood Burning Economics

Franklin was concerned about the cost of house heating. He said, "Much more of the prosperity of a winter country depends on the plenty and cheapness of fuel, than is generally imagined."[46] In his travels in different countries he observed that where wood or coal was expensive, the working people were ragged and lived in miserable hovels, but where fuel was cheap they had the necessities of life and decent habitations. He

Figure 5.11 Modern Franklin stove. From *Wood Heat* by John Vivian. Rodale Press. Emmaus, PA. (By permission of John Vivian.)

wrote, "An English farmer in America with fires in large, open chimneys needs the constant employment of one man to cut and haul wood."[47] Cutting up the wood in lengths for the fireplace was a major task. As Henry David Thoreau said, "Wood heats you twice, once when you cut it and again when you burn it." Franklin considered the greater effectiveness of the Germans' stoves and speculated, "The difference in this article of economy alone shall in the course of years enable the German to buy out the Englishman and take possession of his plantation."[48] At that time Franklin was a loyal English subject, and this worried him. Perhaps his work with stoves helped to prevent that situation from coming about. In colonial New England 30 cords of wood a year might be burned in open fireplaces.[49] But even as late as 1860, with improved stoves, the average American family burned 17.5 cords of wood annually. Today most homes burn oil or gas because they are more convenient fuels that leave no ash. However, there are still many wood stoves being manufactured and used. There are modern, so-called Franklin stoves which give the home occupants the pleasure of viewing the fire and hearing the crackle of the wood burning. They may have doors which can close off the fireplace and gain the higher efficiency of closed stoves (Fig. 5.11).[50] Some have a fire-resistant glass door which when closed still affords sight of the fire. During the Arab oil embargo in the 1970s many people returned to wood stoves—a million were sold in 1978, and many people continue to burn wood.[51] For people who own treed land and a chain saw it may be the cheapest way to heat. Based on the rule of thumb that an acre of land will produce a cord of wood indefinitely, six acres is said to be enough forested land to keep a home perpetually supplied with firewood. Two hardwood trees—oak, maple, or ash—12 to 18 inches in diameter at the base can yield a cord of firewood: Eight to twelve such trees burned in a modern, efficient stove will heat a home all winter in the northern United States.[52] In Vermont and Maine it is reported that 12 percent of all homes are heated entirely by wood and 55 percent partly by wood. Similar figures are estimated for New Hampshire, northern Michigan, and parts of Wisconsin.[53] Even in Florida, where one cord will last all winter, wood stoves are very popular.[54] One-third of the world's population depends on wood for heating.[55]

Franklin once said he wished he could come back in a hundred years to see the progress made in that time.[56] Were he to see us now—comfortably warm in our homes and workplaces on the coldest days—he would be mightily pleased at the advances which his efforts have done so much to initiate.

6

Benjamin Franklin and the French Revolution

King George III and the British government blamed Benjamin Franklin for causing the American Revolution. He didn't. In fact, he spent many years attempting to prevent that rupture. But the French Revolution is another matter.

The French Revolution is one of the great events in the history of the world. According to historians it had its basis in the outdated medieval structure of royal authority. This included the blatant extravagance of the kings and their courts; the excesses of the privileged upper classes of nobility and clergy; the growth of a successful but unenfranchised middle class; the mismanagement and gross inefficiency of the financial affairs of government, in which the burden of taxation fell on the middle and lower classes. All these, along with the unusual droughts and poor harvests that brought poverty and hunger to a large part of the population, contributed to the revolution.

That these were major contributory causes of the French Revolution cannot be denied, but what precipitated this cataclysmic event? It is the premise of this argument that it was the American Revolution and with it the presence and actions of the American ambassador to France, Benjamin Franklin, who resided in that country for nine years from 1776 to 1785, prior to the revolution in 1789. Benjamin Franklin has been credited with many things, but never with influencing the French Revolution.

Let us begin by listing how Franklin influenced the French Revolution:

1. To the common people of France, Franklin brought hope and by example indicated how, through rebellion, they could improve their miserable lives.
2. The nobles and higher clergy saw through him how they might shift power away from the king and into their own hands.
3. The idealists, namely the liberal aristocrats, the professionals, and some members of the lower clergy, felt that Franklin gave them a blueprint for eliminating special privilege and erecting a constitutional government as in the United States. Franklin's closest friends were in that group.
4. And finally, Franklin's unique ability to raid the royal treasury on behalf of his own country tipped the financial scales that made the French Revolution inevitable.

Historians state that the philosophers Rousseau and Voltaire had the greatest influence in causing the French Revolution.[1] This chapter shows that an American named Franklin deserves to share that responsibility.

Liberty, equality, fraternity — the clarion call of the French Revolution: Where did the French find these noble sentiments put into action? Not in England, not in Germany, not in Russia, but in America in the Declaration of Independence, with its emphasis on liberty and equality. And the triumphant Declaration of the Rights of Man and the Citizen, the French Bill of Rights — where did this French document have its origin? Contrary to what we might suppose, it was not in the American Bill of Rights, for that document was approved by Congress in September 1789, one month following the French declaration.

But the French declaration did originate in America. It had its origin in the Bill of Rights of Virginia of 1776 and those of the other American states, when they and their state constitutions were published in France by Franklin, having been translated into French at his request by his friend La Rochefoucald d'Enville.[2] La Rouchefoucald also translated the Declaration of Independence and the U.S. Constitution, documents which Franklin also had a hand in preparing.

The revolutionary ideas in these documents were personified in France by the very visible presence of Franklin himself. A common man, a printer, he wore plain clothes, went bareheaded without a wig, and often wore a rustic fur cap. Imagine such a figure at the royal court amid the courtiers and king in their powdered wigs, lace, silks, and ruffles. Franklin was the acclaimed great philosopher and scientist, who, according to Turgot's famous epigram, had "seized the lightning from the sky and the scepter from tyrants."[3] To Americans the tyrant was the English king, but in France, which was an absolute monarchy, many French people equated "king" with "tyrant."

America had been characterized by French intellects like the naturalist Buffon as a primitive land that had produced only savages, the naked Indians. They believed that the American soil, water, and climate were responsible, so that the animals and even man degenerated by living in America.[4] But then came Franklin, the wizard of electricity and the creator of the universal wisdom of *Poor Richard's Almanac*. How was such a great American to be explained? In his *Almanac*, including "The Way to Wealth," he demonstrates the wit and idealism of Voltaire, and, at the same time, in this acclaimed philosopher the French found the living example of Rousseau's noble savage, the unblemished, superior human being, uncorrupted by civilization, the embodiment of natural wisdom, a man to be admired, revered, and adored.[5]

In France, Franklin was a sensation, a superstar, a combination of Einstein and the pope. People lined the streets to see him ride by in his coach. As John Adams, the future American president, reports: "His reputation was more universal than that of Leibnitz or Newton, Frederick [the Great], or Voltaire; and his character more beloved and esteemed by any or all of them." And there was no one "who did not consider him a friend to humankind." The French people looked to Franklin to do for them what he had done for lightning.[6]

Such a popular man, a revolutionary espousing equality, liberty, and freedom for all, was a virtual time bomb in a despotic state that was still shackled with serfdom and in which the King imprisoned people without charges or a trial. Further, France was a staunchly Catholic country, and the king was a devoutly pious man, while Franklin was Protestant like France's enemy, England. Surprisingly, however, the king and the nobility did not see Franklin as a threat. To them he was by definition a friend, being "the enemy of my enemy." Besides, Franklin, as a celebrated scientist, had been honored for his electrical experiments by the king's predecessor, Louis XV.[7] Furthermore, he was such a personally cordial fellow that no one could think of him as a provocateur or incendiary. He was invited to the royal palace at Versailles to meet the king and queen and was sought as an honored guest at the homes of the best people. The scientists and intellectuals besieged him.

He enjoyed the company of philosophers like Condorcet and Morellet, encyclopedists like Diderot and D'Alembert, the economists Turgot and Du Pont de Nemours, and scientists like Lavoisier and Bailly. At a meeting of the Academy of Sciences Franklin met the great writer and philosopher Voltaire. At the demand of the audience the two men embraced and kissed each other on both cheeks, French style, to the thunderous applause of the attending scientists. This was the same Voltaire who had previously been expelled from France and his writings banned because of his attacks on the injustices of the French government. His watchword was "Crush the Evil Ones."[8] When Franklin and Voltaire embraced, the spectators understood that the two men stood for the same goals.[9] Voltaire died shortly thereafter, and Rousseau one month later, but Franklin was still living and expected to carry on.

Franklin and Voltaire had also come together at the Masonic Lodge when Voltaire was inducted. Franklin had been a lifelong Mason, and he was at home in this "Lodge of the Seven Sisters," whose members were among the most enlightened and boldest men in France. Among them were prominent publishers who readily printed Franklin's wartime propaganda pieces against the British enemy. When the lodge got into trouble with the royal authority and feared it would be closed, lodge members made Franklin Grand Master because of his prestige, believing that he would not be touched, and they were proved correct.[10] Franklin was also a frequent visitor to the many fashionable salons, where he became acquainted with a number of the leading people of France. Wherever he went, he represented America and all the values that revolutionary America stood for: equality, human rights, individual and religious freedom, a free press, and a republican form of constitutional government, with popular election of representatives.

In diplomatic circles Franklin demonstrated his persuasiveness, in the salons his charm. John Adams, Franklin's constant observer, writes that Franklin "has the most affectionate and insinuating way of charming the woman or man he fixes on."[11] Despite his personal disapproval of Franklin, Adams had to admit that Franklin had the charm to soothe "the savage sachem [Indian] in me.[12] Franklin could charm the skirts off the ladies, and some say that is exactly what he did. But in his seventies Franklin may have been more a talker than a doer. The story goes that he liked to shock the ladies by asking them to spend the night with him. When one lady agreed, Franklin was shocked in turn. He quickly recovered and said, "It is July; why don't we wait until December when the nights are longer?" When American Admiral John Paul Jones told Franklin he was eager to learn French, Franklin advised him to learn with a "sleeping dictionary," and the hostess where Franklin was staying was only too happy to oblige Jones.[13]

Everyone knows of Thomas Malthus' famous essay, in which he

predicts the population explosion. In this essay Malthus credits the idea to Franklin, who had written on that subject some fifty years earlier.[14] In the final examination of a university course I taught, one question was, "What did Benjamin Franklin have to do with the population explosion?" A student, who had heard tales about Franklin and the ladies of Paris, wrote, "He caused it!"

This is not to suggest that Franklin's attention to French women was the cause of the Revolution. If that were true, it would have been a far kinder and gentler revolution. Actually, in its earlier, moderate stage, the Revolution met with Franklin's general approval. Because he died in 1790, one year after the beginning of the Revolution, Franklin was spared the later, bloody part that would have caused him much grief and pain. When in 1789, he received news of the violence in the fall of the Bastille, he was concerned about the welfare of his friends but wrote, "The convulsions in France are attended with some disagreeable circumstances, but if by the struggle, she obtains and secures for the country its future liberty and a good constitution, a few years enjoyment of these blessings will amply repair all the damages."[15] In their Revolution Franklin's French friends followed the American example and formulated their own constitution with a one-house legislature like Franklin had in Pennsylvania and had advocated for the United States.

In 1787, after Franklin had returned to America, he received a letter from La Rochefoucald: "France, whom you left talking zealously of liberty for other nations, now begins to think that a small portion of this same liberty will be a very good thing for herself."[16] The same sentiment of impending revolution was expressed in 1787 by Arthur Young, an English traveler in France. He notes "a great ferment in all ranks of men and a strong leaven of liberty, increasing every hour since the American Revolution."[17] Franklin's philosopher friend Condorcet had written "The Influence of the American Revolution on Europe,"[18] and Turgot had said, "America is the hope of the human race and may well become its model." Thomas Morris, the schoolboy son of Robert Morris, the treasurer of the American Revolution, reported that he saw at Franklin's dinner parties in Paris "persons who subsequently became conspicuous actors in the French Revolution."[19]

In 1789, when it arrived, the French Revolution, unlike the American Revolution, was a complex series of convulsions with successive governments and different actors playing leading roles during the various stages. The first stage was a constitutional monarchy (1789–1792); then came a militant republic (1792–1795), with radical zealots' ascendancy to power and the institution of a reign of terror with the execution of King

Louis XVI and Queen Marie Antoinette, many nobles, and political opponents. Then, after several twists and turns (1795–1799), the Revolution ended in 1799 with the seizure of power by Napoleon.[20]

Franklin's friends held power in the early stages of the revolution, but many paid with their lives later on. Among the latter were some of his closest associates: Lavoisier, the great chemist, who at Franklin's request developed a purer saltpeter for America's gunpowder; Le Veillard, Franklin's neighbor, who couldn't bear to see him leave France and accompanied him all the way to Southampton in England; La Rouchefoucald, a duke, the highest rank of nobility next to royalty, who was willing to give up title and privilege for a republic like that in America; Bailly, the astronomer who served with Franklin on a royal scientific commission to investigate mesmerism, an early form of hypnotism; and Condorcet, the distinguished mathematician and philosopher whom Franklin made a member of the American Philosophical Society, the first scientific society in America, which was founded by Franklin.[21] For legally defending the king in court, the famous lawyer Malesherbes and his daughter and grandchildren were executed on the guillotine.[22, 23]

It should be clear that the leaders associated with the gruesome reign of terror were not among Franklin's friends, although they may have had contact with him. Robespierre was a lawyer who had written to Franklin about a case he had involving lightning; Marat, a physician, had requested that Franklin witness his experiment on the nature of fire; and Danton was a member of Franklin's Masonic Lodge. Franklin, however, was a friend of Guillotin, a surgeon whose name was linked to the notorious executioner's instrument, the guillotine, which was used in those political executions. But Guillotin had no part in its use; he had earlier proposed it as more humane, rapid, and impersonal than the traditional axe wielded by the executioner, which formerly had been used to behead criminals.

The effect of the French Revolution on several important friends of Franklin deserves special mention. The first is the Marquis de Lafayette, the wealthy, young idealistic member of the nobility, whose belief in liberty and freedom were to cost him his social position, his fortune, and his freedom. But he won the admiration, love, and respect of the people of both France and America. At the age of twenty, dissatisfied with court life and the tyranny he saw at home, Lafayette decided to go to America to fight on the side of the Americans. Franklin sent a letter to Washington, asking the general to take good care of this fine youth. Washington developed a great fondness for Lafayette, as did Franklin, and later Jefferson. Lafayette fought so courageously in battle that he became an American hero. In 1779, after France had declared itself on America's side, Lafayette returned to France and with Franklin convinced the king to send General Rochambeau and 6,000 troops to fight on the side of the Americans. With this good news Lafayette again joined Washington and helped defeat the British at Yorktown. Back again in France after the peace, he took part in reform politics that preceded the Revolution. Lafayette, the most popular Frenchman in America, became a devoted friend and follower of Franklin, the most popular American in France.[24] When Lafayette asked Franklin his advice on naming his children for America, Franklin responded, "Miss Virginia, Miss Carolina and Miss Georgiana will sound prettily enough for the girls, but Massachusetts and Connecticut are too harsh even for the boys, unless they were to be savages."[25] Lafayette called one of his daughters Virginie and named his son George Washington Lafayette.

Lafayette was a prominent leader of the French Revolution. When the Bastille fell, he gave Tom Paine, who was then in Paris, the keys to the Bastille to take as a gift to Washington. Lafayette was the first member of the National Assembly to call for a Declaration of Rights for the French people. From 1790 to 1792 he was the most powerful man in revolutionary France, as the commander of the national guard. The French Revolution, however, turned out to be quite different from the American Revolution, which had the same government and leaders from beginning to end. The French Revolution was complex, with different governments and different leaders as it proceeded through three stages. From 1790 to 1792, a constitutional monarchy was in place, which instituted the democratic reforms Lafayette had proposed. From 1792 to 1795, the French government was a militant democratic republic. It was broadly represented by a legislative body, the National Convention, but had several political parties hotly vying for power.

When the radical Jacobin party gained control, Lafayette was declared a traitor and had to escape the country, only to be captured by the Austrian army, with whom France was then at war. He was kept in foreign prisons for five years. This actually proved fortunate for him because he escaped the reign of terror by the Paris mob, which was let loose by his zealous, radical enemies and which resulted in the execution of the king and queen and some twenty thousand aristocrats and political opponents of the ruling party.

Disgust with this bloodshed led to a third state of the Revolution, in 1795, the formation of a moderate republic, which ended when Napoleon grabbed power in 1799. Lafayette returned to France in 1799 but refused political office under Napoleon, until 1815, when Napoleon returned from Elba and gave France a liberal constitution. He then served as vice president of the chamber of deputies and continued for the rest of his life to aid other countries in winning independence or reforms for their governments. Lafayette lost his fortune in the upheaval of the Revolution, but the American Congress gratefully voted him $200,000 and huge grants of land in Louisiana and Florida.[26] His name was honored again a century later when, in World War I, the American volunteers were called "The Lafayette Esquadrille," and when the American expeditionary force landed in France, General Pershing made his famous statement, "Lafayette, we are here."[27]

Another friend Franklin sent to America became the greatest revolutionary of his time. He was not French, but English. When Franklin met Thomas Paine in England in 1774, he found they had similar ideas. Franklin sent him to America with a letter of recommendation, as he had done for Lafayette. In America, Paine went to work as a journalist and, in response to Franklin's suggestion, wrote a pamphlet about the political conditions in America in 1775 and 1776, which he titled "Common Sense." This pamphlet electrified America and aroused the populace to the struggle for independence. Paine then wrote "The Crisis," which opened with the stirring words, "These are the times that try men's souls," and gave the people the will and courage to stick it out when the fortunes of war were most bleak. He also served as a soldier and was proclaimed an American hero for his services. After the war Paine went to Europe to sell his invention of an iron bridge. He was armed with letters of recommendation from Franklin, but he got involved in politics in England and tried to stir up a revolution there. William Pitt, the prime minister, said, "If I were to encourage Tom Paine's opinions we should have a bloody revolution." Paine was indicted for treason in England in 1792 but escaped to France, where revolutionary ideas were in favor. The assembly of the revolutionary government honored Paine by making him a citizen of France. He became a celebrated figure in Paris and was elected to the National Convention, a government body of 749 members, in which he was conspicuous by being non–French. Like Franklin's other friends, he opposed the terror, for which he was arrested and put into prison, where he was slated for execution. He was saved only because his door, marked with an X, was swung open and the guard missed seeing it. After nine months, James Monroe, the future president, came to Paris and demanded Paine's release as an American citizen. After much difficulty he was successful. Paine then went back and took his seat in the Convention but soon was disgusted and returned to the United States, where he spent the rest of his life. He wrote two books, *The Rights of Man* and *The Age of Reason*, both of which were revolutionary not only in his time but at any time.[28] In Paris, the French erected a gilded statue of Paine with an inscription that reads: "Thomas Paine, 1737–1809;

Citizen of the World, Englishman by Birth, American by Adoption, French Citizen by Decree."

Another follower of Franklin was Brissot de Warville.[29] Like so many of the French intellectuals, he was influenced by the social contract of Rousseau and the writings of Voltaire. The American Declaration of Independence in 1776 electrified him and made him ardently pro American. When Franklin arrived in Paris, Brissot started thinking realistically of bringing freedom and democracy to France. He wrote, "The dignity of man consists in his liberty, in his equality before the law, in his independence, in his subjection only to those laws to which he has given his consent, in the control he exercises over those he has entrusted political authority."[30] Like Franklin, who became president of the first antislavery society in America, Brissot was an abolitionist who organized an antislavery society in France. Among the members of this society were Franklin's friends Mirabeau, Lafayette, and Condorcet.

Brissot was a member of Franklin's Masonic Lodge in Paris. He met Franklin again in Philadelphia during an extended trip he took to the United States in 1788. He found the old statesman at home surrounded by the books, which Franklin said he still called his best friends. Brissot noted that the pain caused Franklin by the stone and gout had not altered the serenity of his countenance or the calm of his conversation, which had made such an impression on the French people of Paris, but he was now more at ease and "no longer wears that chilling mask of reserve which his diplomatic position formerly forced upon him." He found Franklin surrounded by his family like an "ancient patriarch philosopher who had come down from the high spheres to bring instruction to simple mortals."[31]

Brissot traveled widely in the United States, visiting George Washington, John Adams, and Samuel Adams. He was interested in everything American: the condition of Negroes, maple sugar as a substitute for cane sugar, diseases and life expectancy in the United States, the American debt, and the Quakers and their customs. He had planned for a longer visit but hurried back to France when he heard the news that a revolution was stirring. He writes in his memoirs: "Indignant against the despotism under which France suffered, I traveled to the United States of America to learn there how to carry out in my own country a similar revolution."[32] He cites Franklin's *Poor Richard's Almanac* as an indirect cause of the French Revolution because of its effect on the "enlightenment and aspirations of the French people for liberty."[33]

Back in Paris, he threw himself heart and soul into the Revolution. He published a revolutionary newspaper and became a prominent leader in the Legislative Assembly and the National Convention. He was one of the first to propose that France become a republic and hoped to spread the Revolution across Europe. His political maneuvering allowed him to become head of the liberal party, the Girondins. While he favored the removal of the king from the government, he voted against the death penalty for him. This and the intense bitterness of rival party politics resulted in Brissot's being sent to the guillotine when his party was overthrown by the radical Jacobins. Like so many of Franklin's friends, he became a victim of the Revolution he had led.[34]

Pierre Samuel Du Pont was one of Franklin's oldest and most intimate French friends. He met Du Pont in 1769 on his second visit to France when he was on a lengthy tour of duty in England serving as a spokesman for Pennsylvania and other colonies to the British government. Du Pont was a physiocrat, the name given to members of a group attempting to put economics on a scientific basis. Always open to new ideas, Franklin eagerly fell in with Du Pont and his colleagues. When Franklin arrived in Paris in 1776, their close association continued. Franklin knew how to please people. When Du Pont's son Victor visited Franklin in America in 1787, Franklin wrote about Victor in a letter to Madame Lavoisier, knowing full well that she would tell her friends, the Du Ponts. He said, "I like young Mr. Du Pont. He appears a very sensible and valuable man, and I think his father will have a great deal of satisfaction in him."[35]

Like Turgot, Du Pont was a fiscal conservative and opposed expenditures for war, but because of Franklin, he strongly supported the American cause. Before the Revolution he worked for fiscal reforms in the government but without success. When the French Revolution came, he was active in the States General and was elected president of the Constituent Assembly. When Franklin, in America, heard about the Revolution he wrote Du Pont that he was sorry for the troubles in France but hoped for beneficial consequences. It didn't turn out that way for Du Pont. He was a moderate and, after 1792, when the Revolution turned more radical, he was outspoken in his disagreement. When the mob attacked the palace where the king and queen were residing, he and his son guarded Louis XVI and his family. For this he was forced to go into hiding but was caught and imprisoned, escaping the guillotine only because of Robespierre's fall from power.

For a while Du Pont left public life but became active again in 1795, when he was elected to the Council of Elders. The political tides turned again, and he again found himself in prison. Upon his release he recalled Franklin's stories about America, and in 1799 he emigrated to the United States. However, in 1802 he returned to France and, after Napoleon's downfall, became secretary of the provisional government. When Napoleon returned in 1815, Du Pont left France for good, returning to America, where his sons were now citizens. He did very well in America, for on his first trip he set up with his younger son a gunpowder factory, which was very successful. The son, Eleuthère Irénée, had learned how to make gunpowder in France as a protégé of Lavoisier. Over the years this company, E. I. Du Pont de Nemours, was to become the largest chemical company in the world, the developer of nylon, orlon, teflon, and hundreds of other products.[36]

In France Franklin hobnobbed with the titled nobility and clergy, but at heart he was a democrat with a basic dislike for titles of distinction. As a lad of seventeen, he had written:

> In old time it was no disrespect for men and women to be called by their own names: Adam was never called Master Adam; we never read of Noah, Esquire, Lot, Knight and Baronet, nor the Right Honorable Abraham, Viscount of Mesopotamia, Baron of Carron; no, no, they were plain men, honest country graziers, that took care of their families and their flocks.[37]

In 1784 Franklin saw newspapers sent by his daughter in America telling about an American organization recently started by retired army officers, called the Society of the Cincinnati, with members assuming hereditary titles by eldest sons, like the aristocracy of Europe. He wrote a letter to his daughter vehemently expressing his contempt for the practice, especially in America, where a person's worth depended on what he had accomplished, not on his birth. Franklin argued that while the person first receiving the title might have earned it, his progeny had not and did not deserve it. If one allowed that this practice was proper because the characteristics that made the title worthy were passed down through the blood line, Franklin calculated that in nine generations, the blood would be diluted 512 times through marriages. Further, he maintained that the title made the recipient proud and disdainful of useful labor, as was the case with the nobility in Europe.[38]

In an indirect way Franklin helped provoke sentiment against this medieval practice of hereditary aristocracy, which he felt was the cause of the autocratic rule and economic injustice that existed in France. He told his friend Mirabeau of his opposition to the Society of the Cincinnati. Mirabeau, himself a member of the aristocracy with the title of count, was, like Lafayette, La Rochefoucald, and other titled friends of Franklin, fair minded enough to see the injustice of the financial privileges of the aristocracy, and he fought for reform of the government. Using Franklin's arguments, Mirabeau published a satire that ridiculed not only the Cincinnati Society but also nobility in general, a dangerous undertaking for a French citizen at that time. This satire was circulated widely in France and England. This is the same Mirabeau who in 1789 was the leading orator of the Revolution and was called "the Tribune of the People." [39]

To save him embarrassment, Franklin's letter on the Cincinnati was not published in France during his lifetime, but three months after his death it was published in full as a weapon by the Revolution to destroy the system of hereditary nobility. Franklin himself was used as an argument against the system: He was a self-made man, distinguished for his achievements, and he alone, not his descendants, deserved the honor bestowed upon him.

In the early days of the American Revolution, when the battles were all in favor of the English, Franklin would always respond to French inquiries about the news from America with the words, "Ça ira" [everything will be all right]. He became associated with this phrase, which proved to be accurate in the case of America. In the French Revolution, "Ça ira" became a popular revolutionary song, indicating how much the common people associated Franklin with their own revolution and how much he inspired them. John Adams said they believed Franklin's plans "were to abolish monarchy, aristocracy and hierarchy throughout the world."

When Franklin left France, his position as American ambassador was filled by another revolutionary hero, the author of the Declaration of Independence, Thomas Jefferson. Franklin introduced Jefferson to his French friends who shared his feelings, like Lafayette and Du Pont, who soon became close friends of Jefferson as well. When the French people met Jefferson they asked, "Oh, you have come to replace Dr. Franklin?" To which Jefferson replied, "No, I have come to succeed him. No one could replace him." This reply delighted the French, and it quickly made the rounds of Paris. Jefferson said, "The succession to Dr. Franklin at the Court of France was an excellent school of humility."[40]

The immediate cause of the French Revolution was the bankruptcy of the French treasury. This made it necessary for the king to call a meeting of the States General, which brought the commoners and the liberal reformers into the decision-making process. The commoners, comprising ninety-five percent of the population, had only thirty-three percent of the vote in the States General. They demanded fifty percent, but the king, under pressure from the nobility and clergy, refused, thus lighting the fuse that produced the explosion.

The question is, why was the government bankrupt? It is well known that the king, like his predecessors, was recklessly extravagant. In 1785, with the treasury teetering, the king bought the queen a palace costing millions as a present on the birth of their second child — as if the palace at Versailles, with hundreds of rooms was too cramped. Other available royal palaces included Fountainbleau, the Tuilleries, the Louvre, the Luxembourg, and more. The administration of the government and tax collection were grossly inefficient and fraught with favoritism and fraud. But the push that toppled this financial house of cards was the money spent supporting the American Revolution. This included paying for the French expeditionary force of six thousand men; the naval flotilla of twenty-eight ships with nineteen thousand men and munitions for seventeen hundred cannon; and the weapons, gunpowder, and uniforms to supply thirty thousand American troops. In cash alone, the king gave America 10 million livres* in gifts and 45 million more in loans without collateral.[41] Turgot, the French minister of finance, had warned the king that expenditures supporting the American Revolution would bankrupt the treasury, but the king went ahead anyway.

And who convinced the king to make this historic decision? None other than the amiable ambassador (then called minister plenipotentiary), Benjamin Franklin. He alone must be credited with convincing the French to side with America and to dig into their treasury to finance our war. It was neither John Adams nor any other American in Paris for that matter. The fact is that Vergennes, the French foreign minister, who advised the king in these matters, refused even to speak to any American except Franklin. Adams' strident manner particularly irritated him. Vergennes trusted Franklin, whose agreeable, placid posture produced results with this French aristocrat. Jefferson, who spent two years with Franklin in France, said of him, "He possessed the confidence of that government in the highest degree, inasmuch, that it may truly be said that they were more under his influence than he under theirs."[42] America could not have won the war without French help, and Franklin's success in obtaining it is often hailed as the single proudest achievement in our diplomatic history.

Franklin frequently professed his love for France, and his conduct during the nine years he resided there proved his sincerity. He said he "loved the King as a father." It is not clear whether Franklin meant that he felt like a father to the king or that the king was the father, as father of his country. Although almost fifty years older than the king, in one respect

*One livre equaled about 20 cents in U.S. money in 1790. Consider, due to the lower standard of living then, that money could buy much more than now. For example, a $1.50 loaf of bread today cost two cents then.

Franklin did resemble a son to the king, that is in the traditional role of the son asking the father for money. Franklin pressed the king again and again for funds and was successful in getting them. He committed a diplomatic affront by having secretly negotiated peace with the English without notifying the French allies. He knew that the French had their own political agenda, which could have torpedoed the peace treaty. Although he was chastised by Vergennes, Franklin then had the temerity to go again to the king and ask for more money. Thanks to his remarkable persuasive skill, he got it.[43, 44]

In his book *Franklin the Diplomat*, Jonathon Dull indicates reasons for Franklin's success as a diplomat:

> Franklin's caution, prudence, and common sense paid off in his winning and keeping the confidence of the French government. No blustering Adams or hostile Jay, Franklin's politeness could mask a threat, cover a change of policy, or create a desired impression, while always leaving him a little line of retreat. Such skill could not be learned from books. Adams studied diligently and could not have been less suited to life at the French court; Franklin apparently didn't bother.[45]

To appreciate Franklin's personal presence, consider the fact that Turgot did not protest when the king opened his purse for America. Turgot was a leading member of the French economist school, which was then in vogue among rich bankers and officials. They were aware of France's financial plight and opposed military aid for America because all the money was needed for France's own financial solvency. Furthermore, Turgot and these men were pacifists who opposed war aid for that reason. But Turgot was also a friend of Franklin. According to Bernard Fay, a French Franklin biographer:

> When Turgot was alone he gave his pacifism free reign, but when Franklin was on the scene, his love for America took the upper hand. Thus, Franklin counterbalanced the pacifist theories of the economists and other philosophers, which might have been dangerous for America, simply by his presence. More than this, he turned the enormous influence of this famous school in the favor of America, which was a big step toward the control of public opinion.[46]

Thus Turgot, along with Du Pont, the leaders of the opposition to financial disaster, were completely neutralized by their devotion to

Franklin. When Franklin died in 1790, the French Revolutionary government honored him with more recognition than even his own government had given him. Mirabeau eulogized him in the National Assembly for his great work in the service of liberty. Condorcet eulogized him before the Academy of Sciences, acknowledging Franklin's inspiration for the French to obtain their liberties as America had done. The eminent physician Vicq dAzyr delivered the eulogy to the Royal Society of Medicine, and for the Paris Commune, which played such an important part in the revolution. The eulogy was delivered eloquently by the Abbé Fauchet, with the mayor, a delegation from the National Assembly, and four thousand ordinary citizens in attendance. The printers met and listened to an oration in Franklin's honor, then immediately struck it off in type for distribution to the public. Franklin had never forgotten his trade. He had a private printing press on his premises in Paris and sometimes would visit printers in the city. All the people of Paris celebrated Franklin's name and deeds in the cafes and in the streets.[47] They owed him a great debt; he had shown them the way to obtain their liberty as he done for his own country.

The interesting fact is that Franklin never intended to foment a revolution in France. As a diplomat he never said anything that would offend his royal host and jeopardize his own government's position. He would have been happy to see reforms such as his friends espoused, the institution of human rights and the elimination of special privilege. In his own country he had championed freedom of speech, press, and religion, as well as taxation with representation. These were achieved. He also espoused freedom for the slaves, fair treatment for the Indians, and the right to vote without ownership of property, none of which were achieved. As a practical man he was willing to take half a loaf and wait for more. In France, however, the ingredients for a revolution had accumulated, and his very presence added the little extra heat that made the explosion occur.

French people high and low knew that he stood with them, and the Revolution honored him as one of their greatest heroes. In fact, they made him a saint. When the Convention invented a new calendar, starting in 1793 as year one, and gave new names to the months, the days which previously honored saints were replaced with days honoring Republican heroes, and June 12 was set aside to honor Benjamin Franklin.[48] This revolutionary calendar was terminated by Napoleon in 1805, but Franklin is still remembered in France with affection and appreciation. A statue of Franklin in Paris contains a bas-relief showing Franklin at the court of Louis XVI in Versailles and at the Treaty of Paris in 1783. With words from Mirabeau's eulogy, the plaque reads: "Benjamin Franklin, 1706–1790, the genius who freed America and flooded Europe with light: the sage two worlds call their own."[49]

It was likely more than coincidence that when Lafayette spoke at Boston, Franklin's birthplace, on his triumphal return visit to America in 1825, he chose the symbolism of the electric spark to demonstrate that the liberty he referred to was associated with his old friend Franklin:

> Heaven saw fit to ordain that the electric spark of liberty should be conducted through you from the new world to the old.[50]

7

Benjamin Franklin,
Money Maker

Benjamin Franklin made his money the old fashioned way—he printed it. During his career as a printer, Franklin was authorized to print money for Pennsylvania, New Jersey, and Delaware. In those early days before the American Revolution, each English colony issued its own money and designated a private printer to provide it. From 1728 to1753, and to 1764 with a partner, Franklin printed about 2.5 million paper notes on his hand-operated press.[1] Franklin had competitors, not his fellow printers, but fellows who were not authorized to print money but did so anyway. They were the counterfeiters. To deter these swindlers, Franklin became America's first fighter against counterfeiting, called the world's second oldest profession.

The most serious problem of the eighteenth-century money printers was the counterfeiting of paper money or the alteration of good money to increase its value. Counterfeiting was a serious crime for which the counterfeiter could receive the ultimate punishment, the death penalty, but efforts to prevent it were usually unsuccessful. Franklin gave the counterfeiters fair warning, by printing clearly on each bill the statement, "To Counterfeit is Death."

The crime persisted nevertheless, and methods had to be found to distinguish bogus bills from legitimate ones. One method Franklin devised was to incorporate a mineral, a type of mica, into the paper. Like all other

Figure 7.1 Two Delaware notes with the warning "To Counterfeit is Death."
Left: Printed by Franklin and partner, David Hall. *Right:* Printed by James
Adams. (By permission of Eric P. Newman.)

strategies, this was to make duplication of bills difficult. The counterfeiters did not have access to the manufacture of paper, whereas Franklin
owned several paper mills. Over the years he produced different kinds of
paper to obstruct the cheaters; for example, he supplied two types of poly-
chromed or marbled paper, a lightweight paper produced in 1775 for the
new Continental U.S. $20 bills and a stronger paper in 1789 for smaller
notes issued by the Bank of North America.

Another method Franklin employed was ornamentation. He used
many kinds of type that he had in his print shop; type that he had obtained
from England and that counterfeiters would not likely have. He purposely
mixed several type fonts in one bill: Old English, small pica, old brevier,
great primer, along with crooked letters, planets, flowers, and even his
own homemade ornaments. Other printers followed his lead, using Greek
letters, Hebrew letters, zodiac signs, and so on, to embellish the bills.[2]

One trick of the crooks was to alter genuine bills to increase their
worth several times. Since all the notes of different denominations were
alike except for the printed notation of value, they simply erased the num
ber denominating the value and, by drawing or pasting on a larger number,

made a new, higher-value bill. Thus a two-shilling note could become a fifty-shilling note. Franklin searched his fertile imagination to confound this skullduggery and came up with an unusual scheme, which he used on four different denominations of Pennsylvania notes, to be able to tell whether they had been tampered with. He purposely spelled Pennsylvania a different way on each denomination bill: Pennsylvania, Pensylvania, Pennsilvania, and Pensilvania. Thus, if you were aware of the spelling you could readily determine whether you had been swindled. Raising the value of each bill, one at a time, was time consuming to the average colonial counterfeiter, but he considered it a lot better than farming, his honest alternative.

The real aristocrats among the counterfeiters were the engravers, who could make a reasonable or even an excellent imitation of the real thing and then print it off in great numbers in no time. The engravers were artists, who sculptured metal printing plates. To make it difficult for the engravers, Franklin decorated the bills with elaborate embellishments he obtained from Europe; however, the counterfeiters were resourceful fellows, able to locate the sources of the printer's ornaments and obtain them for their own nefarious handiwork.

Nature Printing

Then Franklin came up with a unique invention, called nature printing, to make the engraver's work much more difficult and time consuming. Nature printing is the production of a printed image of a natural object from the object itself. Franklin didn't invent nature printing; he invented a way to apply it to printing. Centuries earlier, Leonardo da Vinci had produced the image of a botanical specimen when he rolled ink on the specimen and then transferred the image to paper. Over the years this process was used by many others, including Franklin's friend, Joseph Breintnal, who made and sold fine quality nature prints of botanical specimens to museums and collectors (Figure 7.2). Franklin was aware of the process for he had advertised Breintnal's prints in his newspaper. Then, in the 1737 edition of his *Almanac*, Franklin displayed a print of the leaf of an herb called the rattlesnake plant.[3] This leaf identified the plant, which, Franklin explained to his readers, the Indians used to cure a rattlesnake bite. But how did Franklin make this reproduction in the *Almanac*? Until then it had not been possible to reproduce these specimens for a publication when many copies were required. This was because the leaf became crushed after a few copies were made. It was necessary to make a rigid negative of the

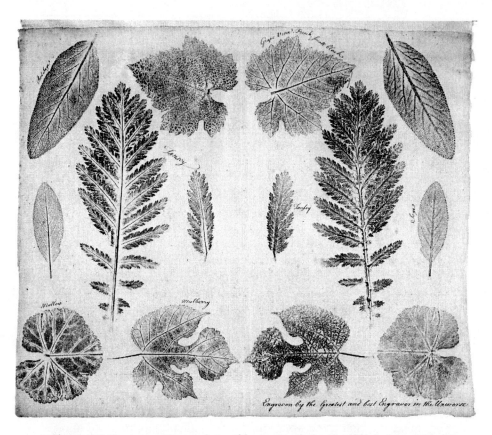

Figure 7.2 Contact nature prints of leaves made by Franklin's friend Joseph Breintnal between 1731 and 1742. (By permission of Library Co. of Philadelphia.)

leaf for use in the printing process, but not for more than a hundred years was that to become possible through the invention of photography.

How then did Franklin do it in the *Almanac*? We are not sure. He may have tried to make a plaster cast of the leaf, but this would not work because he would have had to pour hot lead into the plaster cast to make a plate, and that would crack the plaster. Yet, from an examination of the leaf prints he made, it is evident that a lead plate had been used in printing the leaf. Franklin never revealed how he did it; he kept it a secret. This was unusual, for he published full information on all his other inventions, saying that since he enjoyed the benefits of the inventions of the people who came before him, he paid his debt to society by giving his inventions free to the public instead of patenting and profiting from them. This case,

Figure 7.3 Face and back of 1739 Pennsylvania bill printed by Franklin with new, leaf design. (By permission of Eric P. Newman.)

however, was different since he printed money with the leaf and he did not want to give away that process to the counterfeiters. The reason Franklin used the leaf imprint on paper money was that leaves, like fingerprints, were unique and no two leaves were identical, so no leaf he selected could be exactly duplicated. In addition, the veins in leaves are of tapering thickness making it extremely difficult for the engraver to copy them precisely, and the leaf's texture is complex, making it an ideal design to deter counterfeiters of paper money.

Although Franklin's life and activities have been researched for 200 years, it was not until 1963 that the secret of his invention may have been discovered. Eric Newman, a distinguished numismatist studying America's early paper money, noticed that the leaf imprint had never appeared in print before the 1737 appearance of Franklin's *Almanac*. Then, it appeared only on money printed by Franklin or that of printers he worked with. Leaf prints appeared on New Jersey bills Franklin printed in March 1737, and were used on the money of four other colonies and later for the first paper currency issued at the outbreak of the American Revolution. It was used consistently to protect the Continental currency but was never used after Franklin's death.[4]

In 1963, Ivy N. Steele, a resident of Chicago, did experimental work to fathom Franklin's secret process for leaf printing. She knew that a plaster negative would fracture from the heat when a lead positive was made from it and deduced that Franklin must have included some heat-resistant ingredients like brick dust, pulverized asbestos, or refractory clays in the plaster to keep it from cracking. After this plaster had set, Steele baked out much of the moisture in the mold and used this negative mold to cast a thin, positive lead plate from which the leaf could be printed off in as many copies as desired. Additional castings could also be made from the same negative for multiple usage. Steele tested her hypothesis and concluded that this was the way Franklin made his plates to print the leaf.[5]

Franklin and American Paper Money

The paper money of other printers was influenced by Franklin. For example, they used his warning to counterfeiters, To Counterfeit is Death. One printer in Georgia used his own very original, but enigmatic, version which read:

TIEFRETNUOCEDIVSIYGRELCFOTIFENEBTUOHTIWHTAEDTCAOT.

To make sense out of this puzzle it has to be read backward, then separated into words, and the words rearranged. It then says, "To counterfeit is death, without benefit of clergy, vide act." The last two words come from Latin for "See the act."[6]

Paper money was a late development in the long history of money. First money consisted of many things, such as unusual beads and shells. (The expression "shell out" meaning "to pay" comes from the use of shells as money.) These were replaced by gold, silver, and copper, and then, to save merchants the trouble of having to weigh out the metal with each trade, the metals were stamped into coins of definite size and weight. Only when the metal was considered too bulky, or when it was not in sufficient supply, was paper money resorted to. Benjamin Franklin didn't invent paper money: It was first used by the emperors in China, where (as reported by Marco Polo in AD 1200) it was made from the bark of the mulberry tree. But in the Western world paper money was not used until 1661, when it was used in Sweden for private transactions.

America has the unique distinction of being the first place in the Western world where governments authorized and issued paper money. Canada used paper money in 1685 as a temporary expedient to pay the military when the payroll from France was delayed, but the province of Massachusetts Bay publicly authorized paper money in 1690, and eventually the other colonies followed suit. This was because most of the gold and silver was drained from the colonies to pay for imports from overseas.

At first, paper money was issued to pay for military expeditions such as King William's war and Queen Anne's war, and for major public projects, but eventually it found its way into general circulation.[7] The British government, the colonies' major creditor, frowned on the colonies' use of paper money, fearing it would be depreciated by inflation. Paper money stimulated business, but it did lead to inflation, and America has the dubious distinction of having the first depreciation in value of publicly issued paper, when by 1713, Massachusetts Bay paper money depreciated by 50 percent, and by 1749 by 1,100 percent. Rhode Island and North and South Carolina also had similar problems with the inflation and depreciation of their paper money.[8] The early paper bills were termed "bills of credit" to distinguish them from real money (metal coins), indicating a borrowing for a specific public expenditure rather than the issuance of a circulating medium. Throughout the colonial period in America, Britain put tight restrictions on the colonies' issuance of paper money, at times prohibiting it entirely.[9, 10] Parliament was determined to protect the monetary interests of its merchants regardless of the effect on the economy of the colonies, which eventually became a major factor leading to the Revolution.[11, 12]

In 1728, Pennsylvania had been undergoing an unfavorable balance of trade with England, with money scarce and prices and interest rates high. Tradespeople, workers, and debtors agitated for paper money to relieve the currency shortage, but moneyed people opposed it for fear of inflation. Franklin, a tradesman, worker, and debtor, who at the age of 22 had just started his printing business, entered the controversy with a pamphlet titled "A Modest Enquiry into the Nature and Necessity of a Paper Currency," in which he made a strong case for paper money.[13] True, he agreed, Pennsylvania had little gold and silver as security for its paper money, but it had land. Franklin wrote, "As bills issued upon money security [gold and silver] are money, so bills issued upon land are, in effect, coined land." He made his case, persuading the Pennsylvania legislature to vote to issue paper money. In his autobiography, Franklin commented, his friends in the legislature, "who conceived I had been of some service, thought fit to reward me by employing me in printing the money: a very profitable job and of great help to me."[14]

When he was American agent in London, Franklin attempted to get the British government to relax its rigid position toward the colonial paper money, but without success. Generally, it relaxed only for special government projects or during wartime for the purchase of military supplies. In 1768, however, Franklin was more successful. Lord Hillsborough, British secretary of state for American affairs, although no friend of colonial paper money, admitted he had read Franklin's 1728 pamphlet in favor of colonial paper currency and said if Pennsylvania, New Jersey, and New York submitted applications for issuance of paper money as Franklin had proposed, he would not oppose them as he had done the previous year.[15] This, however, was just a temporary reprieve from the restrictions on the colonies, which became tighter than ever with a series of punitive tax laws, causing the colonies to revolt. Richard Hoober states that the money problems and the British government's blind refusal to assist the colonists in this matter, more than the spectacular events with emotional overtones like the Boston Massacre and the Boston Tea Party, had created deep-rooted resentment on the part of the Americans. He further states, "Through more than forty years, no single person was more influential at home and abroad, in pressing for a solution to the problem than Benjamin Franklin."[16]

During the whole colonial period, the colonists in their assemblies fought back against the restrictions. For example, the New York assembly refused to pay the royal governor's salary for one year until he approved the 1737 paper money issue. In Massachusetts, Governor Shute's salary was reduced because of his unfriendly attitude toward paper money, while later, Governor Shirley had his allowances increased because of his more tolerant position.[17]

Although Franklin favored paper money, he was fiscally conservative and keenly aware of the possibility of inflation and its tendency to depreciate the currency. That is why he wanted the paper to be backed by something of real value, land, if not gold and silver. Later, during the Revolution, when Congress discussed issuing paper money, Franklin spoke in opposition, proposing taxes instead, as a way of raising money to pay for the war. Congress had no stomach for taxation and issued the paper Continentals instead. Franklin later wrote, "I took all the pains I could in Congress to prevent the depreciation by proposing that the bills should bear interest." This was rejected. Then, after the first emission of printed money, he wrote, "I proposed we should stop, strike no more, but borrow on interest those we had issued and ... to fix the value of the principal, the interest should be promised in hard dollars." When this advice was ignored and the currency had been devalued by excessive issuance of printing-press money, Franklin said, "The only remedy now seems to be a diminution of the quantity by a vigorous taxation." Congress did not heed this counsel either.

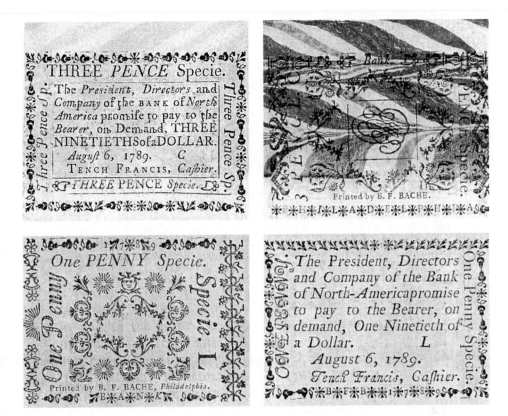

Figure 7.4 Front and back of 1778 one-penny and three-penny, anticounterfeit bills with colored swirls, a process Franklin brought back from France. (Courtesy of Museum of American Financial History.)

After the inflation occurred, Franklin commented that the Europeans were mystified by how America was able to carry on a war so long so successfully with such money. He then philosophized, with tongue in cheek:

> This currency, as we manage it, is a wonderful machine. It performs its office when we issue it: it pays and clothes troops, and provides victuals and ammunition; and when we are obliged to issue a quantity excessive, it pays itself off by depreciation.[19] But this depreciation, tho' in some circumstances inconvenient, has the general good and great effect of operating as a tax, and perhaps the most equal of all taxes, since it depreciated in the hands of the holders of money, and thereby taxed them in proportion to the sums they held and the time they held it which generally is in proportion to men's wealth.[20]

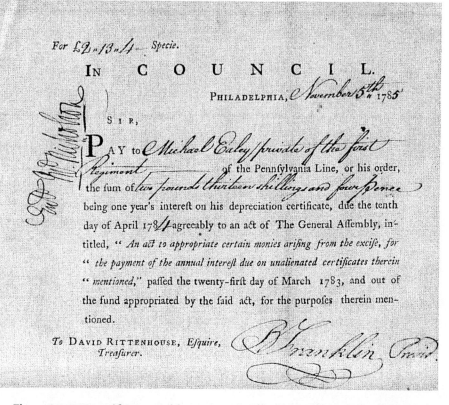

Figure 7.5 1785 certificate payable as money by the state of Pennsylvania, signed by Franklin in his capacity as president of the state, a position no longer in existence. (Courtesy of Museum of American Financial History.)

But one way in which Congress followed Franklin's advice was to put flecks of mica, called isinglass in the paper used to print the money to make it harder to duplicate. When from 1776 to 1785 when Franklin was in France as the representative of the U.S. government to that country, he learned a method for printing paper money with colored swirls, which he used to confuse the counterfeiters. When he returned home, he had his grandson, Benjamin Franklin Bache, whom he had set up as a printer, print some of these types of bills as U.S. money. One such bill had swirls of red, orange, and blue across a cream-colored background (Figure 7.4). When Franklin was made president of Pennsylvania (a position no longer in existence) among his other duties, he signed certificates, like cash, payable by the state of Pennsylvania (Figure 7.5).

Each year in *Poor Richard's Almanac*, Franklin included mottoes and wise sayings to encourage moral and successful living. He believed in these sayings and often quoted them in his letters and other writings. He felt it was important to keep these moral, practical ideas in front of the public, and when the Continental Congress appointed him to the committee to make the paper money he saw to it that the notes served as a billboard to carry these messages. One bill he created had a picture of the sun's rays and a sundial with the caption "Fugio (Latin for the sun saying, 'I fly') Mind Your Business," meaning "Time flies so get on with your business." His *Almanac* for 1748 presented a similar thought, "Lost time is never found." Other messages he proposed are: "The fear of the Lord is the beginning of wisdom," "Keep thy shop and thy shop will keep thee," "He that buys what he has no need of will soon be forced to sell his necessities," and "In a corrupt age, putting the world in order will breed confusion."

Franklin was also responsible for the first American political cartoon, which shows a snake cut into a number of separate pieces, each labeled with the initials of a colony and followed with the message, "Join or Die" (Chapter 1, Figure 1.1). This was his attempt in 1754 to get the separate colonies to join forces to fight the French and Indian War. For the first Continental currency, paper and coins, Franklin employed a similar

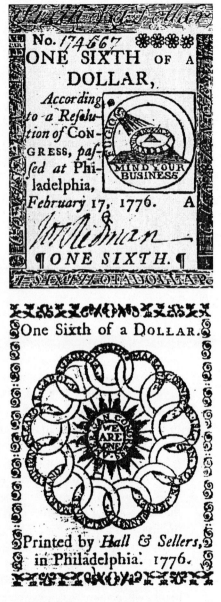

Figure 7.6 (top) "Sundial bill." Face of 1776 continental paper currency with moralistic design by Benjamin Franklin. The image of the sundial is meant to remind the bearer of the bill to get on with his business — time is flying! (By permission of Eric P. Newman.) *Figure 7.7 (bottom)* "WE ARE ONE." Back side of sundial bill with Franklin's sketch signifying the unification of the colonies into the United States. (By permission of Eric P. Newman.)

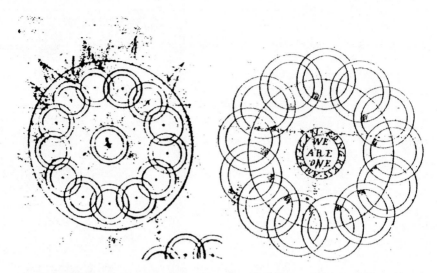

Figure 7.8 Franklin's original sketches for the design of the sundial bill. (By permission of Eric P. Newman.)

concept for a patriotic cartoon showing the unity of the colonies, now become states in a central government. It shows thirteen interlocking circles, each with the name of one of the original states, and in the center is pictured a sunburst. Inside that is a smaller circle around which are the words "American Congress," and in the center of the small circle is the message "WE ARE ONE."[21] Franklin's ingenuity and dexterity is demonstrated by these figures and by his ability to divide a circle into thirteen equal arcs to locate center points to draw the links. The first official coin minted for the new United States government was the 1787 Fugio cent (Figure 7.9), referred to by numismatists as the "Franklin cent," with the same face and back as the bill. During the colonial period there were no American coins, their having been forbidden by England; furthermore, the colonies lacked the necessary gold and silver. Instead, the coins used in the colonies were English, French, Portuguese, and Spanish. The Spanish-milled dollar was a favorite, and to make lower denominations it was cut into eight pieces called "bits" or "pieces of eight," thus two bits equaled a quarter of a dollar, and four bits a half dollar. Similarly, paper bills were cut into smaller pieces when there was a shortage of small-denomination paper money.[23] In this period, before steamships, most shipping and distance transportation was by sailing ships which depended on the wind, a symbol that Franklin depicted in a sketch used for paper currency (Figure 7.10).

Even after his death in 1790, Franklin's influence on U.S. coinage is evident when the mint, in its first coins, produced the large cent, half cent,

Figure 7.9 The Fugio cent, 1787, designed by Benjamin Franklin. This was the first coin issued by the United States government. *Top:* Face and back of a reproduction of the Fugio cent by the Gallery Mint Museum, Eureka Springs, AR. *Bottom:* Face and back of original Fugio coins. (Courtesy of Ken Bressett.)

and dollar coins showing the female liberty head with flowing hair. This depiction was copied from the 1783 "Liberatus Americana" medal designed in France at Franklin's instigation, and he sent the medals to Congress for its approval of the use of this symbol on U.S. coins[24] (Figure 7.11). The Bank of North America — planned by Alexander Hamilton — when created, was responsible for carrying on the war and the relative financial stability of the United States in the postwar period. Franklin also played an important part in the founding of this bank. Robert Morris, supervisor of U.S. finance, in 1781 submitted the plan for the bank to Franklin in France, who obtained capital from eminent Paris bankers to invest in the bank, allowing it to be incorporated on December 31, 1781, by the Continental Congress. In the copper panic of 1789 Franklin again came to the aid of the bank. The only small coins in circulation in Pennsylvania were New York and Connecticut copper coins, as well as genuine and counterfeit English half-pence. In 1788 these coins dropped in value and continued to glut the

Figure 7.10 **Original sketch by Franklin honoring sailors and sailing ships. Used on 1775–1777 continental currency, faces of $20 and backs of $30. Motto: *Vi Ventorum Concitate*, meaning "driven by the wind." (By permission of Eric P. Newman.)**

market until the middle of 1789, when they became unacceptable, their circulation stopped and small trade was paralyzed.

Franklin suggested a solution to his son-in-law, Richard Bache, who was on the board of directors of the bank, namely that the bank should use small paper notes to supply the public's need for change during the interruption in the circulation of copper coin. He also presented a sheet of a very peculiar fabric, which he said would be most suitable for the purpose. He had in his possession only two reams of this marbled paper, which he would give to the bank for this use. The board resolved that Benjamin Franklin Bache, Franklin's grandson, who was now set up as a printer in Philadelphia, would print notes of one-ninetieth and three-ninetieths of a dollar. Why these unusual denominations? Because a Spanish dollar had exchange value of seven shillings six pence, or forty pence in Pennsylvania currency, and one penny was therefore equivalent to one-ninetieth of

Figure 7.11 Liberty head 1793–1795 coins with flowing hair, proposed by Franklin before his death in 1790. Based upon medals by French artist Dupre, celebrating the French Revolution. *Top:* Faces of one-cent coins. *Left:* One-dollar coin. (Courtesy of Ken Bressett.)

a Spanish dollar. To make these notes acceptable, they would be equivalent to specie (metallic money) and payable as such on demand.[25]

In 1779 Franklin wrote home from France proposing for the money "some important proverbs of Solomon, with some pious, moral, prudential or economical precept. The frequent repetition on seeing these good words every time one sees a piece of money might make a lasting impression on the mind." Like his inventions, these innovations were intended to create a better society. In 1864 Congress followed Franklin's advice and put "In God We Trust" on U.S. currency. But the idea for mottoes on paper money did not originate with Franklin. The early settlers in the Massachusetts Bay Colony in their 1690 issue made the plea, "Come over and help us." In 1776, a New York issue pictured a candelabrum with thirteen candles and the motto: "With one and the same fire." Georgia had an emblem with two floating jugs, representing England and America, with the message," If we collide we break." North Carolina had a picture of a rattlesnake with the threat, "Don't tread on me." A most unexpected one from South Carolina read, "Slavery of all kinds is wretched." South Carolina was the most proslavery state but must have been thinking of the British treatment of the colonies rather than their own treatment of the blacks. In any event, the slogan was in Latin, "Misera Omni Servatus," and was not understood by most of the citizens.[26]

The History of Counterfeiting in America

Counterfeiting has been practiced as long as there has been money or any medium of exchange. Larceny is a trait that lies deep in the human psyche and is found in every culture. Even before the invention of money, when one farmer traded a sack of wheat to another for a bag of beans, unscrupulous persons put dirt in the bottom of the sack to increase the weight. When the first English settlers in America traded with the native Americans, both used the Indians' money, wampum, beads made from the inside of shells. There were two kinds of wampum, black and white, the black being worth twice as much as the white. The Indians sometimes counterfeited their wampum by dyeing the white beads black and passing it off on the unsuspecting white men.[27] We often hear how the white men cheated the poor Indians, but Roger Williams, the founder of Rhode Island, complained that Indians counterfeited the wampum, cheating the white men. William Penn, founder of Pennsylvania, was shocked on his arrival in America to find so much counterfeiting going on, not all of it by the Indians.

Coined money was invented about 700 BC by the Lydians, whose king, Croesus, stamped out coins with the figure of a bull on them. Soon opportunists found they could make a neat profit by crafting coins with cheaper metal, which they stamped with a bull's head. One device they used was to coat the base metal with gold or silver to make it look authentic. The receiver of the coin could test it by cutting into its edge to see if it were coated. Genuine coins were then made notched to show that they were the same metal throughout; however, the counterfeiters then notched their coins and plated the notches. In the long history of money, keeping one step ahead of the deceivers has been a problem.[28]

By the sixth century BC, counterfeiting had become so prevalent that in Greece, Solon passed laws decreeing death for counterfeiting, a penalty still in effect in Franklin's time. In England, where most of the American colonists originated, forging money was held to be high treason, and the penalty was that the offender would be dragged to the gallows, not carried or allowed to walk, hanged by the neck and cut down alive; his entrails would be taken out and burned while he was yet alive; his head would be cut off and his body divided into four parts; and his head and quarters would be at the king's disposal. There was, therefore, a precedent for the death penalty in the English colonies in America.

In Franklin's century, America led the world in the art and commerce of counterfeiting. Americans in the eighteenth century demonstrated their genius and ingenuity in this trade by producing counterfeit paper currency a full half-century before the first bogus English note turned up at the Bank of England. An anonymous American commented, "It may be safely stated that the art, as pursued in the United States, is without parallel and ... we can beat the world on this our national specialty—counterfeiting."[29]

Why was this illegal trade so prolific in Colonial America? One reason might be that England got rid of her felons by shipping them to America, with the excuse that she was helping to people this wilderness land. Franklin was so incensed by this practice that he wrote a satire proposing to repay this "favor" in kind by exporting to London thousands of rattlesnakes from America. Among the felons were counterfeiters, and the rest had the necessary ambition to learn the trade. Due to the shortage of metal money, America needed paper money more urgently than Europe, and whereas the production of coins was slow and tedious for the counterfeiters, the printing press made the production of paper money quick and easy. Furthermore, the primitive state of the land made policing and apprehension of violators of the law difficult. They could hide out in the forests and the swamps, and when a violator in Pennsylvania was discovered, he could move his operation to New York or Maryland. There was no central authority and little cooperation among the colonies since each colony printed its own money and had no concern for another colony's money.

Making and passing illegal money was not limited to felons; counterfeiters came from all walks of life in colonial America. They were ministers, physicians, trades people, justices of the peace, and members of the legislature. This motley crew even included women.[30] A wealthy Rhode Island Quaker, John Porter, was one of the establishment types that Franklin spoke about when he said at the Constitutional Convention in opposing the vote for only the wealthy, "Some of the greatest rogues I ever was acquainted with were some of the richest rogues." Porter, a wealthy businessman who was entrusted to sign the official Rhode Island paper money, was a counterfeiter. Because of his prominent position in the community, he was able to visit the plant where the money was printed and inspect the process that was employed. He put this knowledge to good use in his own counterfeiting business, which over the years proved to be very lucrative. When he was finally caught he was able to get off with just a fine because of his wealth and position.[31] The penalty for counterfeiting varied greatly depending on the locality, the judge, and the jury. The lucky ones were merely fined, while others were put in the stocks, had their ears cropped, were branded, or imprisoned. But many other culprits ended their days on the gallows. In a humorous story, a counterfeiter in Massachusetts who was punished by having one ear cut off made his way to Canada. There, with his beaver hat pulled way down, he entered a dry goods shop and asked the clerk, "How much is a length of this ribbon from ear to ear?" When the clerk answered, "Five pence," he said, "All right [putting down the money], give me all the ribbon. I have one ear here and the other is in Massachusetts."[32]

Although counterfeiting started out as a cottage operation, it soon developed into a big-time industry when paper money came into general use. In 1756 a New York newspaper described counterfeiting in Duchess County, "Where tis said a large gang of villains have harbored for a considerable time past, a few of which have a crop [ears cropped] or a brand mark." Another New York paper in 1768 observed, "It is said that there is a clan of these gentry of at least 500, who correspond through all the colonies, as far as North Carolina." One gang printed and passed 12,000 pounds of fake Rhode Island money, an equal amount of New Hampshire bills, as well as 3,000 pounds of New York currency. A New York assemblyman was so upset that he proposed that all New York bills have a picture showing three felons on a gallows or human figures forced into a burning pit.[33] In Virginia, devilishly accurate counterfeit paper money almost brought the colony's business to a standstill. The steward of George Washington's plantation declared that he dared not take money for the corn he had to sell for fear it would be counterfeit.[34]

But as great as the production of bogus bills by the gangs was, it was far outdone by another player in this game, the mother country itself. When the war for independence began, the British government retaliated by introducing a new form of warfare — economic warfare. Its method was to flood the rebellious colonies with counterfeit currency so that their money would become worthless and the Americans would not be able to buy the supplies necessary to continue fighting. The British had their own engravers and printers and also bought the services of renegade Americans who were already printing counterfeit money. There were also many Tory sympathizers who helped by dispersing the bad money throughout the colonies, which were now calling themselves states. After the British forces under General Howe took New York, this city became the base for their operation, and in April 1777, Howe openly published the following advertisement in all the newspapers:

> Persons going into other Colonies may be supplied with any number of counterfeit Congress-notes, for the price of the paper per ream. They are so neatly and exactly executed that there is no risque in getting them off, it being almost impossible to discover that they are not genuine. This has been proved by bills to a very large amount, which have already been sufficiently circulated.
>
> Enquire for Q.E.D. at the Coffee-House, from 11 p.m. to 4 a.m. during the present month.[35]

Many applicants were recruited to pass the phony notes, which they could disperse at a fraction of their nominal value and still make a profit since the cost of production was absorbed by the British government. What's more, as Tories they were doing their patriotic duty. General George Washington fumed when he saw the advertisement. He wrote to the Continental Congress, "No artifices are left untried by the enemy to injure us."[36] Actually, this was a bloodless form of warfare, more humane than the bombs and bullets that were being used. And it was effective. One gang was reported to have passed $50,000 in bad bills, and the organizer of the gang, when captured and condemned to death, escaped to the British lines, where he was rewarded with a commission in the intelligence service. John Langhorne, who later served as governor of New Hampshire, said of him, "Damn him ... I hope to see him hanged. He had done more damage than ten thousand men could have done."[37] Washington complained to John Jay that depreciation of the money was so bad that "A wagon load of money will scarcely purchase a wagon load of provisions."[38] Thomas Paine wrote a letter to General Howe: "You, sir, have the honor of adding a new vice to the military catalogue; and the reason, perhaps, why the invention was reserved for you is because no general before was mean enough even to think of it."[39]

The English people were not enthusiastic about this war against their American relatives, and this was especially true of the merchants who lost their American trade due to the war. Benjamin Franklin, well aware of this sentiment, picked up his pen to write a propaganda piece for distribution abroad, titled "The Retort Courteous." In it he acknowledges that the

British had expertly produced vast quantities of counterfeit money which depreciated the value of U.S. money as they had contrived to do. But the effect was to punish the British merchants because it prevented the American merchants, who were greatly in debt to their British counterparts, from being able to pay their honest debts.[40]

A pro–British item appeared in the April 1, 1777, *Smythe's Journal*:

> The pasteboard dollars of Congress are now refused by the hottest among the rebels themselves. One, who was a member of a committee to punish those who might refuse them, was lately punished for refusing them himself, and, in short, everyone is putting them off from himself, in exchange for almost anything he can get for them. Yesterday, a Connecticut parson, with a parcel of rag money in one of his moccasins was taken at Kings Bridge and brought into New York. He was this morning obliged to chew up all the money, and declare, in the presence of a large assemblage of people, that he will not again pray for the Congress, or the doer of their dirty work, Mr. Washington.[41]

Although British counterfeiting had a severe effect on the American economy, it did not cause the depreciation expected because of action by the Continental Congress. The Congress had to carry on the war, but only the states had the power to tax the people. The Congress could only request money from the states, and there was never enough. Congress, therefore, issued its own paper money, termed "continentals." To pay the bills as the war dragged on, it issued more and more money; a total of $240 million, with the result that the money so depreciated that a continental dollar was "not worth a continental," an expression from then on applied to anything of no value. In 1778 Jonathon Carver, a writer, stated, "The Congress paper dollars are now used for papering rooms, lighting pipes, and other conveniences." Thus, the British were not successful in ruining the American currency — because Congress had done it itself.

How, then, was the American army able to continue the struggle and eventually win the war? The answer: with French money, French credit, French supplies, and French military forces, which Benjamin Franklin, as the American representative in Paris, had been able to obtain.

Counterfeiting in the Nineteenth and Twentieth Centuries

Counterfeiting was alive and well in the nineteenth and twentieth centuries, growing with the growth of the country. After the fiscal fiasco of the Continental Congress, the federal government issued no more printed money until the beginning of the Civil War, in 1861. But there were plenty of paper bills to counterfeit because the states and the private banks, which they chartered, continued to issue it. By 1860, it is estimated that there were notes of 8,000 banks, with counterfeiting flourishing. During the Civil War period, one-third of the currency was counterfeit, with 4,000 different counterfeit notes compared to 8,000 genuine ones. Bank failures were common, and people regularly suffered losses on notes they received and held. To fight this persistent crime, the federal government in 1865 established the U.S. Secret Service in the Treasury Department, which to this day is the greatest defense against this pernicious drag on our economy. Despite the harm and chaos counterfeiting caused, it surprisingly served a useful purpose in the development of America. The pioneers of the early nineteenth century used counterfeit money to buy their lands in the West whenever they could; it served our merchants as currency with which to expand their business during tight money periods and contributed to the development of America in many other ways.[42]

The twentieth century greatly expanded the horizons for the counterfeiters. When the Secret Service checked them in the United States, the culprits crossed the borders to Mexico and Canada and went overseas to Europe and the Middle East. During the twentieth century the United States became an economic power, and U.S. money was used in international trade. Today, the government is concerned mainly with forgers overseas, where about two-thirds of the $608 billion in U.S. paper money is in circulation.[43] The farther from our shores, the less U.S. currency is recognized, and the greater the temptation to counterfeit it. Furthermore, setting up illicit operations outside this country made it easier to evade the tentacles of the Secret Service. In addition to common crooks, international drug traders, terrorists, and rogue nations joined the ranks of the counterfeiters. As a result, it became a much more professional and sophisticated business, and the need to overcome this onslaught was critical.

Today, with machines to check the optical and magnetic properties of each bill to detect counterfeits, the New York branch of the Federal Reserve Bank processes 12 million used notes every day and in 1995 confiscated 360 million dollars of counterfeit paper money. Millions more go undetected. Another reason for the huge increase in fake money was the development of new technology: the color copier, the laser scanner, and the computer, all affordable and available to anyone with the inclination to make a dishonest buck. In former times, the traditional counterfeiter had to buy large, expensive equipment that the law enforcement people could readily monitor and control, but now the new machines are in every office and home. For example, today the counterfeiter doesn't need to shoot a negative; the high-definition laser scanner can replace the work of photography in making printing plates. After the plates have been made, all that is needed is carefully selected ink, fine-quality paper, and an offset printing press. It is estimated that 90 percent of all counterfeits are made this way.[44]

The color copier introduced a new class of criminal, the so-called casual counterfeiter. It's just so easy it's hard to resist, and this kind of criminal is growing rapidly. Of $47.5 million in counterfeit money in circulation in 2001, 39 percent was computer generated compared to 0.5 percent in 1995.[45] Still, only 0.03 percent of all currency in circulation is counterfeit, having leveled off since the introduction of the 1996 redesign. However, the casual counterfeiter usually produces low-denomination bills because larger bills are carefully scrutinized, and the amateur products don't match the genuine bills. The false bills tend to be muddier, the paper and ink don't match exactly, and they have a shiny appearance. In addition, there is the matter of feel: The counterfeits have a flat feel, whereas the genuine banknote has a raised, or three-dimensional feel and look due to the intaglio printing in which ink fills the engraving under 20 tons of pressure and is forced out onto the surface of the paper.[46]

The New Franklin Hundred-Dollar Bill

The big-time counterfeiters, especially those in international operations, don't bother with small notes but produce exclusively the hundred-dollar bill, the largest bill presently in circulation, with the portrait of Benjamin Franklin. The "Franklin 100" was first issued in 1914 and was redesigned in 1929, although Franklin's face on U.S. money goes back at least to the 1830s–1840s, when he was on many notes issued by private banks. He was on a fifty-dollar government note issued in 1874 and, during the first charter period of 1863–1883, a ten-dollar national currency note was issued depicting Franklin flying his kite and drawing electricity from the clouds during a thunderstorm.[47]

In 1996, the government put in circulation a new Franklin 100 with a special mission: to confound and defeat the counterfeiters (Figure 7.12). This was the first of a series of bills of lower denominations with the same mission. For the casual counterfeiter, the bills would have to be difficult to duplicate by color copiers. To counteract the professionals, the bills would have to stymie the intaglio printers. To discourage all the imitators, it would have to be very difficult and expensive to produce a reasonable copy (Figure 7.13). No single feature would suffice; a combination of features would be necessary. This was the challenge for the new hundred-dollar Franklin supernote.[48]

Figure 7.12 Front and back of new U.S. anticounterfeiting, Franklin $100 bill, presently in circulation.

To prevent the old practice of raising the value of bills that Franklin contended with by using mica in the paper or spelling Pennsylvania differently in different notes, the Treasury put colored cotton threads, called security threads, in the paper. But the new threads are different. First, there are two threads that run the length of the paper to denominate the banknote and prevent a one-dollar note from being washed clean of its ink and being raised to a higher value. The security threads dispersed in the paper appear in a different location for each denomination, and these tiny threads also have microprinted on them numbers denoting the bill's value. The microprinted numbers are 42 thousandths of an inch tall, a process that requires great precision, which is monitored by cameras and computers.

To defy the photocopiers, the text is clearly visible in transmitted light but cannot be reproduced by the reflective light of a photocopier. Threads for the new currency also glow red under ultraviolet light. The new bills retain the classic design and colors. Other countries have employed many colors on their bills, but the new systems are so good at reproducing multicolors that the addition of colors was not considered a security asset.[49] The green back of the old nineteenth-century "greenback" was retained, but this bill is made of a secret mixture of pigments that is hard to copy. Another new wrinkle has been added. Some countries have put holograms (three-dimensional images) on their high-value notes, but holograms are easily damaged and cannot stand the folding, crumpling,

Figure 7.13 Concentric lines behind Franklin's portrait and Independence Hall in new $100 bill, like the veins of a leaf, are difficult to replicate.

and rumpling the bills undergo in their lifetime. Instead, a foil was developed that changes color when struck by light from different angles, but since crumpling damages this foil, it was ground to a fine powder and is used as a pigment in the ink on the Treasury seal and the number 100 on the bill. Thus, when the new 100-, 50-, 20-, or 10-dollar bill is tilted, the color of the number in the bottom righthand corner changes from green to black.[50]

There are other new characteristics of the current bills that are so secret the government will not even talk about them. One unique distinction of these 100s, however, is the watermark. Watermarks in the paper have been used in currency as early as Franklin's century, but this watermark is different; it is of Franklin himself. His face is worked right into the three-dimensional structure of the paper and gives a tonal graduation to the feel of the paper. It is the same Franklin image used on the bill (Figure 7.14). The watermark can be seen only when backlighted and cannot be reproduced by a scanner or photocopier.[51]

Figure 14 Watermark (enlarged) of Franklin's image incorporated in paper of $100 bill.

What's Ahead

To keep ahead of the counterfeiters the Treasury decided to redesign bills every seven to ten years. The latest design, inaugurated in October 2003, for the first time in U.S. history on any note, is the Andrew Jackson, twenty-dollar bill with color added — not splashy colors like the colored money of some other countries but the conventional black and green of the old notes plus subtle additions of blue and peach in certain places. The colors have a role in foiling the counterfeiters, but the Secret Service won't reveal what the security features are. They do acknowledge that there are a number of small, yellow "20's" on the left side of the back of the note that are invisible under ordinary light. There are two American eagle symbols of freedom on the front of the note, and the serial numbers appear twice; otherwise it is much like the new 1996 design except for the color additions. New designs for the fifty- and hundred-dollar colored bills are planned for the following years, and what to do about the tens and fives will be decided later. Nothing is planned for the one-dollar bill.[52]

No news yet, but speculation has it that we may in the future adopt a plastic note in place of paper. In 1720, Massachusetts issued notes on parchment to get a longer service life than paper provides and save money. Now, plastic offers to keep the bills in circulation longer, and in addition, it stays cleaner, resists tearing, water, sweat, and oil and can be recycled. Australia converted entirely to plastic bank notes in 1996, and Canada may issue a plastic fifty or hundred within a year. Brazil, Indonesia, and Romania are among the countries that have already issued some of their bills in plastic. A major selling point of a plastic note issued via the Reserve Bank of Australia is a transparent window that is said to make the note impossible to copy on an inkjet printer. Dupont and Exxon Mobil are companies that have patented a technology for manufacturing plastic bank notes, and the U.S. Treasury is seriously testing different polymer compounds for their suitability in substituting for paper as stock for the new bills.[53]

The Franklin Portrait

Before the present Franklin hundred-dollar bill was designed there were suggestions that other historical American figures be honored with this bill. One suggestion was to honor women by selecting an outstanding woman for this large banknote. But the Treasury was determined to maintain tradition and stay with old Ben, whom everybody was used to and would recognize. It did, however, employ an engraving of a different

Franklin painting, the Duplessis, which is in the National Portrait Gallery. The portrait was used by master engraver Tom Hipschen to carve a life-like image into steel. Before beginning this assignment, Hipschen read three books about Franklin as well as his autobiography. He commented, "He was a wonderful character. I mean he was a human being of incredible proportion. I especially like the idea that he began as a tradesman. He was a printer, which is almost the same trade that I'm in." Hipschen was the first artist in over six decades to put an original portrait on U.S. currency, and he went about it with enthusiasm and great care. The job took him a year to complete. While the purpose of the new bill was security, not aesthetics, it would be viewed by many more people than any painting of the world's most famous artists, and Hipschen had this in mind when he did his work. In the first four years approximately four billion of these Franklin one hundreds were printed by the Bureau of Engraving and Printing.

On witnessing the portrait, people commented on what appeared to be a smirk on Franklin's face. Hipschen replied, "I didn't really intend to put a smirk on the portrait, but I did go for a painterly effect, which I think was the best part of the portrait. He's a witty guy and I wanted that to come across." Franklin's new portrait with the Mona Lisa smile is an important security feature of this bill. People readily recognize faces: A special part of the brain enables us to do this. We can distinguish small differences in Franklin's face between a genuine bill and a counterfeit. For that reason the portrait was made 50 percent larger on the new bill than on the old 100. On the new bill the portrait is off center because people frequently fold bills in half, distorting the important facial features in a centered portrait, making it more difficult to detect a fraudulent note. Microprinted on the lapel of Franklin's coat is the text, "United States of America," as an additional security feature.[54] This would have pleased Ben. He was very proud of his new nation and his part in bringing it into being.

For the face of this bill the government chose an icon, an image that everyone would recognize and associate with the world's oldest democracy, a stable government with stable money. Franklin would also serve as a symbol of sound economic policy, with his emphasis on industry and thrift, as indicated by the many banks and investment institutions that have taken his name. His many wise sayings in *Poor Richard's Almanac*, like "A penny saved is a penny earned" and "If you would know the value of money, go and try to borrow some," have become part of the fabric of America.

It is significant that when the government decided to issue the new anticounterfeit paper money, the first bill printed was the Franklin hundred-dollar banknote with his enlarged portrait and his image incorporated in the very fiber of the paper. His efforts embattling the counterfeiters have mostly been forgotten, but this new Franklin bill serves nevertheless as a fitting tribute to this nation's first counterfeit fighter.

8

Detergents,
Emulsions, and Foams

Jehovah parted the waters of the Red Sea; Jesus of Nazareth walked on water in the Sea of Galilee; and Benjamin Franklin of Philadelphia flattened the waves in Clapham Pond with a few drops of oil. The first two events were miracles; the third was science: surface science.

Detergents, emulsions, and foams are modern chemical products that have helped transform our lives. What do these three products have in common? They all owe their activity to surface science. They all exert their action on the surface between oil and water when the two are in contact.

A modern dictionary of surface science, a field that got its name from a unique observation of Franklin, states that Franklin was the first to estimate the thickness of a monolayer of oil on water and used his observation to explain the calming effect of oil on the waves.[1]

This story is as old as ancient history and as new as modern science. It begins in 1757, when Franklin was sent to England to solve some tax problems the people of Pennsylvania were having with the proprietors of that English colony. Franklin's ship joined a fleet of 96 ships bound for Nova Scotia to attack the French fortress at Louisbourg. On board, Franklin noticed something strange about two of the ships:

> In 1757 being at sea in a fleet of 96 sail bound against Louisbourg,
> I observed the wakes of two of the ships to be remarkably smooth,
> while all the others were ruffled by the wind, which blew fresh.

Being puzzled with this differing appearance I at last pointed it out to our captain, and asked him the meaning of it. "The cooks, says he, have I suppose, been just emptying their greasy water through the scuppers, which has greased the sides of those ships a little;" and this answer he gave me with an air of some little contempt, as to a person ignorant of what everybody else knew. In my own mind I at first slighted his solution, though I was not able to think of another. But recollecting what I had formerly read in Pliny, I resolved to make some experiment of the effect of oil on water when I should have opportunity.[2]

The Pliny Franklin referred to is Pliny the Elder, 23–79, a Roman official and author who wrote, "Everything is soothed by oil, and this is the reason why divers send out small quantities of oil from their mouths, because it smoothes every part which is rough." Plutarch, AD 46–120, a Greek philosopher and biographer, also read by Franklin, asked this question: "Why does pouring oil on the sea make it clear and calm? Is it for that the winds, slipping the smooth oil, have no force, nor cause any waves?"[3]

In 1762, when Franklin was on the sea again returning home from England, he made another interesting observation. To light his cabin he had made an oil lamp from a glass tumbler that he filled one-third with water, on top of which he layered an equal amount of oil, added a wick and lighted it. A rope tied to the roof of the cabin supported the lamp. He called this his Italian lamp. Franklin noted with curiosity that as the ship rocked the oil layer on top of the water remained calm but the water layer under the oil was violently agitated, rising and falling. After the oil burned off, the water layer became calm and tranquil even though the rocking continued.

An old sea captain was a passenger on the ship, and Franklin asked him about this phenomenon, but as Franklin reported, he "thought little of it." Instead he told Franklin of the practice of Bermudan fishermen who put oil on the water to smooth it so they could strike fish that they could not see if the water was ruffled by the wind. The captain thought this was the same phenomenon, but Franklin disagreed, stating that in one case the water is smooth until layered with oil and then becomes agitated, whereas in the other it is agitated before the oil is applied and then becomes smooth. The captain had another story, this one about the fishermen of Lisbon who, on returning from a rough sea to the river, when there was a great surf on the bar that would fill their boats in passing through, would pour a bottle or two of oil into the sea to suppress the breakers and allow them to pass safely. Discussing these stories with other sailors, Franklin found confirmation for Pliny's account about divers. He was told that divers then operating in Mediterranean waters carry a small amount of oil in their mouths, which they release to calm the water on the surface. They need as much light as possible for their work, and the refraction caused by the numerous little waves breaks up the light.[4] He also heard that the harbor of Newport, Rhode Island, was always smooth when the whaling vessels were in it. Apparently this was due to the fact that some of the oily blubber from the whales was released into the water when the holds in which it was kept were pumped out into the harbor.[5]

Franklin was eager to do some experimenting on this subject, but unfortunately the time was not right. His entire life involved a struggle for time between his desire for scientific exploration and his sense of duty to his public responsibilities, in which the latter usually won out. He voiced that struggle in a comment about the great scientist Sir Isaac Newton:

> Had Newton been pilot but of a single common ship, the finest
> of his discoveries would scarce have excused or atoned for his
> abandoning the helm one hour in time of danger; how much less
> if she [the ship] carried the fate of the commonwealth.[6]

However, when he returned home he did find enough time to try to explain the action of the Italian lamp. He suspended the same lamp by a rope and swung it to and fro in the air. It acted just as it had on the ship. Without the oil "the water appeared to keep its place in the tumbler as steadily as if it had been ice." But when the oil was layered on top, "the tranquility before possessed by the water was transferred to the surface of the oil and the water under it was agitated with the same commotions as at sea."

He demonstrated this experiment for a number of intelligent persons, who attempted to explain it, but Franklin found these explanations not very intelligible to him. He described this occurrence to his friend Dr. John Pringle in London, a fellow of the Royal Society, who related it to a group of his friends, all of whom he said "were agog about this new property of fluids."[7] For most of the next two years after he returned home, Franklin was busy traveling around the American colonies on horseback, setting up the post office, in his capacity of deputy postmaster general of the British colonies in America. The postmaster general in England was a figurehead, a member of the nobility appointed by the crown in return for some political favor.

In 1764 Franklin returned to his diplomatic duties in England, where he was to remain until 1775, just before the hostilities of the Revolutionary

War broke out. Pliny's account and the stories of the sea captains may have been on his mind, but now with other pressing business they were put on hold, and it was not until around 1770 that he began his experiments with oil on water.

Were Pliny and the others right? In fairness, he said, "it has been of late too much the mode to slight the learning of the ancients. The learned too, are apt to slight too much the knowledge of the vulgar."[8] But after all, Pliny had also written that a tempest could be stilled by throwing vinegar into the air. He thought about these stories he had heard: "I at times revolved in my mind and wondered to find no mention of them in our books of experimental philosophy."

What Happened at Clapham Pond

In 1770, when he was again in England, the time was ripe to put to the test the stories he had planned back in 1757. The place was Clapham, a residential area four miles from the center of London:

> At length being at Clapham, where there is, on the common, a large pond, which I observed to be one day very rough with the wind, I fetched out a cruet of oil, and dropt a little of it on the water. I saw it spread itself with surprising swiftness upon the surface, but the effect of smoothing the waves was not produced; for I had applied it first on the leeward side of the pond where the waves were largest, and the wind drove my oil back upon the shore. I then went to the windward side, where they began to form, and there the oil though not more than a teaspoonful produced an instant calm, over a space several yards square, which spread amazingly, and extended itself gradually till it reached the lee side, making all that quarter of the pond, perhaps half an acre, as smooth as a looking glass.[9]

Thus, Pliny, Plutarch, and the sea captains were right — oil does calm the waters! But not satisfied with this single trial, Franklin was determined to repeat the experiment in different places under different conditions. The famous scientist Lord Rayleigh, writing a hundred years later, said Franklin had almost made a hobby of wave-calming demonstrations. Whenever Franklin had occasion to travel from London into the country-side he took with him a little oil, which he kept in the hollow of his bamboo cane. He performed the experiment at several locations, including Derwent Water (a lake) and High Wycombe, confirming it to his satisfaction. He demonstrated it to friends, one of whom told him about cleaning in a nearby pond a little cup that formerly contained oil. In the cup were some flies that had drowned in the oil. The friend reported, "These flies presently began to move, and turned round in the water very rapidly as if they were vigorously alive, though on examination they were not so." The friend wondered whether the flies somehow had temporarily come back to life, but Franklin disproved that theory with a simple experiment. He took chips of wood and pieces of paper the size of a fly which he cut in the shape of a comma. He soaked them with oil and placed them in the water, whereupon the commas turned around rapidly on the surface of the water just as the flies had done.[10]

Science or Miracles?

One may ask whether Franklin was a serious scientist. He was certainly serious about science, but he was not always a scientist who was serious. He had his playful moments and he loved to play tricks. He used this phenomenon for one of his tricks. He equipped his cane, in which he kept the oil, so that the oil would drip out of its end when he pulled a lever in the handle. Then, in the company of friends, and being near a stream that was being whipped by wind-producing waves, he stopped and claimed very dramatically that with just a wave of his magic cane he could quiet the waves. He walked off a hundred paces along the stream in the direction of the wind, muttered some mysterious incantations, and passed his cane over the stream allowing a few drops of oil to fall imperceptibly into the water. The astonished audience stood in amazement as they saw the waves disappear and the surface of the stream looking like a mirror. After enjoying this sport, Franklin revealed the secret of his cane and explained the experiment that they thought had been a miracle.[11]

One time when he was pouring oil on the rippled water, a farmer, seeing the results, imagined some kind of supernatural influence and asked in amazement, "Tell me, what am I to believe?" Franklin responded bluntly, "Only what you see and nothing else." Later, he commented: "This man, being witness to something extraordinary was ready to believe the wildest absurdities— such is the logic of three-fourths of the human race." In the same vein, he lamented there are everywhere people who "think of inventions as miracles: there might be such formerly, but they are ceased."[12]

Franklin may have heard the story told by the English ecclesiastical historian, the Venerable Bede (AD 673–735), of a priest who was to escort a princess to become the bride of the king. Since a sea voyage was necessary, he asked for the blessing of Bishop Aidan (AD 635–651). The bishop gave him his blessing and some oil with the following instruction: "Remember to pour the oil I have given you on to the sea; the winds will drop at once, the sea will become calm and serene, and will bring you home the way you wish." Bede added: "He who judges the heart showed by signs and miracles what Aidan's merits were." For Franklin, that was then; the age of miracles was past, and the miracles of the present were performed by scientists like himself. Incidentally, it was Bede who introduced the familiar expression "oil on troubled waters," when he said, "A spoonful of oil on the troubled waters goes further than a quart of vinegar."[13]

Interested in demonstrating his experiment for fellow scientists, Franklin with Sir John Pringle visited the home of William Brownrigg, distinguished physician and fellow of the Royal Society of London, who was an experimenter in his own right. The three experimenters went out in a boat on a lake called Derwent Water, where Franklin demonstrated the experiment for them. Subsequently, a clergyman, James Farish, who knew Brownrigg, heard about the experiment, namely, that water which had been in great agitation was instantly calmed after pouring in it only a very small quantity of oil, and it spread to so great a distance around the boat that it seemed incredible. He wrote: "I have since had the same accounts from others, but I suspect them all of a little exaggeration." It was indeed incredible and it did seem exaggerated. As it happened, it was only due to Farish's letter that we know at all about these experiments, for Brownrigg passed on Farish's letter requesting details about the experiments to Franklin, who then replied with a long account of the subject. Brownrigg then took it upon himself to publish Franklin's letter in the "Transactions of the Royal Society" in 1774, where it was widely read and talked about.[14]

The Letter Writer

It was not unusual for Franklin to write a long letter about something that interested him. He was an avid letter writer who may have spent half his time writing letters and making copies (handwritten, of course) of them, which he kept in letter books. Yale University's Franklin Papers Project has published over thirty volumes of Franklin's correspondence to date and expects the number to approach fifty when completed. Franklin may have written more on oil and water, but unfortunately a number of his letter books were lost or destroyed when the British troops took over his house in Philadelphia during the Revolutionary War.

Franklin liked letters as a form of writing, and most of the writing we have of his is in that form. Even his autobiography is written as a letter to his son. He did not write books; his book on electricity is a series of letters describing his work written to Peter Collinson, his correspondent in London, who had them published by the Royal Society for the benefit of other scientists. They were then collected and published as a book by an enterprising printer to make money (that is for himself, for it is doubtful that Franklin received any money for the sale of his widely circulated book on electricity).

Franklin probably became enamored of letter writing when as a youth of sixteen he took on the fictitious persona of an elderly widow named Silence Dogood to write a series of comic essays in the form of letters commenting on life in Boston. These he surreptitiously slipped under the door of the newspaper owned by his brother, who would never have accepted them if he had known who the author was. The essays were very successful, and from then on Ben felt comfortable with this form of writing. In conversation also, Franklin was more at ease one on one, or with just a few friends, whereas in a crowd he was almost always silent, making speeches only when absolutely necessary.

The letter to Brownrigg suggests Franklin's style, his mixture of homespun and humor with science. Brownrigg's letter is dated January 27, 1773, and Franklin's reply is dated November 7 of that year. Franklin must have decided to reply with a lengthy essay on the subject, and he had to find the time to do it; yet an apology was due. He wrote, "Our correspondence might be carried on for a century with very few letters, if you were as apt to procrastinate as myself. Though an habitual sinner, I am now quite ashamed to observe that this is to be an answer to your favor of January last."

He delays responding to the scientific inquiry by referring to his visit at the Brownrigg home and his giving Mrs. Brownrigg a recipe for making parmesan cheese:

> I suppose Mrs. Brownrigg did not succeed in making the parmesan cheese, since we have heard nothing of it. But as a philosophess, she will not be discouraged by one or two failures. Perhaps some circumstance is omitted in the recipe, which by a little more experience she may discover. The foreign gentleman who had learnt in England to like boiled plum pudding and carried home a recipe for making it, wondered to see it brought to his table in the form of a soup. The cook declared he had exactly followed the recipe. And when that came to be examined, a small but important circumstance appeared to be omitted. There was no mention of the bag.[15]

(Apparently, the ingredients for making the cheese, like those for the plum pudding, were supposed to be put into a cloth bag, which filtered off the liquid while retaining the solid cheese.)

To the Ocean

Franklin's letter about oil on water, published by the Royal Society, appeared as things were heating up prior to the American Revolution, and Franklin was well known as a leader on America's behalf. It was in this vein that James Boswell, the renowned English author, wrote in 1775 to the Reverend William Temple, an American sympathizer, "Franklin has written upon stilling the waves of the ocean by oil, as I see you would quiet the turbulent Americans by lenient measures." Now, after amazing scientists and lay people alike by his demonstrations in ponds and lakes, Franklin was ready for the ultimate test, the effect on the waves in the ocean.

In his trials Franklin had found that he could suppress the waves if he could go to the windward place where they arise. He realized, "This in the ocean can seldom if ever be done. But perhaps something may be done on particular occasions to moderate the violence of the waves when we are in the midst of them, and prevent their breaking where that would be inconvenient." Franklin considered the case where seafarers wished to go ashore but were prevented from landing by a violent surf breaking there. Perhaps if the sailors scattered oil to and fro, the waves might be depressed sufficiently to permit a landing, and the expense of the oil might be justified.

At a demonstration at Green Pond in London, Franklin was accompanied by Count William Bentick of Holland along with his son, Captain John Albert Bentick of the Royal Navy, and Jean Allernand of the University of Leyden (Leiden) in Holland. Captain Bentick happened to be commander of a naval ship stationed at Portsmouth and was very much interested in the demonstration. He arranged for Franklin and a retinue of his friends to make an ocean trial at Portsmouth and to experiment off the shores near Spithead He provided boats and accompanied them on the test. The friends included two members of the Royal Society who had sailed with the famous Captain James Cook, discoverer of Australia and Hawaii, on his trip around the world. In Cook's account of his trip, he mentioned islands he had wanted to land upon but could not because of the violent surf breaking on the shore, and these adventurous men of science were eager to see if Franklin's experiment would make it possible to accomplish such a feat. They went out in Captain Bentick's ship, the Centaur, accompanied by a longboat and a barge. It was a very windy day with the foam flying over the waves rolling toward shore. Franklin explained:

> Our disposition was this: The longboat was anchored about a quarter of a mile from the shore; part of the company were landed behind the point (a place more sheltered from the sea), who came around and placed themselves opposite to the longboat where they might observe the surf and note if any change occurred in it upon using the oil. Another party, in the barge, plied to windward of the longboat, as far from her as she was from the shore, making trips about a half a mile each, pouring oil continually out of a large stone bottle through a hole in the cork, somewhat bigger than a goose quill.[16]

It is always difficult to report negative results of experimental research. Therefore, the negative results are often not reported or are interpreted so as to give them a positive spin. Franklin was always honest, reporting the bad with the good. He was not doing research for the money, and his reputation was secure. He said of this experiment: "The experiment had not in the main point the success we had wished, for no material difference was observed in the height or force of the surf upon the shore." But those in the longboat observed a track of smoothed water the whole length of the distance in which the barge poured the oil and gradually spreading in breadth. Though the swells were not flattened, they were smoothed, and their surface was not roughened or wrinkled by the smaller waves, with very few whitecaps, whose tops turn over into foam. Franklin observed that a small sailboat on its way to Portsmouth turned into that smooth tract and "used it from end to end as a piece of turnpike road."[17]

The experiment was not the success he had hoped for, but it was not an unqualified failure. Franklin noted that reporting an unsuccessful experiment could be useful, providing hints for improvement in future trials. Actually Franklin's report did stimulate further efforts, which confirmed his findings and found practical application, as he had wished. The large swells could not be prevented but a boat might ride them without capsizing, if the smaller top waves that curl over and splash into the boat could be prevented.

In trying to understand the phenomenon he had observed, Franklin recognized that the large waves were raised by another power, such as the mechanical impulse produced when a stone was thrown into a pool of still water. Once started, they continue for a long time, as a pendulum continues swinging long after the force that started it is removed. Oil would not prevent these waves, but it might help in preventing their enhancement by the wind. He wondered whether this enhancement might have been reduced if he had conducted his experiment farther out in the sea and he had used more oil. Unfortunately he never got to run these further tests, for the waves of political unrest were demanding his complete attention. Within a year he was sailing the ocean again, but this time back to America, shortly to sign the Declaration of Independence.

The Sea Captains

The publicity given to Franklin's trials on wave damping acted like the mechanical impulse he described with the stone dropping into the water to start a wave motion. Scientists studied the subject, but what would have delighted Franklin even more, after his experience at Portsmouth, had he lived to learn of them, were the practical results reported by sea captains who tried this method of quelling the waves. An extensive report by the U.S. Bureau of Navigation in 1886 reported on the effects of the use of oil at sea. It is titled "The Use of Oil to Lessen the Dangerous Effect of Heavy Seas" and relates the experiences of about one hundred sea captains who tried this method. While Franklin was disappointed that his ocean trial was not as successful as he had expected, the captains were unanimous in their enthusiasm.

When Captain Robertson of the British steamer *Elstow* ran into a gale off Newfoundland, he hung bags filled with linseed oil over the side of his ship, which allowed the oil to drop slowly into the sea. He remarked, "They had a wonderful effect on the high seas, taking the dangerous curl off of them and preventing so much water from coming on board." W. H. Langford, chief master of the bark *Ascalon*, reports encountering a heavy gale off the Australian coast with a heavy, breaking sea and the vessel shipping large quantities of water, doing great damage; two oil bags were hung over the side," which had a wonderful effect of subduing the breaking power of the waves, and from that time until the finish of the gale no water of any consequence was shipped." On the homeward passage, a fierce gale with a tremendous sea was again encountered off Cape Horn. He applied the bags of oil and said, "I firmly believe that had it not been for their use the ship would never have lived through the night." W. G. Whitmore reported commanding a ship in a terrific gale followed by a tremendous sea breaking over the stern of the ship, to the danger of the ship and crew. A short time after applying the oil, "the effect was wonderful, for what was a heavy running and dangerous sea was reduced by the use of the oil into what a seaman would call blind rollers, quite harmless to a ship: in fact the effect was so marked that it appeared by looking astern that the vessel was passing through a lane of smooth water." The testimonials were all similar to that of Captain George E. Lane, who stated, "I followed the sea constantly over thirty-five years from cabin boy to master. During that time I had occasion to use oil several times, always to good advantage." Captain Charles Moore reported that his chief officer, who had not seen oil used previously, "was simply amazed" and now declares that when he is master he will always stock oil for this purpose.

Two accounts are worthy of particular notice. One from R. H. Berrilt, pilot of *Port Adelaide*, tells of the rescue of a lifeboat from the ship *Abberton* from London: "There were twenty-four all told in the boat for eighteen days, no food nor water left, and they were all but gone. They attributed their safety to the fact that the chief officer put a keg of oil in the boat before leaving the ship, he having previously used it crossing Shield's Bar. They had a heavy gale after leaving the ship, and one and all stated that nothing but the use of oil saved them." The other story relates to a shipwreck. Captain Amlot of the British steamer *Barrowmore* reported on approaching the wrecked ship *Kirkwood* that the sea was very heavy, but he noticed that around the wreck the sea was much smoother. He maneuvered through the smoother water, lowered his lifeboat and in two trips rescued the crew of twenty-six men. In explaining the smooth sea, the rescued men explained that they did not come prepared with bags of oil, but showing their ingenuity, they remembered in the cargo cans of canned salmon and poured oil from these cans into the sea to prevent the waves from breaking over them.[18]

With the record of success of the sea captains, one wonders why oil wasn't used in the World War II allied invasion of France. The water in the crossing was so rough that the soldiers became terribly seasick. In addition, many landing craft capsized, resulting in great loss of life.

Introducing John Shields

The history of wave stilling would be incomplete without mentioning the Scottish industrialist John Shields. Shields was ignorant of the reports of Pliny, Franklin, and the sea captains, but he independently discovered the phenomenon when oil from his linen mill ran into a pond on a windy day, and he saw an opportunity to make money. Being of a practical turn of mind, he ventured that oil might be useful in aiding ships entering harbors during stormy weather. After some experimentation, in

1879 he patented a process for piping oil into the harbor. At his own expense he tested his process in Peterhead and Aberdeen harbors. At Peterhead, on a very stormy day, a schooner making for the harbor was signaled not to enter, as it was unsafe. In less than a half hour after oil was pumped in, "the sea was as smooth as glass, although undulating," and a tug steamed in with the schooner. In Aberdeen, an observer reported, "the gale and sea was most violent, the effect of the oil was very pronounced ... when the influence of it on the crests of the waves was most apparent, reducing them to rollers only." Shields appealed to Parliament to subsidize further demonstrations. The members gave the subject serious discussion and decided that this was a matter for private business, and they could not justify saddling the taxpayers for this effort. The engineering problems in securing the pipes in the harbor during stormy weather and the further consideration of the cost of the oil finally led Shields to give up this enterprise, promising as it had seemed.[19]

The Monolayer

As interesting and useful as these wave-calming results may be, they are not what caused Franklin to be mentioned in the dictionary of surface science. Wave calming was old stuff, as old as Pliny, and even older. It was Franklin's being the first to estimate the thickness of a monolayer that resulted in his notice in the dictionary. This observation, it is stated, was used by him to explain the calming effect of oil on waves, but it is the observation related to the thickness of a monolayer that caused C. H. Giles, a leading researcher in surface science, in referring to Franklin's experiment at Clapham Pond, to write, "Undoubtedly this test is the first recorded scientific experiment in surface chemistry." That was another of many firsts for Franklin. Surface chemistry, now an important science, is responsible for a great many of our technological achievements in different fields.

Always inquisitive, Franklin wanted to know not only how something worked but why and ultimately whether it could be of any use. Regarding the action of oil on water, he said, "I think it a curious inquiry, and I wish to understand how it arises." It is his following observation which led him to be regarded as the first in surface science and for others to follow through with great scientific discoveries:

> In these experiments, one circumstance struck me with particular surprise. This was the sudden, wide and forcible spreading of a drop of oil on the face of the water, which I do not know that

anybody has hitherto considered. If a drop of oil is put on a
polished marble table, or on a looking glass that lies horizontally;
the drop remains in its place, spreading very little. But when put
on water it spreads instantly many feet around, becoming so thin
as to produce the prismatic colors, for a considerable space, and
beyond them so much thinner as to be invisible except in its effect
of smoothing the waves at a much greater distance. It seems as if
a mutual repulsion between its particles took place as soon as it
touched the water, and a repulsion so strong as to act on other
bodies swimming on the surface, as straws, leaves, chips, etc.
forcing them to recede every way from the drop, as from a center,
leaving a large clear space. The quantity of this force, and the
distance to which it will operate, I have not yet ascertained, but
I think it a curious inquiry, and I wish to understand whence it
arises. [20]

Franklin never did get around to pursuing this matter, but calling
attention to it was enough. What he had observed was a monomolecular
film of oil; the oil had spread on the water until it was only one molecule
thick, ultimately thin, the most it could spread and still be intact (Figure
8.1). The fact that all matter is made up of atoms and molecules was not
known in Franklin's time, so he could not have been expected to explain
what he saw as a monomolecular film. That was not recognized for another
hundred years. Observing that just one teaspoon of oil had affected an
estimated half-acre of the pond, he could have calculated the thickness of
the film. If he had done so, he would have known that the thickness of the
film was less than one ten-millionth of an inch (10^{-7} centimeters, or one
ten-thousandth the thickness of a human hair, or that fraction of an inch
as a second is to one-third of a year) and that the oil dropped in the water
had expanded to an area ten million times its original size. We know today
how incredibly tiny a molecule is; then how can those molecules in a

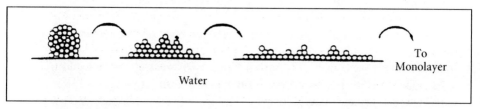

Figure 8.1 Molecules in a drop of oil as they spread out on water to become a
monolayer. When they are in a monolayer the attractive force between molecules tends to keep the film intact; however, a strong mechanical force can break
up the film.

spoonful of oil cover such a great surface? The answer is that there is an incredibly large number of molecules in that teaspoonful of olive oil, namely one thousand million million million of them.[21] While he didn't mention the kind of oil he used, it is assumed that Franklin used olive oil or a similar plant or animal oil since petroleum oil did not come in general use until the late-nineteenth century.

"After Franklin's publication we find many authors discussing wave damping by oil, during the nineteenth and twentieth centuries." Giles, who stated this, is referring to seventeen authors of scientific investigations, and he gives references to their work.[22] Among those who made significant contributions in this area were Thomas Young, John Aitken, Lord Rayleigh, Agnes Pockels, William Hardy, and Irving Langmuir.

Thomas Young, 1775–1829

English physician Thomas Young was among the most brilliant and versatile men of science of his day; he discovered basic principles explaining the theory of light and the ocean tides, and he deciphered the Rosetta stone, which permits us to understand Egyptian hieroglyphics. Among his accomplishments is the measurement and description of surface tension, which plays an important part in Franklin's oil-in-water experiments.[23] All liquids have a force at the surface that acts as a skin, binding the surface. If one fills a glass with water to the brim and then carefully adds a little more water, before the water spills over the sides, the glass will be filled over the brim with a convex surface of water. This is because the surface tension holds the molecules of water at the surface more tightly than the molecules in the water below. Another impressive demonstration of this skinlike surface is that a needle placed very gently flat on top of the water will float, even though it is seven times as heavy as the water. One way to float a needle on water is to place a piece of tissue paper on the water surface and the needle gently on the paper. When the paper gets wet it will sink, leaving the needle floating on the water. The needle is simply lying on that "skin" and will sink immediately if it is disturbed. Water has the highest surface tension of most common liquids, and surface tension is intimately involved in the oil-on-water phenomenon.

Surface tension exists because all the water molecules have an affinity for each other, but the molecules below the surface, being much greater in concentration than those gaseous water vapor and air molecules above the surface, exert a stronger force, causing the surface water molecules to be pulled inward (Figure 8.2). The liquid is forced to adjust itself to give

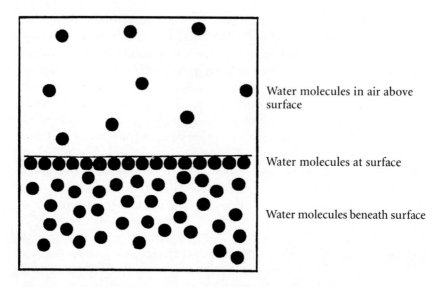

Water molecules in air above surface

Water molecules at surface

Water molecules beneath surface

Figure 8.2 The greater concentration of molecules in the liquid water compared to the lower concentration of molecules in the air over the water surface results in a greater attractive pull inward on the surface water molecules. This causes the liquid to adjust to give the minimum surface area. The water molecules at the surface are thereby compressed to produce a tight, membranelike surface, known as surface tension. The oil molecules oriented on the surface of the water as shown in Figure 8.4b lower the surface tension.

the minimum surface area and the surface water molecules to be tightly bound together in a sort of a skin. This is why raindrops are spherical, since a sphere contains the largest volume of any shape within the smallest surface area.

John Aitken, 1839–1919

In previous times many of the scientists were not professionals employed by major companies, universities, or research institutes as occurs today but were amateurs who had the financial resources to support themselves without working. Dr. John Aitken, like Benjamin Franklin, was an example of a scientist who pursued his interest in science just for the satisfaction of it. His investigations were in the field of meteorology, where he was the first to recognize the role of solid particles in the formation of rain and the conditions necessary for the formation of dew. In the drawing room of his house he set up his laboratory and workshop, where he conducted his experiments. Being a Scotsman, he had heard about Shield's experiments in wave damping and decided to try to explain why oil diminished the wave action. Performing experiments in small troughs of water, he concluded that the oil film worked by reducing the surface tension of the water.

Aitken disagreed with part of Franklin's explanation of how the oil damps the waves, namely that the oil film greases the waves so the wind cannot catch on them and instead slides over them. He compared oil and water, each alone in pans with wind blowing over them and found that the oil alone is more easily driven into waves than the water, but when the oil is put on the water, the water is much quieter than the oil alone. On his finding that the oil reduces the surface tension of the water, Aitken said, "Paradoxically as it may at first sight appear, it is nevertheless true that the weakening of the surface film by the oil is a source of strength to the surface of the water, and enables it to resist the action of the wind." Thus this effect would prevent the formation of small waves on the surface of the large ones and thereby prevent the formation and breaking of their crests. Franklin's explanation was therefore correct at least in this respect. Aitken used several methods to measure the ability of various oils to lower the surface tension of water, and he determined the oil's wave-checking activity. He found that those oils which lower the surface tension the most are best in wave checking. The oils he found most effective are sperm oil, followed by linseed oil and rapeseed oil, with cod-liver oil and olive oil less effective, and mineral oil least effective.[24] The sea captains had much the same results, with fish oils best, followed by vegetable oils, and petroleum oils last in the list. The light, refined petroleum oils were no good, but the heavy crude oils were better.

Lord Rayleigh, 1842–1919

Like Aitken, Lord Rayleigh (John William Strutt) was a wealthy amateur who provided himself a laboratory at his own expense. Although born into a world of wealth and privilege, Rayleigh became no playboy or idler. He was a member of the House of Lords by heredity but preferred science to politics and worked on a theory of sound, on optics and color vision, and also on mathematical and statistical problems. He explained why the sky is blue and the setting sun is orange-red. He also discovered the gaseous element argon, for which he received the Nobel prize in 1904. To add to his credits, he served as president of the Royal Society and as chancellor of Cambridge University.[25]

Rayleigh's interest in surface science, so the story goes, came about when the lady who served him tea always put a teaspoonful of water in the saucer. When asked why she did this, she replied, "So that the cup don't slip!" This somehow made him think of Franklin's experiments with oil on water. He had a high regard for Franklin and said of him, "no soberer inquirer ever existed." He repeated Franklin's experiment, carefully measuring the area of the film, and now that molecules were known, he was the first to conclude that the oil was spread one molecule thick — to a monomolecular film (Figure 8.1).

Rayleigh developed a method for testing oil on water in a small laboratory container. He used shavings of camphor which skipped rapidly when placed on water but made no motion when the surface was covered by oil. With these bits of camphor in his experiments, Rayleigh could tell how much oil on the water stopped their motion, which let him know the amount of oil to just fill the container and produce a monomolecular film. To explain why the oil film prevents the formation of waves, he likened the oil film to an inelastic membrane floating on top of the water which hampers its motion, under which condition the waves cannot be generated unless the forces are much greater than usual.[26]

Agnes Pockels, 1862–1935

When he had just published his papers on surface phenomena, Rayleigh received a letter from a young woman in Germany whom he had never met. He called his wife to translate the letter. The message was on a subject he was then studying, the action of oil on water. It begins:

> My Lord, — Will you kindly excuse my venturing to trouble you with a German letter on a scientific subject? Having heard of the fruitful researches carried on by you last year on the hitherto little understood properties of water surfaces, I thought it might interest you to know of my own observations on the subject. For various reasons I am not in a position to publish them in scientific periodicals, and I therefore adopt this means of communicating to you the most important of them...

The letter ends:

> I thought not to withhold from you these facts which I have observed, although I am not a professional physicist; and again begging you to excuse my boldness, I remain, with sincere respect,
>   Yours faithfully,
>   Agnes Pockels[27]

This letter is considered a landmark in the history of surface science. Most investigators in this area have cited the Pockels' work in their publications, but few have known anything about her. The letter introduces the most unusual case of Agnes Pockels, who was probably the first important woman scientist, preceding even Madame Marie Curie of radium fame. Without a college education, without encouragement, and without a laboratory, she did fine, quantitative research making important scientific measurements. She received no recognition from scientists in Germany — it was a man's world, and a woman's place in it was raising children. Her parents wouldn't pay for her advanced education; that was for her younger brother, who became a physicist, so she borrowed books to educate herself. As the daughter, she was assigned to prepare the meals for the family, manage the household, and take care of her sick parents, which she continued to do all of her life. It was in the kitchen at the age of eighteen or nineteen that her attention became focused on the greasy dishwater, and she began experimenting. The kitchen became her laboratory. She was twenty when she invented the slide trough, the basis for her measurement of the oil film. She did all her work alone since the German scientists took no notice of the work of a woman, particularly an uneducated woman. Pockels, who never married, was thirty when she had the courage to write to Lord Rayleigh about her work.

When Rayleigh read her letter he was astonished that a young woman had done this work. Could Agnes be a man's name in Germany? He wrote to Agnes and she replied, "With regard to your curiosity about my personal status, I am indeed a lady!" Rayleigh was so impressed by the work described in her letter that, although she had no credentials whatever, by using his influence with the editor of *Nature*, Britain's most prestigious science journal, he was able to have the letter published. That gave her recognition, and the German journals subsequently published her further work.

In her experiments Pockels made surface-tension measurements with pure water and observed that they were difficult to reproduce. She found that even dipping her finger in the water reduced the surface tension, apparently due to the oil on the skin. She measured the surface tension with a homespun device — a button suspended on a string. The button was lowered to the liquid surface, and the force to pull it off was measured. Her greatest accomplishment was to develop a trough in which the surface could be swept to control the area of the surface film so that quantitative measurements could be made. In his later experiments Rayleigh adopted this device, and in 1939 the noted scientist Langmuir stated that this primitive measuring device laid the foundation for nearly all modern work with films on water, and even today it is the standard tool of surface scientists. Pockels used her device to study wave damping, by mechanically initiating wave action and counting the number of waves produced relative to the amount of oil. By the measurements, she showed that a coherent film, insufficient to cover more than a small fraction of the surface, damped the ripples, and further increasing the surface with oil further damped them, until the whole surface was covered, when no further damping occurred. This experiment showed that a monomolecular film is all that is necessary for maximum effect. Agnes Pockels had the satisfaction of receiving recognition during her lifetime. At the age of 70 she was awarded an honorary doctor's degree for her achievements by the Carolina-Wilhelmina University in Brunswick, Germany.[28]

William Hardy, 1864–1934

Making use of Pockels' method, in 1926 Sir William Hardy said, "Without exaggeration the immense advances in the knowledge of the structure and properties of this fourth state of matter which have been made during this century are based upon the simple experimental principles introduced by Miss Pockels." William Hardy was a distinguished scientist, president of the Royal Society, who had shed light on the friction between surfaces and the nature of lubrication. He was a Welshman, trained as a biologist, who had turned his interest to the new field of biophysics, the physics of biological activities. Since the composition of all living organisms is largely water, and since oils are produced by plants and animals, he wanted to understand how they functioned in living organisms. He studied the structure of protoplasm and gels, the stability of emulsions and foams, and ultimately the nature of surface forces and films. He postulated for the first time the orientation of polar molecules on surfaces, the result being that "the surface of two different fluids would attract or repel one another according to the sign [electrical charge] of their surfaces."[29]

Hardy took notice of Franklin's experiment and remarked, "His discussion is worth reading. It has the spacious dignity and charm which the hurry and speculation of today have of necessity banished from scientific papers." (Hardy would be truly shocked if he experienced the tightness and brevity required of papers now, three-quarters of a century later, when there are so many people working and publishing in the science arena.) Regarding Franklin's observation that two ships in the convoy had smooth wakes, Hardy noted that tallow was used in those days to coat the bottoms of vessels to keep them free of barnacles, which slow their progress in the water, and suggested that these two ships could have been recently tallowed. Tallow, of course, is an animal fat or grease that is chemically similar to oils from other natural sources. As to Franklin's explanation of wave damping, Hardy says it is entirely based upon friction; the oil makes the wave smooth so the wind cannot catch on it. He adds, "I confess Franklin's explanation did not appeal to me at first, but I believe he is right."[30] He wrote:

> The comparative safety of a "smooth" is due not [to] the fact that the seas in it are sensibly smaller than those outside of it, but to the fact that they have been deprived of their viciousness. Now the viciousness of a sea, the degree of danger it carries to the mariner, is measured by its instability. It is when the head of the sea topples over and becomes a mass of water moving with a high velocity that it is dangerous. Within the limits of a "smooth" produced by oil the seas cease to break, or to "crackle" as Cornish fishermen say. The wind not only drives a sea forward by its horizontal pressure, but also draws the crest upwards by friction against the surface of the wave.
>
> If the friction between the air and the water be greatly reduced, [due to the oil on the surface] the wind fails to lift the crest of a wave to the point at which it is blown bodily over by the horizontal pressure. The wave then sinks down to a relatively harmless "swell" ...
>
> When there is no oil film a great wave carries countless ripples and wavelets each of which gives the wind a direct thrust on the surface. It is to the suppression of ripples and wavelets that the characteristic smooth appearance is due, and when they cease to be formed the chief "catch" of the wind upon the sea is lost.[31]

Irving Langmuir, 1881–1957

Hardy knew he didn't have the whole story and that the surface-tension phenomenon had something to do with it. His earlier postulation of the orientation of polar molecules was confirmed by Dr. Irving Langmuir, who added another important piece to the puzzle. Langmuir was neither a university professor like Hardy nor a self-supporting amateur like Rayleigh, but rather one of the new breed of industrial research scientists. He was an American employed by the General Electric Company and was the first American since Franklin to make a major step in solving the oil-on-water mystery. Langmuir was a physical chemist who developed the gas-filled incandescent lamp, made discoveries responsible for the radio

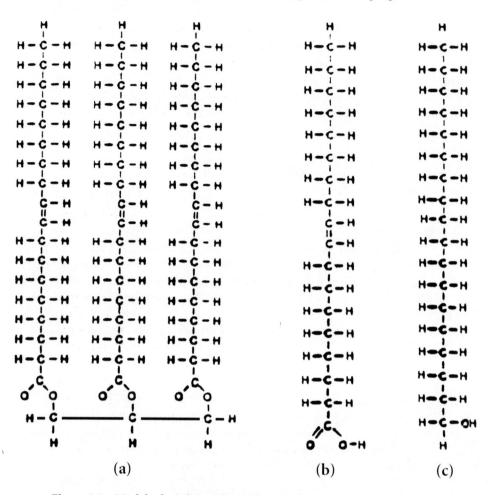

(a)   (b)   (c)

Figure 8.3a Model of triolein (olive oil) containing 3 molecules of oleic acid attached side by side to a molecule of glycerol.

Figure 8.3b The organic chemist's model of oleic acid, the major component of olive oil. With 18 carbon atoms in a chain, 17 of them are connected to hydrogen atoms (H) and another carbon atom (C), making this long tail of the molecule a water-hating (nonpolar) hydrocarbon repelled by water. The eighteenth carbon is attached to water-loving (polar) oxygen atoms, making this head of the molecule attracted to water.

Figure 8.3c Model of molecule of cetyl alcohol, used as a monomolecular film to retard the evaporation of water. Like oleic acid this molecule has a long, 18-carbon-chain hydrocarbon tail and an oxygen-containing head. The difference is that the head of the oleic acid molecule is an acid (carboxyl) group, as exists in citric acid and acetic acid (vinegar), whereas the head of the cetyl alcohol group is an alcohol group, as exists in ethyl alcohol and in sugar.

vacuum tube, discovered atomic hydrogen and utilized it in a process for atomic-hydrogen welding of metals. Apart from these achievements, he is better known by the public for his discovery of cloud seeding for producing rain. Charles Tanford, a well-known surface scientist who has written a most enjoyable history of surface science combining science and biography, *Ben Franklin Stilled the Waves*, says, "Scientifically Irving Langmuir represents the pinnacle of surface chemistry."

"Chemistry" is the key word. Langmuir's predecessors were physicists, and now a chemist was needed to apply his special ability to this jigsaw puzzle. Aitken found that oil lowers the surface tension of water — but why? Rayleigh said the oil acts as a membrane over the water — but how? Hardy postulated the orientation of polar molecules on surfaces of two different fluids and that attraction and repulsion has to do with electrical charges. Each man had added a piece to the solution of the puzzle. Langmuir in 1917 showed that each oil molecule of vegetable and animal origin (not mineral oil) has a polar (water-attracting) and nonpolar (water-repelling) end, and each end is oppositely charged. By allowing the oil to spread over water to a monomolecular film, as Franklin had done, Langmuir was able to calculate the shape of the molecules, their length, width, and thickness, and to visualize their orientation at the oil-water interface. By accurately knowing the area covered by the film and the quantity of oil employed in the film, he measured the thickness of the film and concluded that it was monomolecular. And then knowing "Avogadro's Number," namely, a figure that gives the number of molecules in a certain weight of any pure chemical depending on the total weight of the atoms in that molecule, he was able to compute the dimensions of various molecules of different oils and related chemicals.

The chemical composition of the oils, in terms of the different atoms they contain and the number of atoms in their molecules had been known for some time. The structure of these "organic" molecules in terms of how these atoms are connected to each other in the molecule was generally accepted. For example, pure olive oil, called triolein (Figure 8.3a), contains three molecules of oleic acid (Figure 8.3b) hooked up together in this large molecule of triolein. Each molecule of oleic acid is, in turn, made up of 18 atoms of carbon, 34 of hydrogen, and 2 of oxygen, with the carbons connected to each other in a long chain, with hydrogens attached to the carbons, and the oxygens at the end. Using other "fatty" (derived from fats) acids that contain a similar atomic makeup and structure but with carbon chains of 16, 18, or 26 carbons, respectively, Langmuir found with his calculations from their films that their molecular length roughly corresponds to the length of their carbon chains. Where organic chemists had

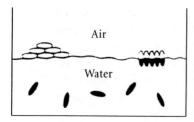

Figure 8.4a (left) Molecules such as hydrocarbons (pictured white) are repelled by water and do not dissolve in the water. Molecules like sugar (pictured black) are attracted to water and dissolve in it. Oils like olive oil, which have both water-attracted (polar) and water-repelled (nonpolar) components in the same molecule, orient themselves on the surface of the water, with the polar part in the water and the nonpolar part in the air.

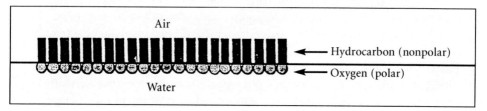

Figure 8.4b Oil molecules oriented with oxygen heads in the water and the hydrocarbon tails in the air.

pictured the three molecules of oleic acid in the triolein molecule connected side by side, Langmuir's measurements of the width of the triolein molecule found it to be approximately three times that of the width of each individual oleic acid molecule, thus confirming the organic chemists.[32]

Lubricating oil, called mineral oil and derived from petroleum, is made up of molecules exclusively containing atoms of hydrogen and carbon and are therefore called hydrocarbons. Natural oils and fats derived from vegetable and animal sources partially resemble the hydrocarbons due to their long carbon chains with their attached hydrogens. Both natural oils and petroleum oils are insoluble in water due to their long hydrocarbon chains. However, the oxygen atoms at the end of the hydrocarbon chain in the natural oils have an affinity for water, which contains oxygen (H_2O) and orient the oil molecule with the water-attracting "polar" oxygen end in the water and the "nonpolar" hydrocarbon chain, repelled by the water, oriented in the air away from the water (Figure 8.4a and 8.4b). This orientation with the oxygen atoms of the oil molecules in the water surface interrupts and interferes with the tight bonding of the surface water molecules, thus lowering the surface tension, as Aitken had discovered for oil on water. Soap, which is made from natural fats and oils, has one end which is "hydrophilic" (water loving) and the other end "hydrophobic" (water hating). It thus lowers the surface tension of the water, allowing the water-soluble dirt to more easily dissolve in the water and the oil-soluble dirt to be removed by the oil-loving hydrocarbon part of the soap molecule. Synthetic detergents, usually made from petroleum, have molecules which have an oil-soluble end and a water-soluble end and act like soap. The difference between these detergents and olive oil is that the detergents are soluble in water, while the oil is not soluble but has only a connection to the water.

For his brilliant work, Langmuir was awarded the Nobel Prize in 1932, the first recipient for research in surface science. Tanford in his book calls our attention to something surprising — Langmuir did not know of Franklin's work, which he had so well elucidated. After his Nobel award he was invited to give a lecture at the Franklin Institute in Philadelphia, created in honor of Philadelphia's proudest son. In the lecture he failed to mention Franklin's experiments, and even more surprising, no one at the Franklin Institute or in the audience informed him of the fact.[33]

Another area of Langmuir's investigation, which Franklin would have applauded, was his study of the effect of monolayers to retard the evaporation of water. He found that a monolayer of cetyl alcohol (Figure 8.3c), a chemical related to the oleic acid in olive oil, having a long hydrocarbon chain with polar oxygen atom in its head, effectively retards the evaporation of water.[34] This finding led to the use of a monolayer of cetyl alcohol on reservoirs, where tests showed it is up to 50 percent effective in slowing the evaporation of water, a finding of great importance, considering that water is our most precious resource and our ever-increasing demands for it in agriculture, industry, and air conditioning, as well as for drinking, bathing, sewage transport, and swimming pools. This technique for water conservation has been tested in the dry, western United States, where water loss from evaporation equals 15 million acre feet per year. Problems occur due to winds blowing the film onto the shore and boats breaking up the monolayer, but it is expected that this method will become more important in the future as the shortage of water becomes critical. The application of films to prevent the evaporation of water is also being investigated for water droplets in fogs used to protect fruit trees against frost and in mines to prevent fires and explosions. It is being tested for coating vegetables and meats, where drying results in spoilage.[35] For all his accomplishments in surface science, Langmuir was to receive yet another honor: The American Chemical Society named a journal on surface science after him.

Thickness of the Monolayer

Franklin never calculated the thickness of the monolayer. He could have; he was adept at calculations, having devised mathematical puzzles, called magic squares, and once when his friend the itinerant preacher George Whitefield preached from the top of the courthouse steps to the people standing in the field, Franklin experimented to find out how far the preacher's voice would reach. Walking to the rear of the semicircle where the preacher could be heard, and allowing a figure of two square feet per listener, Franklin calculated that 30,000 people could be reached. He was thus reconciled to newspaper accounts that Whitefield had preached to 25,000 people in the fields, and to the ancient stories he had read of generals haranguing whole armies, which he sometimes doubted.[36]

No doubt his duties in government took precedence over his scientific amusements and kept him from performing the thickness calculation. But scientists who repeated the experiment did the calculation, and it is interesting to compare Franklin's results, computed by Giles,[37] with theirs.[38]

Name	Date	Film Thickness
Franklin	1774	10×10^{-8} cm
Rayleigh	1890	16×10^{-8} cm
Pockels	1892	13×10^{-8} cm
Langmuir	1917	13×10^{-8} cm

It is astonishing to see how close Franklin's results come to those of the scientists. They had done their experiments under controlled laboratory conditions with exactly known areas and precisely measured amounts of oil, whereas Franklin's experiments were done outside with a teaspoonful of oil (what size, how full?) and just an estimate of the area affected. Davies and Rideal have a calculation of 25×10^{-8} cm (25 angstroms) for Franklin's results, which is a negligible difference when considered in the context of their statement: "As long ago as 1765 Benjamin Franklin observed that olive oil spreads over water to a thickness of 25 Angstroms. This was indeed the first conclusive proof of the ultimate indivisibility of matter and of the atomic theory: the monomolecular layer cannot become thinner than this, since 25 Angstroms is the length of the hydrocarbon chains."

Applications of Surface Science

Since Franklin's first surprising observation, surface science has now developed to become a full-fledged field of knowledge with many applications. Household detergents are synthetic soaps and, like soaps, operate at the surface between oil and water. Emulsions are made up of particles of different surface-active substances dispersed in each other like cream, which is an emulsion of oil (butterfat) in water (milk). Many cosmetics and drugs are dispensed as emulsions. Foams are formed at the interface of a liquid and air. They can be hardened to make sponges or to produce styrofoam for cups and lightweight insulation.

Oil films are used on water to prevent the breeding of mosquitoes and on solid surfaces to provide lubrication. Oil films for mosquito prevention function by reducing the surface tension of the water, causing mosquito larvae, pupae, and emerging adults to drown. For this purpose a monomolecular film of compounds of a long-chain (fatty) alcohol is employed (Figure 8.3c).[40] For the lubrication of metals, a relatively viscous (multimolecular) oil film is usually employed to decrease the friction between moving parts. This film prevents the seizure of the metal surfaces when there is no lubricant or when the oil film is too thin. A mixture of hydrocarbons and polar fatty acids like oleic acid are used (Figure 8.3b). Lubricating greases are made from these fatty acids and "soaps." Soaps are usually long-chain fatty acids combined with a polar metal atom. In mining, the froth flotation process is employed, in which the crude ore is finely ground with water and a surface-active chemical is added that allows only the pure ore particles to be wetted and transferred by air bubbles to a foam and then floated off for separation.

There are very many applications of monomolecular films on different surfaces. Catalysts of great importance to industry utilize solid film surfaces, and efficient computer chips are examples of these. A most important finding is that the cells of our body depend on surface membranes, which contain films of fatty chemicals of polar and nonpolar composition. These serve to control the selection of water-soluble and nonsoluble nutrients for penetration of the cell and for other materials that need to be secreted or excreted. Such now familiar names as cholesterol and lecithin are among these fatty chemicals, called lipids, which make up these membrane films. Certain oil-soluble medicines or, if present, poisons are absorbed because of these oily membranes. We purposely utilize some of these poisons for killing harmful cells like bacteria and cancer. Anesthetics used in surgery pass through these membrane films and produce narcosis because of their oil solubility, but they pass out again so we recover. The lipid membranes also serve as a waterproof bag to keep water-soluble materials necessary to the cell from leaking out. They do not, however, function alone; the cell membranes contain protein molecules that play a part, but they, like the lipids, also have water-attracting and water-repelling ends to orient them at the surfaces.[41]

The Italian Lamp

Our friend Franklin's observation of oil on water has gone a long way, but his Italian lamp never got as much attention as his observation at Clapham Pond. Explanations have been offered for the damping of the waves, but how can the peculiar turbulence of the water under the oil in the Italian lamp be explained? Giles suggests the following: The oil lowers the surface tension of the water so less energy is required to disturb the surface between the water and oil than the surface between oil and air. Then there will be more agitation in the water than in the oil. Further, because there is only a small difference in the weight (specific gravity) of the water and oil, any partially or wholly detached drops of water resulting from the motion will readily rise into the oil layer and fall back only slowly, causing the water surface to show considerable irregularities.[42, 43]

Wave Damping Revisited

N. K. Adam did not agree with the lubrication explanation of oil damping on waves in the wind given by Franklin and supported by Hardy, namely that the oil prevents the wind from gripping the water surface like it does on a clean surface.[44] Having examined the motion on the surface and layers slightly below the surface, he points to Aitken's measurements showing that oil films do not diminish the actual amount of motion caused by the wind to the water. He suggests instead that a clean surface, having no surface film, is blown in different directions with varying force by a gusty wind and that this appears to be the main, exciting cause of irregular, interfering ripples. The oil film offers resistance to compression of the molecules and distributes the motion uniformly over large areas, greatly diminishing the excitation of ripples.

Dinesh Shah, an internationally respected surface scientist at the University of Florida, proposes that in the case of waves, the lowering of the surface tension relieves the stress due to the stretch between their troughs and crests, thus tending to level the waves and keep them from breaking.[45] This functions well for shallow waves, as has been shown, but there is insufficient energy to materially affect the deep ocean waves caused by high winds and geological disturbances in the ocean floor.

It is well known that oil with good spreading power is essential for effective damping of waves. But why does the oil spread on water and not on a sheet of glass or marble? The molecules of water are in constant motion parallel to the surface, diffusing long distances, and, because of the water-attracting chemical groups in the oil molecules, the water and oil molecules adhere to each other, breaking the surface "skin" of the water, which lowers the surface tension. This releases a great amount of energy, furthering the process. The molecules of oil that have left the drop to form a film stick to the water surface, and the diffusing motions go on continually beneath the drop. The oil molecules that spread out first are continually being pushed our farther by the surface pressure of those first leaving the drop. In the case of a sheet of glass, a few oil molecules may diffuse a little way along the surface, but being less stable on the surface than in the drop, they soon return to the drop and do not stick to the surface.[46]

To bring the practical use of wave damping with oil up to date, one might ask, what is the practice in stormy seas today? Telephone calls to two Coast Guard stations resulted in the answer, "We never heard of it." Calls to the U.S. Coast Guard Academy and the U.S. Naval Academy produced the same answer. Some responded that oil can't be used because it is a pollutant and is prohibited. On the other hand, Captain Robert Meurn of the Merchant Marine Academy, in his recent book, "Survival Guide for the Mariner," comments, "Oil on seas that are breaking has a calming effect that is little short of miraculous, and it doesn't take much."[47]

Further investigation revealed what has happened to produce this confusion. In 1974, the Inter-Governmental Maritime Consultative Organization held an international conference in London, "Safety of Life at Sea," which called for the use of oil in all lifeboats, each vessel to contain 4.5 liters (1 gallon) of fish, animal, or vegetable oil.[48] However, as of July 1986, new instructions were given that lifeboats were to be constructed with a rigid cabin structure with a canopy to prevent breaking waves from getting into the boat. All new ships must follow this practice. Old ships must continue to use oil, and safety guidelines recommend but do not require new ships to carry animal or vegetable oil "to calm the surface or take the top off the waves."[49] Because they are biodegradable, these oils are not pollutants.

Catching Up Again with Franklin

Franklin was disappointed in the results of his ocean experiment, but he shouldn't have been. He had hoped the waves would disappear, as in the pond, but he realized why that was not so and observed that the oil kept the waves from breaking and flooding the boat, which proved to be the action that provided safety for the ships. Aitken's results show that the oils most effective in wave damping are fish oils and that the least effective are the hydrocarbon oils derived from petroleum. These findings agree with those of the sea captains, who found that the heavy petroleum oils are much better than the light oils, like kerosene. The effectiveness of the heavy oils can be explained by the fact that they contain oxygen compounds (phenols) and nitrogen bases (amines), which give them surface orientation, whereas the refined oils are made up of only hydrocarbons, which have no hydrophilic groups and do not orient their molecules at the surface. Hydrocarbons, therefore, do not form a monolayer.

After his years in England lobbying for America and occasionally pouring oil on water, Franklin went home and joined the Revolution. He was there less than a year when the Congress, making use of his diplomatic experience, sent him to France to obtain that country's help in the war, which he was successful in doing. When the war was finally won, he negotiated the Treaty of Paris, the peace treaty between Britain and the United States. It was then that he received a letter from Christopher Baldwin, a friend from London who had been with him in earlier years at Clapham Pond. The letter reads:

> Look my dear sir at the place from whence this letter is dated [Clapham Common]. Have you forgot it? I am sure you have not.... Have you forgot the many pleasant hours you have passed here? No, you have not. Have you forgot your throwing oil in the pond ... instantly smoothing the troubled water? ... Impossible! Tis you my dear sir who have troubled the mighty ocean! Tis you who have raised billow upon billow and called into action kings, princes, and heroes! And have poured the oil of peace on the troubled wave and stilled the mighty storm![50]

To bring this story forward to today's world, when you use detergents to wash your dishes and clothes, or when you pour a flavored emulsion of oil and water (salad dressing) on your lettuce and tomatoes, or when you admire that sturdy head of foam on a glass of beer or lemon meringue pie, you will smile and think of Benjamin Franklin.

9

The Hypnotist

Can you name a famous Viennese physician who practiced hypnotism and psychotherapy but whose nontraditional healing methods caused great controversy in the medical establishment? If you say Sigmund Freud you would be correct. But if you answer Franz Anton Mesmer, a Viennese physician who lived 100 years before Freud, you would also be correct. While Freud is known for psychoanalysis, Mesmer was famous for animal magnetism. Unlike Freud, Mesmer has been forgotten, but he still lingers in our language. We say, "the speaker mesmerized the audience" and "he has a magnetic personality."

A biographer of Mesmer has this to say about the man:

> Franz Anton Mesmer is one of the most extraordinary figures in medical history. And very likely the most controversial. He has been called the father of psychotherapy as well as of Christian Science, the discoverer of hypnosis, the progenitor of clairvoyance, telepathy and communication with the beyond; and he has been denigrated as a rogue, a charlatan, an arrogant pursuer of social and monetary favor, a meretricious magician. In his day it was asserted that he had sold his soul to the devil. More subtly, he has been cast as a visionary who unwittingly stumbled upon a discovery the value of which he was not able to see.[1]

Mesmer was born in 1734 in Germany near Switzerland to a middle-class Catholic family. He had an excellent education in Vienna, obtaining a doctor of philosophy degree; then six years later he became a doctor of

Figure 9.1 The glass armonica, a musical instrument invented by Benjamin Franklin. It employs glass bowls which are rotated by a foot pedal, and tunes are produced by pressing wet fingers against the edges of the bowls.

medicine at the age of thirty-two. Everything so far in his life was conventional, except for his medical-degree dissertation titled "The Influence of the Planets on the Human Body."[2]

A tall, handsome, ambitious man, Mesmer married a wealthy widow, a member of the Austrian aristocracy, ten years his elder, with a ten-year-old son. He settled down in Austria to a life of luxury as lived by the aristocracy at the time of Queen Maria Teresa. Mesmer was an accomplished musician who played several instruments including Benjamin Franklin's invention, the glass armonica. In 1746 the composer Gluck had given a concert using a number of glass tumblers filled with different amounts of water to give different tones when he rubbed the rims with his finger. A well-known performer with these glasses, Marianne Davies, played in London, where Franklin saw her and was captivated by their sound. He invented an instrument with rotating bowls in place of the glasses, which made it possible for the performer to play chords using both hands and more than one finger, as was necessary with the glasses.

Davies switched to Franklin's instrument and played a concert in Vienna before the emperor and empress, where it was heard by and made a great impression on Mesmer, who bought one and learned to play it, becoming most proficient at it.[3] It was his favorite instrument. He would use it in his work, and it was a companion to him all his life. Mesmer enjoyed musical sessions, inviting friends to join him in them at his spacious house. Leopold Mozart, father of the composer Wolfgang Amadeus Mozart was a friend and frequent house guest, bringing with him young Wolfgang and his sister. Mozart was fascinated by Franklin's armonica, and Wolfgang learned to play it, later composing music for it.[4]

Despite his high living, Mesmer was a serious physician who did not neglect his medical practice. This practice was quite ordinary: He treated all illnesses but had a special interest in nervous diseases. He pursued his private practice from his home, where he maintained an office, a dispensary, and a research laboratory. One of Mesmer's patients was a young woman named Francisca Oersterlin, familiarly known as Franzl, who was a permanent house guest of the Mesmers. She was a cheerful, friendly person who enjoyed doing favors for others but unfortunately suffered from periodic fits of terrible hysteria.

Mesmer described her symptoms: "Her hysterical fever caused convulsions, spasms of vomiting, inflammation of the intestines, inability to make water, agonizing toothache and earache, despondency, insane hallucinations, cataleptic trance, fainting, temporary blindness, feelings of subluxation, attacks of paralysis lasting for days, and other terrible symptoms."[5]

The sieges always ended with a regular climax of convulsions and unconsciousness, after which Franzl would begin to breathe regularly again and gradually regain her normal composure. Mesmer treated her using all the standard methods of that time, which included drugs, bleeding, purging, and blistering, but to no avail. The Mozarts were very fond of Franzl, and Leopold Mozart wrote to his wife about her condition. On July 21, 1773, he wrote, "We found Franzl in bed, very much emaciated." On August 2 he wrote, "Franzl is now recovered." And on August 12, "Franzl has again been dangerously ill and blisters had to be applied to her arms and feet. She has knitted a red silk purse for Wolfgang." On August 21, "Franzl has had a second relapse and has again recovered. It is amazing how she can stand so much bleeding and so many medicines, blisters, convulsions, fainting fits. She is nothing but skin and bones."[6]

Search for a Theory and a Cure

Mesmer's frustration with Franzl's case led him to develop his own theory and treatment of disease, particularly of nervous disorders. In so doing, he went back to the dissertation he had written for his medical degree, which called upon ideas of Paracelsus, the famous German alchemist and physician of the Renaissance. Paracelsus believed in a cosmic fluid that had healing properties. He used magnets to concentrate this cosmic fluid in his patients to cure them. Mesmer also borrowed from the "Irish stroking doctor," Greatracks, who acquired great fame in curing people by laying his hands on the afflicted part, stroking the stricken area, applying holy water and praying. Mesmer considered himself a modern scientist, so he incorporated only the touching and stroking aspects of Greatrack's procedure, not the religious part. In the grand cosmological theory that Mesmer developed, he envisioned a universal fluid force like gravitation or magnetism that affected the human body, especially the nervous system. This fluid, which he termed "animal magnetism," was necessary for the body's well-being, and anything that interfered with it would cause disease. Thus, there was only one cause of disease and only one remedy.

To test his theory, Mesmer obtained magnets and placed them on parts of Franzl's body when she was having one of her attacks. He noted that she felt volatile currents moving within her body in the direction of the magnets, after which the attack was alleviated. He repeated the experiment with the same results. He felt that he had generated artificial tides in her nervous system and was controlling the flow of the universal fluid by the use of the magnets. In later experiments he found that he could obtain the same reaction from Franzl and from other patients suffering from nervous maladies when he used wood or other nonmagnetic materials, or even touched them himself. He interpreted this to mean that he himself, although nonmagnetic, was acting as a magnet, and thus was in effect an animal magnet, capable of magnetizing people and objects just as an ordinary magnet magnetizes iron.

By continual treatments with his new method, Mesmer cured Franzl of her hysteria and terminated her psychosomatic symptoms. In 1780, Mozart visited the Mesmers and reported on seeing Franzl. "I hardly recognized her, she is so large and fat. She has three children, two girls and a boy."[7] Following this success, and having similar results with other patients, Mesmer assured himself that his theory was correct. Hypnotism then being unknown, he did not know that he had hypnotized his patients, whose ailments were amenable to the power of suggestion. He immediately publicized his results expecting to receive the commendations of his fellow professionals and was crushed when, instead of the praise he expected, he was totally rejected by the medical community, who considered his theory absolute nonsense and who found other explanations for his successes. The general public on the other hand was not so skeptical and was ready to believe in the results; thus his office was swamped with patients hoping to be cured. Of course, not all his patients were cured, but he was successful enough to be convinced that he had something very important to offer the world. Unable to convince the medical community in Vienna of the credibility of his work, he departed for Paris, hoping his discovery would be appreciated by the broad-minded physicians of that great city.

Paris

Paris was the place to go. It was agog for science. Just a century ago, Newton's laws, made intelligible for the French by Voltaire, explained the movement of the planets in their orbits; Benjamin Franklin, who had tamed the terrible lightning, was now living in their city, and the brothers Montgolfier had sent men in balloons to heights only dreamed of before. Mesmer's reputation had preceded his arrival in Paris in February 1778. Although the medical community treated him with great reserve, the Parisians were enthusiastic in their welcome and interest. People of all classes rushed to his clinic in the hope that his new revolutionary procedure would end their suffering. Among his patients were many ladies of fashion, some of whom were not ill but merely curious. To Mesmer's delight, a few physicians who came to observe his procedure were so impressed by what they saw that they volunteered to assist him. The most distinguished of these was Charles Deslon, a young member of the Paris Faculty of Medicine and the private physician to the brother of King Louis XVI. Deslon was completely converted to Mesmer's method and became his chief assistant, an important asset to Mesmer's chance for success in persuading the doctors of Paris to accept his findings.[8]

Mesmer's strategy was to win over the scientists first, hoping the doctors would follow. He would present his discovery to the members of the French Academy of Sciences, who were eminent scientists. As scientists they understood physics, including the cosmos, gravitation, electricity, and magnetism. In order to prepare his official meeting with the Academy, Mesmer arranged a dinner with Benjamin Franklin, who was in France and was a member of the French Academy. Franklin had conducted experiments on the effect of electricity on paralyzed people and was interested in learning about Mesmer's procedures, so Mesmer had sent him his report on animal magnetism. With his musician friend, Madame Brillon, whom John Adams (also in Paris) called "one of the most beautiful women in Paris and a great mistress of music," Franklin visited Mesmer to hear him play the glass armonica. Unfortunately for Mesmer, Franklin had since received a devastating letter about Mesmer's medical procedure from Jan Ingenhousz, physician to Queen Maria Theresa of Austria and friend of Franklin, who had personally witnessed the procedure: "I hear that the Vienna conjuror Dr. Mesmer is at Paris ... that he still pretends a magnetical effluvium streams from his finger and enters the body of any person without being obstructed by walls or any other obstacles, and that such stuff too insipid to get belief by any old woman, is believed by your friend Le Roy." At the dinner the conversation was strained: Mesmer and Franklin talked affably about Franklin's glass armonica, but Franklin was reluctant to discuss Mesmer's medical work. Mesmer was hoping to get Franklin's endorsement of his procedure. This occasion proved to be a foreshadowing of Mesmer's meeting with the members of the academy. Afterward, Madame Brillon said to Franklin, "In heaven Mesmer will content himself with playing the armonica and will not bother us with his electrical fluid."[9]

The Scientists and the Doctors

According to Mesmer, the members of the academy were disorderly and seemed to have closed minds about his theory of animal magnetism. They insisted that he give them an immediate demonstration of his procedure. To comply, he bandaged the eyes of a patient and made a few passes under his nose. Then, when the patient was told by Mesmer that he smelled the odor of sulfur, the patient agreed that he did, although no sulfur was present. Similarly, when given a cup of water, he said he tasted different flavors, which Mesmer had suggested to him. This was a classic case of hypnotism, but neither Mesmer nor the members of the academy understood it. Instead, the members were skeptical of the demonstration, suspecting trickery, and they claimed that it was too intangible to sustain Mesmer's theory of scientific medicine.

Not easily discouraged, Mesmer decided next to approach the doctors. He was afraid the Paris Faculty of Medicine was too much like the hostile Vienna Faculty, so he applied to another medical organization, the Royal Society of Medicine. This society arranged for two of its members to visit Mesmer's clinic and observe his cures. In his clinic they saw Mesmer place his hands on a patient's shoulders, then run his hands down her arms to the finger tips, hold her thumbs for a moment, and then repeat the process. He explained that he was setting up a flow of animal magnetism in her extremities. This procedure produced gasping with palpitations in the patient, followed by convulsions before she recovered. This patient was suffering from epilepsy, and coincidentally she had been treated without success by one of the observing doctors. That doctor was not interested in seeing Mesmer controlling her epileptic fits when he had failed, and he reported that patients who said they had been cured by Mesmer were actually only pretending to be epileptic, paralyzed, or blind. Both of the doctors claimed that what they had witnessed was a useless, immoral spectacle.[10]

Upset and angry but not defeated, Mesmer insisted that the society send another delegation of observers to his clinic. They agreed and sent a trio of distinguished French physicians. Mesmer carefully selected his patients in order to make the best impression. During the next two months he with Deslon showed the examiners cures that should have served as absolute proof of the validity of his method. They had made the paralyzed walk, the blind see, and the deaf hear. But again Mesmer failed to convince his audience. The doctors merely stated, "The facts are undoubtedly amazing, but they are inconclusive." It was not in Mesmer's nature to give up, but now he changed his tactics. He wrote his *Memoir*, explaining in detail his theory of animal magnetism, and for the next few years he devoted himself completely to the patients who thronged to his clinic. His system in the clinic consisted of the séance, the trance, and the crisis.

The Séance, the Trance, and the Crisis

Mesmer was certain that with the continuing success of his practice the validity of his method and theory would be assured. To attain this success, he carefully screened patients, avoiding those patients whose ailments were organic, causing physical damage to the tissues, and selecting those patients whose ailments originated in the nervous system. He was aware that imagination and suggestion also played a part in the healing process, and he did his best to provide the proper mystique. In his clinic the elegantly decorated rooms were dimly lit; the odor of exquisite perfumes wafted in the air, and strains of ethereal music emanated from a glass armonica. A doctor who heard the music said it sent a "shiver up my spine." Heavy drapes covered the windows so that no light or sound from the outside could intrude. In addition, Mesmer and his assistants spoke only in whispers.

He had found that the effect he was trying to produce was contagious, passing from one patient to another. So he conducted séances with as many as 30 patients arranged in a circle around a large wooden tub (called a baquet) that was filled with water, powdered glass, and iron filings. The baquet had iron rods protruding at regular intervals which were jointed so a rod could be held by each patient. Mesmer explained that the baquet captured and concentrated the flow of the magnetic healing fluid and transported it through the iron rods to the patient. His method was said to allow the diagnosis and treatment of any illness and required no preparation, except "extreme cleanliness and abstinence from tobacco."[11]

Dressed in purple breeches, a coat with ruffles, and a powdered wig, Mesmer carried an iron rod in his right hand and walked about from patient to patient. He would point the rod at the patient to let the healing fluid flow through him and the rod to the patient and put his left hand on the part that was ailing, to direct the animal magnetism to where it was needed. The patients were excited by the feel of his hand. As the process continued, there was heavy breathing among the patients, nervous coughing, shuddering, trembling, convulsive motions, and hypnotic trances, with each patient stimulating the others to greater intensity, until the entire group became hysterical.

When patients with convulsions became violent they were taken and individually treated in a room with padded walls. Mesmer maintained that this final stage, termed the crisis, was absolutely necessary to effect the cure. One of Mesmer's disciples showed that the crisis was not really necessary, but Mesmer stubbornly insisted that there could be no cure without the patient having been transported through the whole process, terminating in the crisis.

Mesmer described reactions in patients he said he had cured. With an asthmatic patient, he said, "I pointed my wand at his chest. His breathing immediately stopped and he would have fainted if I had not ceased." With a paralytic woman: "As soon as I pointed the wand at her left side, Mademoiselle Belancourt staggered and fell on the floor with violent convulsions." And with a neuralgic man: "When I pointed my rod at him, this caused him to tremble wildly; his face became flushed; he fainted and fell back on the sofa unconscious." The patient's convulsions were marked by reactions including violent, involuntary movements of the limbs and whole body, throbbing in the chest, rapid blinking eyes, crossed eyes, piercing cries, tears, hiccups, and uncontrollable laughter.[12]

An army officer, Charles du Hassay, described his condition and

Mesmer's treatment, which Mesmer used as a testimonial to the Royal Society of Medicine. Hassay was suffering from a series of ailments: fever, trembling, protruding eyes, and partial paralysis. "My gait," he wrote, "was that of an elderly drunkard, not that of a man of 40." When treated by Mesmer with animal magnetism, he said he felt intense sensations from head to foot. "I went into a crisis that my body seemed to be turning to ice. Then I felt intense heat causing much fetid sweating." The crisis lasted more than a month. "Four months later, I can stand erect and stable on my feet. I'm not suffering any pain. I have excellent digestion and appetite. In short, I am entirely free of any infirmities."[13]

The Queen

Deslon, Mesmer's associate, wrote a book on mesmerism in which he refers to his own illness, namely, that since childhood he had stomach pains and headaches which were not alleviated with any treatment until he found Mesmer's. By 1781, Mesmer, having received such testimonials, decided to push for the recognition he deserved. This time he ignored the unappreciative doctors and scientists and went straight to the top, to Queen Marie Antoinette of France. She was like him, Austrian, the daughter of Queen Maria Theresia, and was reached through two of his enthusiastic patients, Princess de Lambelle and the Duchess de Chaulnes, who were intimate with the queen.[14] Mesmer had been threatening to leave Paris as he had left Vienna, to go where he would be appreciated. After his threat, he was besieged by hordes of the sick who had heard of his cures, and the titled ladies advised the queen that his loss would be a disaster for the people.

The queen turned the matter over to her minister, Count de Maurepas, to act in her behalf. In March 1781, Maurepas met with Mesmer and Deslon at the Royal Palace at Versailles and offered Mesmer a cash settlement if he would remain in Paris: namely, an annual pension of 20,000 livres, plus 10,000 livres additional for a school of animal magnetism, in which the government would be able to enroll three students. Amazingly, Mesmer turned down the offer, suspicious that the government's students would be spies who would report on him. He told Maurepas that his only demands apart from the money was official endorsement of animal magnetism by the government and that only he would choose the students. Maurepas was astounded at the temerity and ingratitude of this man in rejecting such a generous offer and substituting instead his own demands, and Maurepas faithfully reported this unfavorable incident to the queen.[15]

Totally disregarding strict diplomatic protocol, Mesmer wrote directly to the Queen as an equal, attempting to persuade her to champion his method. Insulted by his audacity in disrespecting her position, she ignored him. He was fortunate that he wasn't sent to the Bastille for he crassly had his letter printed. For his part, Mesmer made good on his threat and left Paris as earlier he had left Vienna. He settled down in the little town of Spa in Belgium, known for its mineral springs and therapeutic baths, where he set up his clinic and took the baths.

Society of Harmony Universal

Some of his devoted patients followed him from Paris, among whom were a lawyer, Nicolas Bergasse, and a banker, Guillaume Kormann. Both of them, so delighted with Mesmer's treatment of their mental depression, decided (with Mesmer's approval) to expand his marvelous gift to humanity, which had failed to be recognized by the entrenched professionals. They created a secret society, which they called the Society of Universal Harmony, and invited membership on the payment of a fee to Mesmer, for which he would teach the members the practice of animal magnetism in order to enable them to be practitioners in their own establishment.

This enterprise was so successful that within two years there were several thousand paying members of the society in 24 lodges in cities in France and other countries.[16] Among the members were some notable people like the Marquis Lafayette, who had fought in the American Revolution under Washington; Jaques Brissot, who visited Franklin when the latter returned to Philadelphia; and Franklin's older grandson, William Temple Franklin, who was serving as Franklin's secretary in France. On leaving Paris to go to America, Lafayette wrote George Washington about his great enthusiasm for animal magnetism and told Washington, "Before leaving, I will obtain permission to reveal to you Mesmer's secret, which, you may believe, is a great philosophical discovery." When Mesmer learned that Lafayette had written to Washington, he sent Washington a letter telling him of the extensive benefits his discovery would bring to humankind. Washington was somewhat confused by all this and wrote a polite but noncommittal letter telling Mesmer how much he appreciated the honor of the anticipated advantages to be obtained from Mesmer's discovery. In America, Lafayette spoke to the American Philosophical Society about the invisible power of animal magnetism but was not at liberty to tell how it worked, leaving the scientists unimpressed.[17]

Now feeling vindicated, Mesmer moved back to Paris and founded an institute, which served as a clinic, medical school, and head lodge of the Society of Universal Harmony. He attracted an able and enthusiastic staff to assist him and became fabulously successful, famous and wealthy, being supported by a large following of the public. His triumph, however, only served to arouse his detractors, who considered him at best a quack and at worst, a charlatan, a sorcerer, and a thief who presented a grave danger to medicine and the people of France. They counseled the king to thoroughly investigate Mesmer and his entire operation.

The king acquiesced, appointing an official commission under the direction of the Academy of Sciences and Faculty of Medicine. Because of his fame as a scientist and a diplomat, Franklin was appointed to head the commission. Other members included the famous chemist Lavoisier, who had explained combustion and founded modern chemistry; Guillotin, the surgeon who recommended the use of the decapitating machine (named after him) as a merciful means of execution; Le Roy, a physicist and close friend of Franklin; Bailly, the leading French astronomer; and DeBary, a noted mathematician.

Because Deslon, who had been private physician to the king's brother, the Count d'Artois, and was a well-respected French doctor rather than a foreigner like Mesmer, he was selected by the king to present the case for mesmerism to the commission. Deslon was now independent of Mesmer, having established his own clinic when Mesmer had left Paris for Spa.[18] Mesmer was highly indignant that someone other than himself, who was the discoverer of animal magnetism, should be selected to defend it. He wrote to Franklin expressing his objections, but without avail.

The Investigation

In March 1784, in the first stage of the investigation, the commission visited Deslon's clinic and carefully observed the paraphernalia he employed: the baquets, wands, musical instruments, and clothing. They witnessed the characteristic phenomena of the treatment: the twitching, convulsions, trances, crises, and cures. The fact that these cures occurred was acknowledged, but the explanation given for them was disputed. Franklin could not come to Paris since he was ill suffering from gout, so the commission held the second stage of the investigation at Franklin's house in the country.

There, the commissioners, Franklin, his secretary, his grandson, and Madame Brillon were all magnetized by Deslon but failed to exhibit any symptoms. A woman was blindfolded, and one of the commissioners, pretending to be Deslon, magnetized her as Deslon had done with his patients. She immediately fell into a fit of trembling with spasms and pain. People were magnetized by Deslon while he faced them, but the results were not reproduced when he magnetized them without their knowledge. Many subjects said they experienced beneficial effects when they were led to believe that they were being magnetized. A classic example was the case of a 12-year-old boy whom Deslon had brought with him. On entering Franklin's garden, Deslon magnetized an apricot tree and stated that it would affect anyone who touched it. The boy was blindfolded and led to four unmagnetized trees, one after the other. Benjamin Franklin Bache, Franklin's younger grandson, who was also in France at the time, describes the results:

> When the boy touched the first tree he coughed nervously and began to perspire. With the second tree, he felt a pain in his head, which increased at the third tree. He then announced that he knew he was closer to the magnetic tree, while in fact he was even further from it. At the fourth tree he stopped short and fainted, whereupon Deslon carried him into the house and revived him.[19]

The Report

In August 1784, the commission sent its report, signed by Franklin and the commissioners, to the king. It was believed to have been written by Bailly or Lavoisier. In brief, it states:

> Having demonstrated that the imagination without magnetism produces convulsions and that magnetism without imagination produces nothing, the Commissioners have concluded there is no proof of the existence of animal magnetic fluid. This non-existent fluid is consequently useless. The violent effects that one observes in public treatment stemming from the touching, come from the activated imagination and that unconscious imitation that causes us to repeat what strikes our senses, in spite of ourselves.[20]

Lavoisier, a brilliant and astute scientist, comments on the problem of drawing conclusions in medicine:

> It is in medicine that the difficulty of evaluating probabilities is greatest. Since the life principle in animals is an always active force

continuously tending to overcome obstacles, since nature left to itself cures many illnesses, then when remedies are used it is infinitely difficult to determine what can be attributed to nature and what to the remedies. Also, whereas most people consider the cure as proof of the remedy's effectiveness, a wise man regards it as a result of a lesser or greater degree of probability, and this probability can become certainty only after large numbers of related facts have been collected.[21]

Today many medical experiments are run by the "double blind" procedure, in which half the patients receive the treatment and the other half receive a facsimile (placebo) without the treatment, but neither the doctor nor the patients are aware which are which until the results are evaluated mathematically without bias by statistical analysis.

The Royal Medical Society of Paris decided that it should also have a part in this medical matter. They petitioned the king and obtained permission to conduct their own investigation of Deslon. They appointed a committee of four, who concluded that animal magnetism was useless and even dangerous, and they recommended that the members of the society be forbidden to practice its methods. However, one member, Antoine de Jussieu, director of the botanical gardens, dissented and issued a minority report. He was convinced that there is an unknown fluid or force which he believed is conveyed by animal heat "emanating continuously from one body to another, developed, augmented, or diminished by physical or moral [psychological] means." Some believe he showed a deeper insight than his colleagues and anticipated later psychological theories.

Shortly after the report was completed, Franklin wrote to his elder grandson, who was a follower of Mesmer:

The report makes a great deal of talk ... and some feel that consequences may be drawn from it by infidels to weaken our faith in some of the miracles of the New Testament. Some think it will put an end to Mesmerism, but there is a wonderful deal of credulity in the world and deceptions as absurd have supported themselves for ages.[22]

One year later Franklin wrote to Ingenhousz:

Mesmer continues here and still has some adherents and some practice. It is surprising how much credulity still subsists in the world. I suppose all the physicians in France put together have not made so much money during the time he has been here, as he has done. And we have now a fresh folly. A magnetizer pretends that he can by establishing what is called a Rapport between any person and a somnambule, put it in the power of that person to direct the actions of the somanmbule by a simple strong volition only, without speaking or making any signs; and many people daily flock to see this strange operation![23]

It is likely because of Franklin's involvement in the Mesmer case that the Medical Society of London elected him to their membership, although it was an institution otherwise restricted to physicians.

Mesmer angrily responded to the reports, stating that he alone and no one else was qualified to represent animal magnetism to the commission. He appealed to the government to give him an impartial examination, but his appeal was refused. He wrote to Franklin saying, "I have the world for a judge.... I will be vindicated by posterity."

In May 1784, Thomas Jefferson arrived on the Paris scene to relieve Franklin as American ambassador. Although Jefferson was not involved in the Mesmer affair, he could not help learning about it since it was then the talk of Paris. Besides, since Jefferson had a keen interest in scientific matters he must have discussed it with Franklin and Lafayette, who held opposite opinions on mesmerism. Jefferson, however, was not indecisive in his opinion, as he expressed it to a correspondent:

Reasonable men if they ever paid any attention to such a hocus pocus theory, were thoroughly satisfied by the Report of the Commissioners. But as the unreasonable is the largest part of mankind, and these were the most likely to be affected by this madness, ridicule has been let loose for their cure. Mesmer and Deslon have been introduced on the stage.[24]

The ridicule Jefferson refers to appeared in pamphlets, engravings, and even in an opera. One picture shows Franklin and the commissioners holding the report, a blindfolded, partly dressed woman falling out of a tub, and Mesmer with Deslon flying away, Mesmer on a broomstick, Deslon on a winged donkey.[25] Lavoisier proposed that the academy send up a balloon carrying a dummy with a wooden tub on its head and have it drop anti–Mesmer leaflets. In another arena, Mozart composed the comic opera, Così Fan Tutte, in which two young men decide to test the integrity of their lovers. Dressed as Muslims so as not to be recognized by the young ladies, they offer the ladies great wealth if they will marry them. Turned down, they test the girls further by pretending to take poison and to be dying for want of their love. In comes a doctor — really the maid in disguise — who is holding an enormous magnet that she says comes directly from the hands of Dr. Mesmer. She rattles off medical-sounding erudition in mock Latin and then goes over the "dying" men with wild mesmeric motions. They convulse, twisting and turning and banging their heads on the floor, after which they are well again. All of this is rendered comically ridiculous with appropriate acting and singing.[26]

The Secret Report

Right after the commission had made its public report, it made another report for the king alone, which remained secret for 15 years. This report dealt with the sexual nature of animal magnetism. It pointed out that mesmerism had a greater attraction for women than for men. They are more sensitive, and with regard to the touching of women, it said, "Touch them in one point, and you touch them everywhere.... Women are like musical strings ... let one begin to vibrate, all the others share the motion." It reported that while under treatment, the older women were simply put to sleep, but the younger ones received delightful titillations. It maintained most of the women drawn to magnetism were not really ill but came for treatment because they were bored. They have enough charm to act on the doctor; thus the danger is reciprocal. The commissioners were especially concerned about the individual treatment the female patients received when sitting face to face, with the magnetizer squeezing her thighs between his knees while his hands caressed her eyes, cheeks, and arms. "Then he lightly applied his hands to the abdomen and left them there for a moment. They lean closer. Their faces almost touch. Their breath mingles. Judgment is suspended.... Her face becomes flushed...."

The commissioners were worried about the sustained proximity, the indispensable touching, the communication of personal heat, "the meeting of eyes [that] are nature's known ways ... for bringing about the communication of sensations and affection. It is not surprising that the senses are inflamed...." Or when, after the séance, the agitated, helpless woman was taken into a private room. They concluded that the whole procedure was not only fraudulent but immoral as well.[27] The commissioners had no proof for these morality charges, but they had suspicion and imagination. It must have come as a surprise to them to find that there were no complaints registered against Mesmer or his young assistants by the patients. Either nothing untoward happened to the women, or they had no objection to what did happen.

Following the report, the Faculty of Medicine formally outlawed employment of animal magnetism in medical practice; however, most of those practicing animal magnetism were not physicians, and they continued to treat patients. Mesmer left Paris and visited lodges of the Society of Harmony in other cities in France, where he was accorded the honor and respect he felt he deserved. But, being proud and single minded, unable to compromise or share credit, he feuded with the leaders in the organization and even attacked Deslon, his closest and most devoted follower, for presuming to represent animal magnetism to the commission. Deslon died in 1786, when, committed to his belief in Mesmerism, even when deathly ill, he refused any other treatment.

Retirement

In his retirement Mesmer lived well on the money he had made, traveling widely, then settling in Switzerland near Lake Constance. He wrote his final book on animal magnetism in which he discusses man, morality, electricity, light, fire, gravitation, and other phenomena involved in the flow of animal magnetism in the cure of illnesses. In 1812 a member of the Berlin Academy of Science paid him a visit and then published a 350-page manuscript with the title *Mesmerismus*. In 1813 another book, *Critical History of Animal Magnetism*, was published. Mesmer always retained his unaltered faith in the scientific basis of animal magnetism, but in his old age he delved into such occult questions as "How can a sleeping man see objects at a distance, and how can he predict future events?" Also, "can animals foresee the future?" Mesmer maintained that they could.[28]

In his Paris days a gypsy told him he would die in his 81st year, and approaching that age he moved to Germany to be near his relatives when the end arrived. He rejoined the Catholic Church when his priest assured him that there was no conflict between Catholicism and animal magnetism. Unlike Deslon, he discussed his deteriorating physical condition with physicians. He enjoyed listening to and playing music, especially on the glass armonica. He did not allow any feelings he might have had against Franklin for preventing his enjoying that instrument, and on his deathbed he requested the priest play it for him. He died on March 5, 1815, in his 81st year, as the gypsy fortune teller had predicted. The members of the Berlin Academy came and placed a large marble monument on his grave.[29]

Mesmerism

Mesmer outlived many of his followers and antagonists. Lavoisier and Bailly among the commissioners and Brissot of the followers ended their days in the 1870s in the French Revolution on Guillotin's machine. Franklin died in 1790. The Mesmer investigation was his last important activity in France before going home, where he helped write the Constitution and finished work on his autobiography. Mesmerism survived the commissioners, the physicians, and Mesmer himself. As late as 1856 a medical journal titled *The Zoist: A Journal of Cerebral Physiology and Mesmerism* was published in London. Mesmerism gradually branched out, changing in several ways.

Bergasse, Mesmer's friend and cofounder of the Harmony Society, along with Lafayette and Brissot, were political and social reformers, influenced by Rousseau, as well as being followers of Mesmer. Bergasse had written extensively, extending mesmerism from the medical to the educational, political, and philosophical areas. This helped spread mesmerism and its reputation.[30] In Germany, Goethe, Fichte, and Schopenhauer acclaimed Mesmer and his work. The philosopher Schopenhauer went so far as to assert: "From a philosophical standpoint Mesmerism must be regarded as the most significant discovery made at any time."[31] While in America, Edgar Allan Poe was a firm believer in mesmerism and used it in several of his fantastic, horror tales.[32]

The Society of Universal Harmony set up to spread Mesmer's method had collapsed in 1789, but thanks to Bergasse's effort it was restored in 1815 as the Society of Mesmerism and was reorganized again in 1842. In its later years mesmerism was taken up not only by mystics and fortunetellers, but also by utopian socialists.[33]

Did Benjamin Franklin change his mind and become a supporter of mesmerism? According to Robert Owen, the answer could be yes. Owen was a Welsh, idealistic industrialist and mesmerist who founded the celebrated utopian community of New Harmony in southern Indiana. In 1853 an article appeared in the *Journal du Magnetisme* in which Owen reported that Franklin and Jefferson had reconsidered and weakened their previous conviction against mesmerism. How did Owen come to this conclusion? Franklin died in 1790 and Jefferson in 1826. Had Owen been told by someone who knew them, or had he discovered unknown letters of theirs? No, he tells us that the information came from the gentlemen face to face, in 17 or 18 séances he had with them.[34]

In 1838, Charles Poyen, coming from France, demonstrated animal magnetism in the United States. One of his converts was Phineas Parkhurst Quimby, who worked cures but became convinced that his patients were curing themselves. This led him to the conclusion that illness was a delusion inflicted by a person on himself; thus animal magnetism or any other medical treatment was useless. A person cured himself by positive thinking. One of his patients was Mary Baker (later Mary Baker Eddy), who added Bible reading to Quimby's method and founded Christian Science. Eddy was fiercely opposed to animal magnetism, calling it esoteric magic and writing against it in her book, *Science and Health*. Even in 1969, when a Christian Science writer asking the question, What is animal magnetism? answered it, "The Sum Total of Evil."

In 1875, Madame Blavatsky borrowed Mesmer's cosmic fluid and founded the Theosophical Society, devoted to disseminating the mysterious wisdom of the East. She wrote, "Mesmerism is the most important branch of magic; and its phenomena are the effects of the universal agent which underlies all magic and has produced in all ages so-called miracles." According to her system of belief, it is this universal cosmic agent that allows for reincarnation.

Émile Coué was another graduate of the school of Mesmer. He was a French pharmacist who developed his own method of healing, which he called autosuggestion and was similar to Quimby's system. Coué's formula for happy, healthy living was for everyone to repeat the words "Every day and in every way, I am getting better and better."

Despite the fact that he had been rejected by the scientific communities in Vienna and Paris, Mesmer always considered himself first and foremost a scientist. It is fitting, therefore, that his major legacy should be in science. Although the commissioners had destroyed his grandiose theory, and other practitioners of Mesmerism had shown that the séance and the crisis, along with the paraphernalia of the baquet and the wand, were superfluous, the trance and the cures were real, leading to discoveries in hypnotism and psychotherapy. Mesmerism in the hands of a London surgeon was used to anesthetize a patient to prevent pain by putting him in a trance before performing an operation. This method preceded surgeons' use of the anesthetics ether and chloroform.

The procedure called somnambulism by Puységur, a follower of Mesmer, created great interest. It involved putting a patient in a trance, and although apparently asleep, he readily followed instructions as if awake. In 1819, a book, *On the Cause of Lucid Sleep*, was written and in 1823, another book, *Treatise on Somnambulism*, appeared in print discussing this phenomenon. Mesmer's theory of a fluid, whether cosmic or otherwise, as being necessary for the phenomenon, was gradually discarded but had its formal demise with the appearance of the publication *The Rationale of Nervous Sleep, considered in Relation with Animal Magnetism*, by James Braid in 1843.

Braid, a surgeon in Manchester, England, conducted many experiments on mesmerism and concluded that the phenomena that observers witnessed were due to effects on the nervous system and brain of the subject. He replaced the word mesmerism with hypnotism, a word he coined from the Greek word for "sleep" to describe his new meaning for it. He said, "I have now entirely separated hypnotism from animal magnetism." He disavowed the popular notion that the ability to induce hypnosis was connected to the magical passage of a fluid or other influence from the operator to the patient.

Braid reported successfully treating paralysis, rheumatism, and aphasia by hypnotism. He explained that to be hypnotized required that the patient be cooperative. Then when the patient concentrates on an object or the operator's hands and, due to psychological fatigue, the mind is cleared, a stupor is developed, and the trance is produced. Braid emphasized that hypnotism is psychological rather than physical, and his findings are said to have led to the development of the field of neuropsychiatry.[35]

In France, French hypnotists were led by J. M. Charcot, who influenced Freud. In 1880, Sigmund Freud hypnotized neurotic patients to help them recall disturbing events they had forgotten. He eventually discarded hypnosis in favor of free association, although contemporary psychoanalysts consider hypnosis as an adjunct to psychoanalytic practice. Freud emphasized many times that psychoanalysis was the heir to hypnotism as hypnotism was to mesmerism.[36] Hypnotism was used to combat neuroses in soldiers during World Wars I and II and has been widely used by practitioners as an aid in medical practice and psychotherapy. Hypnotism is also used in criminal investigations to help defendants recall events they might otherwise not remember.

Modern research has indicated that the hypnotic state represents an altered state of consciousness, and there are electrical changes in brain activity when a person is hypnotized. Everyone today knows about hypnotism, but Mesmer, who gave it its start, is largely forgotten. Vincent Buranelli, whose excellent book *The Wizard from Vienna* tells the story of Franz Anton Mesmer, has credited Mesmer with leaving his stamp on psychiatry, psychosomatic medicine, personality studies, and group therapy. Buranelli calls Mesmer the Columbus of modern psychology.[37]

Benjamin Franklin would not have recognized the word "psychology," but as an experienced politician and diplomat he was familiar with its application. This is well documented in his letter to a doctor who asked him for his opinion on animal magnetism. The letter arrived before the commission had begun its examination of the subject, and Franklin replied:

> As to the animal magnetism so much talked of, I am totally
> unacquainted with it, and must doubt its existence till I can see

or feel some effect of it. None of the cures said to be performed by it have fallen under my observation and there being so many disorders which cure themselves, and such a disposition in mankind to deceive themselves ... and living long having given me frequent opportunities of seeing certain remedies cried up as curing everything, and yet so soon after totally laid aside as useless, I cannot but fear that the expectation of great advantage from the new method of treating diseases will prove a delusion.

That delusion may, however ... be of use while it lasts. There are ... a number of persons who are never in health, because they are fond of medicines and, by always taking them, hurt their constitutions. If these people can be persuaded to forbear their drugs in expectation of being cured by only the physician's finger or iron rod pointing at them, they may possibly find good effects, though they may mistake the cause.[38]

10

America's First Senior Citizen

William Bradford, Roger Williams, John Winthrop, Cotton Mather, John Woolman, and Jonathan Edwards were all distinguished Americans who preceded Benjamin Franklin. However, if you were to ask any educated person anywhere in the world about these people, the chances are they would know little or nothing about them, but they would certainly know something about Benjamin Franklin. Franklin is remembered for his many contributions during his long lifetime. He was by far the eldest of the founding fathers. He was 26 years older than George Washington, 29 years older than John Adams, 37 years older than Thomas Jefferson, 45 years older than James Madison, and 51 years older than Alexander Hamilton, all of whom he worked with in the founding of the United States.

Upon Franklin's death the editor of the Scottish newspaper *The Edinburgh Review* wrote, "Franklin must be considered higher than any of the others which illustrated the 18th century." High praise, but in considering whether to credit Benjamin Franklin as America's first senior citizen, it would be well to review some of his accomplishments.

Franklin was trained as a printer and practiced that trade. He printed a newspaper, books, his famous *Poor Richard's Almanac*, government documents, and paper money. He was so successful in business that he was able to retire when he was 42 years old. He had founded the first police force and the first fire department in Philadelphia; he also established the first fire insurance company, the first lending library, the first public hospital, the first scientific society, and the first political science society in America. He established an academy in Philadelphia which later became the University of Pennsylvania. Formerly a slave owner, he became the president of the first antislavery society in America.

In his political and governmental career, he served as a member of the Philadelphia city council, clerk and speaker of the Pennsylvania Assembly, agent in England for Pennsylvania and other American colonies, member of the Second Constitutional Congress, ambassador to France, delegate to the Constitutional Convention, and president (governor) of Pennsylvania. He assisted in writing the Declaration of Independence, the Constitution of the United States, and the Treaty of Peace with Britain.

Franklin served as postmaster of Philadelphia, as deputy postmaster general of North America under the British, and then as the first postmaster general of the independent United States. He joined the Freemasons, becoming Grand Master of Masons of Pennsylvania and then Grand Master of the mid–Atlantic province of Masonry. In Paris, he was asked to join the leading Masonic lodge, of which he became head.

Franklin's research in electricity made him famous and served as a basis for later developments in that field which impact our lives today. In the area of medicine, he wrote extensively on the subjects of exercise, fresh air, nutrition, and colds. His best-known inventions include the Franklin stove and house heater, the lightning rod, and bifocal eyeglasses. The glass armonica, a musical instrument he invented, was very popular in Europe for many years; Mozart and Beethoven wrote music for it. He also invented a device he called his long arm, which he used to reach books on the top shelf of his library. Until recently it was employed in grocery stores to reach cans on the top shelves. It is now sold in medical supply stores for people with arthritis who have trouble raising their arms.

Franklin was the first American to be recognized and honored both in America and Europe. In America, he received honorary degrees from Harvard, Yale, and William and Mary, and in Britain, doctor's degrees from St. Andrews and Oxford universities. He was elected to membership in honorary societies in England, France, Spain, Belgium, Holland, Germany, and Russia. Franklin's life covered most of the eighteenth century, and he knew many of the important people of his time.[1, 2] He says in his autobiography that he had been in the presence of five kings and had sat down to dinner with one of them.

Five American presidents were among Franklin's acquaintances: Washington, Adams, Jefferson, Madison, and the young John Quincy Adams. He sent to America from Europe some of the greatest heroes of the Revolutionary War: Thomas Paine, Lafayette, John Paul Jones, von Steuben, and Pulaski. In England he knew and dealt with famous prime ministers, William Pitt, the elder and the younger, and the distinguished members of Parliament, Edmund Burke, John Foxx, and William Wilberforce, among others. English scientists he knew were Joseph Priestley, the discoverer of oxygen; Henry Cavendish, the discoverer of hydrogen; Matthew Boulton, who made James Watt's steam engine successful; James Cook, who discovered Hawaii and Australia; and Jeremiah Dixon and Charles Mason, who surveyed the Mason-Dixon line in America. French scientists of his acquaintance were Antoine Lavoisier, the famous chemist; Jacques Charles, of Charles' law of gases; the Montgolfier brothers, the first balloonists; and Joseph Guillotin, for whom the guillotine was named. Other acquaintances were physician-scientist Erasmus Darwin, grandfather of Charles Darwin; John Fitch, inventor of the steamboat; and A. Volta, who invented the chemical battery.

Franklin knew portrait artist Charles Wilson Peale; sculptor Jean Houdon; Josiah Wedgewood, maker of fine pottery; John Baskerville, creator of fine printing type; and David Garrick, famous actor. He knew the writers James Boswell, Edward Gibbon, and Noah Webster of dictionary fame. In philosophy, his acquaintances included the Englishmen Adam Smith, David Hume, and Jeremy Bentham; and the Frenchmen Diderot, Voltaire, and Condorcet. In the clergy, he knew the Puritan preacher Cotton Mather, the evangelist George Whitefield, and the first Catholic bishop of America, John Carroll.[2]

The Senior Citizen

"In old age," Franklin said, "the spirit is interior, it looks out the window at the stir of those who pass by without taking part in their disputes." But this did not apply to him. At age 74 he told a friend, "Being arrived at 70, and considering that by traveling further in the same road I shall probably be led to the grave, I stopped short, turned around, and walked back again; which having done these four years, you may call me 66. Advise those old friends of ours to follow my example. Keep up your spirits and that will keep up your bodies; you will no more stoop under the weight of age than if you had swallowed a handspike."[3]

As a retiree at 50, Franklin was a busy young man. In Philadelphia, he introduced a successful program of street paving, cleaning, and lighting. He designed the streets to be raised at the center and gradually curve down to the edge, so that the rain would wash the debris off the street, to be carried away by the current of water produced at the edges when it rained. He was appointed military commissioner and conducted military inspections at Carlisle, Pennsylvania, and in New York. With other commissioners for Indian affairs, he met with the Indians of the Delaware tribe in Easton, Pennsylvania. In Virginia on post office business, he met George Washington and also received an honorary degree from William and Mary College. He was elected a fellow of the British Royal Society and a member of the Society for the Encouragement of Arts, Manufacturers and Commerce in London.

In 1766, at the age of 60, he was in London, where he was sent by the Pennsylvania Assembly to get the British government to force the Penn family to pay taxes on their vast property in Pennsylvania. Except for the years 1762 to 1764, he remained in England from 1757 to 1775 trying to negotiate the increasing problems of the colonies with the British government. While in England he made many important friends in government and science. He traveled to France, Belgium, Holland, Germany, Scotland, and Ireland. During this time he acquired more honorary degrees and became known as Doctor Franklin. The book on his experiments in electricity was published in several additions and was distributed all over Europe.

At age 70, he had just arrived in France as representative of the government of the new, independent United States. Just a few short months before, he had signed the Declaration of Independence and was reported to have told the other signers, "We must all hang together, or most assuredly, we will hang separately."[4] If a British warship had captured him as he sailed across the ocean, his jest would have come true for him. When his doctor was concerned about the danger of this voyage, Franklin responded, "I am old and good for nothing; perhaps the best use such an old fellow can be put to is to make a martyr of him."[5] As a senior citizen who was financially well off and comfortable, with a loyalist son who was the governor of New Jersey, Franklin could easily have sat out the American revolution rather than risk his life and fortune in becoming a rebel. But, like Washington and Jefferson and his other younger compatriots, he was determined to do what was right.

He remained in France for nine years, during which time he was able to persuade the king to provide the money and military needed for the American victory. He was very popular in France with people from the king on down. They put his picture on everything — painted medallions, snuff box covers, all kinds of bric-a-brac: He wrote his daughter that his face was as well known in France as the man in the moon. His wife had died while he was in England, so as a widower he was very popular with the ladies. Two in particular received his special attention. He proposed to one of them, a widow, but she refused him, deciding to remain true to the memory of her departed husband. The other was already married. John Adams, who was also in Paris, commented, "Although 70, he hasn't lost his taste for beauty." The romances, if indeed they were such, were literary rather than physical, with letters instead of kisses.[6] We must be thankful for that because we are able to read these delightful, flirtatious missives, whereas the kisses would have left nothing for us to enjoy.

On Franklin's 80th birthday he was back at home in Philadelphia with his daughter, son-in-law, and grandchildren in a house he had built while he was still in England. On the trip across the ocean, his eighth and last such trip, he studied the Gulf Stream and produced the first map of that waterway. Of lesser worldwide significance, he invented a dish for serving soup that would not spill its hot contents on the passenger during a storm at sea. He received a grand reception upon his arrival in Philadelphia and was elected president of Pennsylvania. He met with the local printers and members of the fire department that he had founded, wearing his old fire helmet.

The most important activity of his last years was his contribution to the creation of a federal government for the United States at the Constitutional Convention. He also established the Society for Political Enquiries, the first political science society, and presided over meetings of the American Philosophical Society and the Pennsylvania Society for the Abolition of Slavery, the first abolitionist organization in America. In addition, he continued his work on his autobiography when he was so ill he was laid up in bed and could not go out. He settled his affairs, made out his will, and died at the age of 84.

Young Man and Old Age

As a young man Franklin showed great respect for older people. When his parents died, both having lived to a ripe old age, he honored them by erecting a large tombstone in the Boston cemetery on which he had inscribed the achievements of their lives. On his first trip to England, as a youth of 18, he boarded with an elderly lady who, he said, knew one thousand anecdotes and they were "so highly amusing to me that I was sure to spend an evening with her whenever she desired it." In a garret of this lady's house was a maiden woman of 70 years who lived alone like a nun, giving most of her meager income to charity. He described her as a woman who was "cheerful and polite and conversed pleasantly," impressing him greatly.[7]

In one edition of his annual *Poor Richard's Almanac*, he published the "Way to Wealth" or "Father Abraham's Speech." In it Franklin assembled many of the wise sayings and proverbs he had included in earlier editions of the almanac calling for practical, moral living. He had old Father Abraham relate these maxims in his conversation with young people. According to Franklin, these aphorisms contained the wisdom of the ages and nations. Father Abraham was described as "a plain, clean, old man, with white locks" who responded when asked, "Pray Father Abraham, what do you think of these times? Won't these heavy taxes quite ruin the country?" With maxims from *Poor Richard's Almanac* opposing idleness, wasted time, and laziness, and favoring industry, frugality, and so on, Father Abraham replies, "Lost time is never found," "Keep thy shop and thy shop will keep thee," and "Now I have a sheep and a cow, everybody bids me good morrow."

The old man's speech was so successful that it was printed separately and distributed all over the colonies, the British Isles, and France. It was reprinted hundreds of times in English and at least 15 times in other languages. Not all of the sayings that the young Franklin put in *Poor Richard's Almanac* were on such a sober subject as increasing wealth. Some were just for fun: "Keep your eyes wide open before marriage, half shut afterwards" and "He's a fool that makes his doctor his heir." Some of them related to senior citizens:

"A long life may not be good enough, but a good life is long enough."

"All would live long, but none would be old."

"An old man in a house is a good sign."

"Many foxes grow gray, but few grow good."

"Old boys have their playthings as well as young ones;
the difference is only in the price."[8]

Another side of the young Franklin's view of old women is seen in a humorous piece he wrote for the entertainment of his friends in a men's club. It was found among his writings long after his death, and because of its risqué nature it was suppressed for some 50 years before it appeared in print. It was in the form of a letter, titled "Advice to a young man on the choice of a mistress." In this piece a young man writes that he is single and wishes advice on the choice of a mistress. Franklin replies that he should seek marriage, but if that is not possible, he says, "In all your amours you should prefer old women to young ones." He then proceeds to give his reasons:

1. Because as they have more knowledge of the world and their minds are better stored with observations, their conversation is more improving and more lastingly agreeable.

2. Because when women cease to be handsome, they study to be good.... They learn to do a thousand services [from] small [to] great, and are the most tender and useful of all friends when you're sick.... And hence there is hardly such a thing to be found as an old woman who is not a good woman.

3. Because there is no hazard of children, which irregularly produced may be attended with much inconvenience.

4. Because through more experience, they are more prudent and discrete.... The commerce with them is therefore safer with regard [to] your reputation.

5. Because in every animal that walks upright, the deficiency of the fluids that fill the muscles appears first in the highest part: the face first grows lank and wrinkled; then the neck; then the breast and arms; the lower parts continuing to the last as plump as ever. So that covering all above with a basket, and regarding only what is below the girdle, it is impossible of two women to know an old from a young one.

6. Because the sin is less.

7. Because the compunction is less.... Having made a young girl miserable may give you frequent bitter reflections; none of which can attend making an old woman happy.

8. And lastly, they are so grateful!

Franklin finishes the letter with "But still I advise you to marry directly."[9] It should be emphasized that Franklin did not publish this letter but used it privately to amuse the members of his club.

Family Relations

When he was 50, Franklin wrote a letter of condolence to his niece after the death of a relative: "I condole with you, we have lost a most dear and valuable relation, but it is the will of God in nature that these mortal bodies be laid aside when the soul is to enter into real life." He wrote that we are now in an embryo state and that we are not completely born until we are dead and take our place among the immortals. "We are spirits ...

bodies should be lent us, while they can afford us pleasure, assist us in acquiring knowledge, or doing good to our fellow creatures.... When they become unfit for these purposes and afford us pain instead of pleasure ... It is equally kind and benevolent that a way is provided by which we may get rid of them. Death is that way." He noted that we may choose a partial death; for example, we may willingly remove a tooth because the pain goes with it, and so it is with death, that all suffering ceases. He concludes with "Our friend and we are invited abroad on a party of pleasure that is to last forever. He is gone before us; we could not all conveniently start together, and why should you and I be grieved at this, since we are soon to follow, and we know where to find him."[10]

A year later, Franklin heard from his younger sister that their older sister was reluctant to move to a new house where she could receive better care. He replied as follows: "As having their own way is one of the greatest comforts of life to old people, I think their friends should endeavor to accommodate them in that, as well as anything else. When they have long lived in a house, it becomes natural to them; they are almost as closely connected with it as the tortoise with his shell; they die if you tear them out of it. Old folks and old trees, if you remove them, it is ten to one that you kill them."

He added, "I hope you visit sister as often as your affairs will permit and afford her what assistance and comfort you can in her present situation. Old age, infirmities, and poverty, joined, are afflictions enough. The neglect and slights of friends and near relations should never be added. People in her circumstances are apt to suspect this, sometimes without cause; appearances should therefore be attended to ... as well as realities."[11]

Franklin received a letter from his niece on a happier note. It was a story about the ridiculous antics of an old man in her town. As she told it, cupid had shot an arrow into the heart of this 81-year-old blind man, who had buried his wife just a month ago: "Nothing would do but he must have another wife. He immediately set about recollecting what beauties he had formerly." His first choice was the niece's mother, but that didn't work out, and, after several vain attempts, he settled on another lady. He sent his grandson to visit the lady and told him to be sure to make a low bow and give her his grandfather's love, asking her to visit him. She did, and when she came into the room, he blindly reached for her and clasped her in his arms, almost stifling her with kisses. "He begged she would retire with him to the chamber, where we must leave them an hour or two." When the lady came down, "they say her cap, handkerchief, and apron are very much discomposed."

The preliminaries being settled, he desired the announcement of the wedding to be made the next morning. His son tried to persuade him to delay it for a week out of respect for the memory of his recently departed wife. The old man replied that he would then lose "a world of happiness with the lady in that time" and insisted on the next day, and so it was.[12]

In his reply to his niece's letter, Franklin stated, "Let us not be merely entertained by this tale; let us draw a small moral from it. Old age ... is subject to love and its follies as well as youth. All old people have been young; and when they were, they laughed as we do at the amours of age." They imagined that this would never happen to them, but "let us spare them, lest the same case should one day be ours." Speaking to his niece, Franklin said

> I see you begin to laugh already at my ranking myself among the young! But you, my girl, when you arrive at fifty, will think no more of being old than does
> > Your affectionate uncle,
> > Benjamin Franklin[13]

Retirement Franklin Style

At the age of 58, while still on duty in England, Franklin said that he sought "that retirement and repose with my little family, so suitable to my years." With his Puritan upbringing Franklin believed with Poor Richard that time is money and that idleness taxes us more heavily than government. Yet, in his old age he liked to indulge in games of chess and cards. This bothered his conscience and he remarked, "I have indeed now and then a little compunction in reflecting that I spend time so idly; but another reflection comes to relieve me, whispering: 'You know that the soul is immortal; why then should you be such a niggardly of a little time, when you have a whole eternity before you?' So, being easily convinced and, like other reasonable creatures, satisfied with a small reason, when it is in favor of doing what I have a mind to, I shuffle the cards again, and begin another game." To a friend he wrote: "We are grown gray together, and yet it is too early to part. Let us sit till the evening of life is spent. The last hours are always the most joyous. When we can stay no longer, it is time enough then to bid each other good night, separate, and go quietly to bed."

At 60, he recalled those happy years in Philadelphia doing scientific experiments and yearned to be back doing that again. But he didn't retire. At 68, he appeared to be slowing down: "I am apt to indulge the indolence usually attending age, in postponing such business, from time to time, though continually resolving to do it." However, when the he left England, he found himself fully immersed in the activities of the Continental Congress, and at age 74, in Paris, he complained, "I have been too long in hot water, plagued almost to death with the passions, vagaries, ill-humor and madness of other people. I must have a little repose." At 77, after the peace treaty with England had been signed, and the Congress did not approve his request to come home, he wrote, "It seems my fate constantly to wish for repose but never to obtain it." Two years later, when he was allowed to come home, he wrote a friend that he was going home to die. "I am going home to go to bed. Wish me a good night's rest."[14]

But he didn't die. When he got home he was asked to serve as president of Pennsylvania, and he accepted this new assignment. Why did he do it? He wasn't sure himself. He wrote one friend that he hoped to be of some further benefit to his people. He told Tom Paine that he did not have the firmness to refuse the request of the different, opposing parties to try to reconcile them. But he seemed to be nearer the truth when he told a friend in England that he was overwhelmed by the enthusiastic reception he received and succumbed to "some remains of ambition, from which I had imagined myself free." He said he hoped to be able to bear the fatigue for one more year and then retire.[15]

A year later he wrote, "I enjoy here everything I could wish for, except repose. And that I may soon expect, either by cessation of my office ... or by ceasing to live." Yet, when his annual term was up he ran for another and did even better in the election than the first time. He was elected without a single dissenting vote and could not refuse, saying that he would decline a third term. True to form, when he was nominated for the third term, he accepted and was reelected. He confided to his sister why he seemed never to have had the resolve to say no. "I must own that it is no small pleasure to me ... [that] I should be elected a third time by my fellow citizens without a dissenting vote ... to fill the most honorable post in their power to bestow. This universal and unbounded confidence of a whole people flatters my vanity."[16]

At age 81, he noted, "I seem to have intruded myself into the company of posterity when I ought to have been abed and asleep."[17] His post had a limit of three terms, so he was not subject to further temptation, and before being called to serve in the Constitutional Convention he was able to enjoy what he called "private amusements," which he listed as conversation, books, his little garden, and cribbage. But Franklin could not be idle, and another of his private amusements was building. Philadelphia was growing rapidly, so houses were a good investment. "I had begun to build two good houses next to the street instead of three old ones which

I pulled down," he told his sister, and he also made an addition to his own house. Within the year the three houses were finished, and he was ready to begin two others. The new addition to his house included a dining room 30.5 ¥ 16 feet, which would seat 24 persons, and above it his library, which was lined to the ceiling with books. Each book was numbered by his private system and placed on the shelf so he could find it easily. It was the largest private library in America with over 4,000 books. He said, "I hardly know how to justify building a library at an age that will so soon oblige me to quit it, but we are apt to forget that we are grown old, and building is an amusement." He wrote a friend, "Building is an old man's amusement. The advantage is for his posterity."[18] In his house he had the first flush toilet in America and a shoe-shaped bathtub with a reading stand so he could read and soak for hours.[19, 20]

Franklin was indeed comfortable at home. As he said, "I live in a good house which I built 25 years ago ... made still more convenient by an addition since my return. A dutiful and affectionate daughter with her husband and six children compose my family.... My rents and incomes are amply sufficient for all my present occasions, and if no unexpected misfortunes happen.... I shall leave a handsome estate to be divided among my relatives." In reply to an inquiry from England about amusements in young America, Franklin replied, "We have assemblies, balls, and concerts, besides little parties at one another's houses, in which there is sometimes dancing and frequently good music. So that we jog on in life as pleasantly as you do in England."[21]

At the Constitutional Convention

The delegates to the convention were outstanding Americans. They were well educated, successful men. Jefferson referred to them as an "assemblage of demigods." Franklin, at 81, was the grandfather of the group. He was different in other ways, too. Someone described the members as "well bred, well fed, well read, and well wed." Franklin was like them in only two respects; he was well fed and well read. No one who has seen his portrait would deny that he was well fed, and his library would attest that he was an avid reader. He could not, however, be described as well bred; his father had barely made a living as a candle maker. And he was not well wed; his wife was the daughter of a carpenter who died in debt. Franklin had only two years of formal schooling, and his success and position in life were all due to his own ability and effort.

Benjamin Rush, Franklin's doctor and fellow signer of the Declaration of Independence, commented about Franklin at the convention: "Dr. Franklin exhibits daily a spectacle of transcendent benevolence by attending the convention punctually and even taking part in its business and deliberations."[22] This he did in spite of his medical problems. Visitors to the convention who had the opportunity to meet with Franklin at his home have given us an intimate, informal look at our first senior citizen.

Manasseh Cutler, a clergyman from Massachusetts, visited Philadelphia during the convention and sought out the delegates. He especially wanted to meet Franklin. "There was no curiosity in Philadelphia which I felt so anxious to see as this great man, who has been the wonder of Europe as well as the glory of America." He imagined he was going to be in the presence of a European monarch but instead saw "a fat, trunched old man in a plain Quaker dress, bald pate, and short white locks, sitting without his hat under a tree." Franklin rose from his chair, expressed joy in seeing Cutler, and welcomed him to the city. Cutler recorded in his diary, "His voice was low, but his countenance was open, frank, and pleasing." Tea was served under the tree by Franklin's daughter, who had three of her children about her. The children, Cutler noticed, did not respond to their mother but appeared "to be excessively fond of their grandpa."

Since Cutler was a botanist and a member of the American Philosophical Society, Franklin showed him a two-headed snake that was preserved in a bottle of alcohol, a glass machine for exhibiting the circulation of the blood in the arteries and veins, and a rolling press he had invented for copying letters. He saw Franklin's library with shelves going up to the ceiling and the "long arm" he used to reach books on the upper shelves. Cutler was even more impressed with Franklin's "great armed chair with rockers, and a large fan placed over it, with which he fans himself, keeps off the flies, etc., while he sits reading, with only a small motion of his foot." Cutler also saw other curiosities of Franklin's invention, but in his opinion they could hardly be compared to this air-cooled, bug-repelling, foot-energized, dandy rocking chair.

Cutler expressed his pleasure at meeting Franklin: "I was highly delighted with the extensive knowledge he appeared to have of every subject, the brightness of his memory, and clearness and vivacity of all his mental faculties, notwithstanding his age. His manners seem to diffuse an unrestrained freedom and happiness. He has an incessant vein of humor, accompanied with an uncommon vivacity, which seems as natural and involuntary as his breathing."[23]

Another visitor to Franklin one morning was Andrew Ellicott, a young surveyor and mathematician, who was introduced by David Rittenhouse, Franklin's scientific friend in Philadelphia. Ellicott recorded in his diary,

"I found him in his little room [study] among his papers.... His room makes a singular appearance, being filled with old philosophical [scientific] instruments, papers, boxes, tables, and stools." Franklin received his visitor warmly and discussed the thinly settled lands in the West. Franklin then arose and put some water on the fire. He was apparently preparing to shave, and Ellicott commented, "Not being expert through his great age, I desired him to give me the pleasure of assisting him. He thanked me and replied that he ever made it a point to wait upon himself, and although he began to find himself infirm, he was determined not to increase his infirmities by giving way to them. After his water was hot, I observed his object was to shave himself, which operation he performed without a glass and with great expedition. I asked him if he ever employed a barber. He answered, no, and continued nearly in the following words; 'I think happiness does not consist so much in particular pieces of good fortune that perhaps accidentally fall to a man's lot, as to be able in his old age to do those little things which, was he unable to perform himself, would be done by others with a sparing hand.'"[24]

Another way in which Franklin differed from his fellow delegates was his 50-year-long service in government including experience in city, state, national, and international affairs. On political matters he showed great wisdom. His experience told him that, in his dealings with his fellow citizens, if he were to ask favors of them they would readily refuse him. "So that I find little real advantage in being beloved, but it pleases my humor." On the subject of public office, he said, "I have long been accustomed to receive more blame and more praise than I have deserved. It is the lot of every public man."[25] "Popular favor is very precarious, being sometimes lost as well as gained by good actions."[26] "A man who holds a high office so often finds himself exposed to the danger of disobliging some one in the fulfillment of his duty, that the resentment of those whom he has thus offended, being greater than the gratitude of those he has served, it always almost happens that, while he is violently attacked, he is feebly defended."[27] When Congress showed its ingratitude by indefinitely holding the money it owed for his service in France due to suggestions by political enemies that he had pocketed government money, he wrote, "I know something of the nature of such changeable assemblies and what effect one or two envious and malicious persons may have on the minds of members."[28]

He commented that the popularity of a man in public life resulted as much from circumstances beyond his control as well as from his own performance. During the war a long series of defeats had created such an appetite for good news that a small victory would be magnified into a great one, and "the man who procures us a bonfire and a holiday would be almost adored as a hero." At the convention he warned his fellow countrymen about "the two passions, which have a powerful influence in the affairs of men." He was referring to ambition and avarice, "the love of power" and "the love of money," which when combined might have the most violent effects.[29] Fortunately, at his age and station of life, he had neither and was thus able to earn the confidence of the delegates.

He once remarked, "Wise and good men are the strength of a state." With men like that, any kind of government would serve the people. He said, "I do not oppose all that seems wrong, for the multitude are more effectually set right by experience than kept from growing wrong by reasoning with them." He was confident that America was on the road to improvement because "we are making experiments."[30] He was convinced that experiments in politics would be just as fruitful as experiments had proved to be in science; therefore he formed and became the first president of the Society of Political Enquiries, which, for political science, paralleled his American Philosophical Society for science. "The arduous and complicated science of government" should not solely be "left to the care of practical politicians or the speculations of individual theorists." America was not only a good place to perform new experiments in government, but it was also the greatest experiment in this new field of political science, and Franklin was confident of its success.

Disposition and Happiness of an Octogenarian

Franklin was always a friendly, outgoing young man; his disposition did not change as he grew older. Benny Bache, Franklin's grandson, wrote in his diary that his grandfather, unlike other old people, was always in a good mood. "All among us may be happy," Franklin said, "who have happy dispositions, such being necessary to happiness even in Paradise."[31]

At 75 years, when he was asked whether he was happy, Franklin replied, "I become more so every day.... First poor, then rich, I have always been content with what I have, without thinking of what I have not. But since I have begun to age, since my passions have diminished, I feel a well-being of mind and heart that I never knew before and which is impossible to know at the age of these young people." At 81, he wrote to an old companion, "You give me joy in telling me that you are on the pinnacle of content. Without it, no situation can be happy; with it, any. One means of becoming content with one's situation is comparing it with worse. Thus, when I consider how many terrible diseases that human body is liable to, I comfort myself that only three incurable ones have fallen to my share, viz. the gout, the stone, and old age and these have not yet deprived me of my natural cheerfulness, my delight in books, and enjoyment of social conversation."[32]

When he was approaching his 83rd birthday, his niece asked him about his health. "You kindly inquire about my health. I have not of late much reason to boast of it. People who have a long life and drink to the bottom of the cup must expect to meet with some of the dregs. And those notwithstanding, I enjoy many comfortable intervals in which I forget all my ills and amuse myself in reading or writing, or in conversation with friends, joking, laughing, and telling merry stories, as when you first knew me, a young man about 50."[33] An eyewitness reported that Franklin's illness kept him confined to his bed for most of his last two years, and if all the comfortable intervals he mentioned were added together, they would not amount to two months. His doctor stated that Franklin retained "the fullest and clearest possession of his uncommon mental abilities and not unfrequently indulged himself in those *jeux d'esprit* and entertaining anecdotes which were the delight of all who heard them."[34]

Health

Through most of his life Franklin was a vigorous, healthy person who took great interest in the subject of health. One of the first books he printed in his own shop was titled *Every Man his own Doctor, or the Poor Planter's Physician*. He believed that fresh air was essential for good health and slept with the window wide open, even though it was then believed that the night air was harmful. He also favored vigorous exercise and did an experiment with a doctor taking his pulse as he engaged in various forms of aerobic activity. He told John Adams, "I walk every day a league in my chamber, I walk quick and for an hour.... I make a point of religion of it."

At the age of 82 when he was unable to do any other exercise he lifted dumbbells. "For the use of it, I have in 40 swings quickened my pulse from 60 to 100 beats in a minute, counted by a second watch."[35] He said, "there is more exercise in one mile's riding on horseback than five in a coach; and more in one mile's walking on foot than five on horseback; to which I may add, that there is more in walking one mile up and down stairs than five on a level floor."

It may be of interest that Franklin is the only Founding Father to be honored as an athlete. His bust is on display in the Swimming Hall of Fame in St. Petersburg, Florida. As a boy Franklin was fond of swimming. He read a book on the art of swimming and taught himself different strokes.

He invented swim fins for his hands and feet in order to swim faster. He once used a kite to propel him across a lake. On his first trip to England, at the age of 19, he taught a friend to swim and, at the urging of some wealthy men who wanted him to teach their sons to swim, he considered starting a swimming school. However, he was homesick for America and returned home instead. He tells of his method to overcome people's fear of the water. He dropped an egg to the bottom in waist-high water and had the beginner reach for it, ducking his head into the water, thus knowing that he was perfectly safe. In England at 19, he swam the Thames River from Chelsea to Blackfriars, about 3.5 miles, and when almost 80, in France, he swam across the Seine River when teaching his grandson to swim.[36]

Franklin joked about his three ailments, the gout, the stone, and old age, by reciting the "Old Man's Song," a song he had sung many times in his youth:

> May I govern my passions with an absolute sway,
> Grow wiser and better as my strength wears away,
> Without gout or stone, by a gentle decay.[37]

He regretted, "I had sung that wishing song a thousand times when I was young, and now at fourscore that the three contraries have befallen me — being subject to the gout and the stone, and not being yet master of all my passions." Of the three maladies, the stone was the most painful and constant. It did not bother him "except in standing, walking, or making water." He said that "observing temperance in eating, avoiding wine and cider, and daily using the dumbbell, which exercises the upper part of the body without much moving the parts in contact with the stone, I think has prevented its increase." To reduce the frequent urgency to make water and relieve the pain of it, he ate a small portion of blackberry jelly, about the size of a pigeon's egg, at bedtime.[38] Even if it didn't work, it was less harmful than other medicines of the time and much better tasting.

Autobiography

Franklin was 65 when he began his autobiography. He had spent a few weeks with his good friends the Shipley family at their home in the country, where he had delighted them with anecdotes of his life in America. They insisted that he write these down. That became the first part of his life's story, and when he was 78, in France, he picked up the pen again at the urging of friends there but soon dropped it. He told a French friend who tried to persuade him to continue, "You are a hard taskmaster. You insist on his writing his life, already a long work, and at the same time would have him continually employed in augmenting the subject, while the time shortened in which the work is to be executed."[39] Franklin had never given his autobiography high priority, and other activities were always consuming his time. But at 82 time was short, and infirmities kept him from other business. At 60, he had said, "Life, like a dramatic piece should finish handsomely. Being now in the last act, I begin to cast about for something fit to end with."[40] That may have been in his mind when he began writing again. Illness and death prevented his telling his story beyond 1758, when he was 52. However, the rest is history, and we have at least the satisfaction of learning about his early years, which otherwise would have died with him.

As he read what he had written, he discovered that he liked it: "If a writer can judge properly his own work, I fancy ... the book will be found entertaining, interesting, and useful; more so than I expected when I began it."[41] At that time he saw himself "yielding to the inclination so natural to old men of talking of themselves and their own actions."[42] But this way, he remarked, no one would have to listen; they would be free to read or not. And finally, he admitted, "I might as well confess it, I shall gratify my own vanity." He said that whenever he had heard the words, "Without vanity, I may say, but some vain thing immediately followed. Most people dislike vanity in others whatever share they have of it themselves, but I give it fair quarter whenever I meet with it, being persuaded that it is often productive of good to the possessor and to others who are within his sphere of action. And therefore, in many cases it would not be altogether absurd if a man were to thank God for his vanity among his other comforts of life."[43]

The autobiography, even though incomplete, was a legacy to the American people. Millions read it, and for the following century, except for the Bible, it was the best-seller in America. It was translated into many languages, published in many editions, and in the nineteenth century had greater influence than any other book in the English language. It portrayed in Franklin's life the possibility of upward mobility in America and was an inspiration to the wave of immigrants who crossed the ocean in hope of a better future here. Franklin showed them how he did it; they could do it, too.

Final Days

On a trip from Europe to America Franklin wrote, "I am going from the old world to the new and I fancy I feel like those who are leaving this world for the next; grief at the parting, fear of the passage, hope for the future." But Franklin approached death without fear or apprehension. "I look upon death to be as necessary to our constitution as sleep. We shall rise refreshed in the morning." Actually, he looked forward to the great unknown with curiosity. He did not believe that the destiny of humankind was oblivion in a dark, endless void. Neither did he believe in a heaven with angels and harps, or a hell with devils with pitchforks. He joked about heaven, "How happy are the folks in Heaven who, 'tis said, have nothing to do but talk with one another except now and then a little singing." In the past he had investigated the unknown with experiments. Now, in the words he had used when he began his kite experiment, "Let the experiment be made!" He explained, "The course of nature must soon put a period to my present mode of existence. This I shall submit to with less regret, as having seen during a long life a good deal of this world, I feel a growing curiosity to be acquainted with some other."[44] He mused about his friends who had departed "to join the majority in the world of spirits. Every one of them now knows more than all of us they have left behind. It is to me a comfortable reflection that since we must live forever in a future state, there is a sufficient stock of amusement in reserve for us to be found in constantly learning something new to eternity, the present quantity of human ignorance infinitely exceeding that of human knowledge."

When he considered his senior years, he had the satisfaction of knowing they had been productive. He said, "Had I gone at seventy, it would have cut off twelve of the most active years of my life; employed, too, in matters of greatest importance." He was not totally satisfied, however, in leaving this world. He expressed this thought: "I have sometimes almost wished it had been my destiny to be born two or three centuries hence. For invention and improvement are prolific and beget more of their kind.... Many of great importance now unthought of will, before that period, be produced; and then I might not only enjoy their advantages, but have my curiosity gratified in knowing what they are to be." In speculating on the future, he wrote: "We may perhaps learn to deprive large masses of their gravity, and give them absolute levity for the sake of easy transport [airplanes]. Agriculture may diminish its labor and double its produce [now done]. All diseases made by sure means be prevented or cured, not excepting even that of old age [much progress]." And then he added, "O, that moral science were in as fair a way of improvement that men would cease to be wolves to one another [no comment]."[45]

One of the afflictions of Franklin's old age was the death of good friends. His dear friend Bishop Shipley preceded him by one year. When he heard the news, he wrote to Shipley's daughter, "Your reflections on the constant calmness and composure attending his death are very sensible. Such instances seem to show that the good sometimes enjoy, in dying, a foretaste of the happy state that they are about to enter." Franklin knew that his own time was short, and he wrote his good-bye to George Washington, who was then serving his first term as president. "For my own personal ease I should have died two years ago, but though those years have been spent in excruciating pain, I am pleased that I have lived them since they brought me to see our present situation. I am now finishing my 84th [year] and probably with it my career in this life, but in whatever state of existence I'm placed hereafter, if I retain any memory of what has passed here I shall with it retain the esteem, respect, and affection with which I have long been, my dear friend, yours most sincerely, Benjamin Franklin."[46]

In March 1790, Thomas Jefferson, on his way to New York to serve in President Washington's cabinet, stopped at Philadelphia to see Franklin. Franklin was delighted to see him and to hear news of his friends in France. Jefferson said that he had heard that Franklin was preparing a history of his life. Franklin responded, "I cannot say much of that, but I will give you a sample of what I will leave," and he handed him a copy of his autobiography.[47] Ezra Stiles, president of Yale University, also paid Franklin a visit, asking for a portrait to hang at Yale next to that of the founder. Franklin said that he didn't have a suitable one, but Stiles could have one painted. However, the artist "must not delay setting about it or I may slip through his fingers." Stiles, a minister, also wanted to know Franklin's opinion of the divinity of Jesus. Franklin replied, "It is a question I do not dogmatize upon, having never studied it, and think it needless to busy myself with it now where I expect soon an opportunity of knowing the truth with less trouble."[48]

Before ending the game of life, Franklin had just one more card to play. As president of the Pennsylvania Antislavery Society, he sent a petition to Congress in February 1790, calling for an immediate end to the slave trade. Franklin had once been a slave owner but later saw the injustice of it and actively opposed it. Along with Jefferson, he tried, unsuccessfully, to inject words of opposition to slavery in the Declaration of Independence. Again, at the Constitutional Convention he considered an antislavery statement but was persuaded that such a stand would endanger passage of the Constitution. Now, with the Constitution in place and Congress in operation, he felt it safe to try again to eliminate this evil from the nation. In March, the committee considering the petition reported that Congress had no authority to interfere in the internal affairs of the states.

The petition had caused such a violent, irrational outburst by members from the Deep South that Franklin felt it necessary to respond. His response, which was published in the newspapers, was a parody of a speech in the House by James Jackson of Georgia.

In this parody, which appeared three weeks before his death, Franklin pretended to have discovered a hundred-year-old document from Algeria in which Sidi Mehemet Ibrahim, a member of the legislature, or Divan, was speaking about a petition from an antislavery organization. Even in Franklin's time, North Africans were capturing and enslaving Europeans, who were Christians. In fact, when he was in France Franklin had a visit from a Frenchman who had been captured by North Africans and kept a slave for many years. It was uncanny, Franklin wrote, how closely the arguments of Mr. Jackson about the blacks paralleled the statements of the Algerian about the Christians. Then Franklin listed the arguments of the Algerian, explaining why it was necessary for the good of the country to continue enslaving Christians and keeping them in bondage. The satire was sharp and pointed; it was the last arrow from Benjamin Franklin's bow.[49]

Franklin died on April 17, 1790, at the age of 84. The immediate cause of death was an infection of the lung cavity. When his daughter had said she hoped he would recover and live many more years, he replied, "I hope not." When he was advised to change his position in bed so he could breathe more easily, he said, "A dying man can do nothing easy."[50] His present afflictions, he had said, were but a trifle when compared to the long life of health and ease he had enjoyed. He added, "and it is right that we should meet with something to wean us from this world and make us willing, when called, to leave it. Otherwise the parting would indeed be grievous."

His will begins with these words: "Benjamin Franklin of Philadelphia, printer, late Minister Plenipotentiary from the United States of America to the court of France, now President of the State of Pennsylvania." First, he was plain Benjamin Franklin, printer — the fancy titles took second place.

Twenty thousand people attended his funeral, half the city of Philadelphia, and it was the largest funeral in America to that time. In the funeral procession were all the men in the Pennsylvania and Philadelphia governments, all the clergy and members of their churches, the firemen, the printers, members of the American Philosophical Society, the Society for Political Enquiries, the College of Physicians, the University of Pennsylvania, and just ordinary citizens. In Congress, Madison gave a tribute calling Franklin a native genius, an ornament to human nature, precious to science, to freedom, and to his country. In veneration of his memory the members of the House wore the badge of mourning for one month. The French revolutionary government also declared a period of mourning for their great friend, whom they revered as a symbol of liberty and humanity.[51]

Near the end, Franklin admitted that he may have made mistakes but added, "Whether I have been doing good or mischief is for time to discover. I only know that I intended well and I hope all will end well."[52] At present, with over two centuries having passed, it is safe for us to say, "You did well, Ben, you did well."

Notes

1. BENJAMIN FRANKLIN'S GREATEST INVENTION

1. Bernstein, Richard B., *Are We to Be a Nation? The Making of the Constitution.* Cambridge: Harvard University Press, 12, 1987. Also Mathews, L. K., "Benjamin Franklin's Plans for a Colonial Union, 1750–1775." American Political Science Review 8(3): 296 (Aug. 1914).

2. Lemay, Leo J. A., editor, *Benjamin Franklin Writings*, 973–74. New York: The Library of America, 1987. Hereafter called Lemay.

3. *Papers of Benjamin Franklin*, Vol. 4, 118–119. Yale University Press, New Haven, CT. Hereafter called *Papers*.

4. Lemay, 969.

5. *Papers*, 4, 117–118.

6. *Ibid.*, 120.

7. Van Doren, Carl, *Benjamin Franklin*, 229. New York: Viking Press, 1938. Hereafter called Van Doren.

8. *Papers*, 4, 119.

9. *Papers*, 5, 65, footnote 2.

10. *Ibid.*, 96–97.

11. Lemay, 1421–22.

12. *Papers*, 4, 117.

13. Brands, H. W., "The First Ameri-can," 231–32. New York: Doubleday, 2000.

14. *Papers*, 5, 274–75.

15. Matthews, see note 1, 397.

16. *Papers*, 5, 335–38.

17. Van Doren, 221–22.

18. Lemay, 446.

19. *Papers*, 4, 393.

20. *Ibid.*, 387–92.

21. Lemay, 389–401.

22. *Papers*, 5, 443–47, 449–51.

23. Van Doren, 233.

24. Lemay, 1431.

25. Bernstein, see note 1, 15.

26. Newman, Eric P., "Sources of Emblems and Mottoes for Continental Currency and the Fugio Cent." *Numismatist*, 1589, 1597 (Dec. 1966).

27. *Papers*, 5, 443–47.

28. *Ibid.*, 449–51.

29. Lemay, 1441.

30. Bradfield, Elston G., "Benjamin Franklin: A Numismatic Summary." *Numismatist*, 1348 (Dec. 1956).

31. *Papers*, 5, 449–50.

32. *The Writings of Benjamin Franklin*, vi, 311–12, Albert Henry Smyth, editor. London: McMillan, 1907. Hereafter called *Writings*.

33. Lemay,747.
34. *Papers*, 22, 40–41.
35. Madison, James, "Notes of Debates in the Federal Convention of 1787," 5. Athens, OH: Ohio University Press, 1966.
36. *Papers*, 22, 120–21.
37. *Ibid.*, 125.
38. *Papers*, 22, 120–25. Also the Avalon Project at Yale University.
39. *Writings*, vi, 459–62.
40. Van Doren, 721.
41. Block, Seymour S., "Benjamin Franklin, His Wit, Wisdom, and Women," 355, 364. New York: Hastings House, 1975.
42. Van Doren, 743.
43. *Ibid.*, 747–49.
44. Block (ref. 39), 356–57.
45. *Ibid.*, 360–62.
46. Lemay, 1139–41.
47. Madison (ref. 33), 659.
48. Lemay, 1019–20.

2. The Mystery of Polly Baker

1. Shepherd, Jack, *The Adams Chronicles*, 76–77. Boston: Little Brown. 1975.
2. Mueller, Gehard O. W., "Inquiry into the State of a Divorceless Society." *University of Pittsburgh Law Review*, 18: 570 (1957).
3. Hall, Max, *Benjamin Franklin and Polly Baker*, 3–4. Philadelphia: University of Pittsburgh Press, 1960.
4. *Ibid.*, 157–60.
5. *Ibid.*, 35–36.
6. *Ibid.*, 37.
7. *Ibid.*, 43.
8. *Ibid.*, 50–59.
9. *Ibid.*, 59–61.
10. *Ibid.*, 67–69.
11. Aldridge, A. O., *Franklin and His French Contemporaries*, 95–104. New York: New York University Press, 1957.
12. Hall, 138–42.
13. *Ibid.*, 144–46.
14. *Ibid.*, 148–49.
15. *Ibid.*, 150.

16. *Ibid.*, 152–53.
17. *Ibid.*, 151–52.
18. *Ibid.*, 153.
19. Jefferson, Thomas, *The Writings of Thomas Jefferson*, xviii, 171. Thomas Jefferson Memorial Association of the United States, Washington, D.C., 1904.
20. Hall, 94–96.
21. Lemay, 5–42.
22. *Ibid.*, 49–50.
23. Nolan, J. B., *Benjamin Franklin in Scotland and Ireland*, 235. Philadelphia: University of Pennsylvania Press, 1938.
24. Crane, V. W., *Franklin's Letters to the Press*, Introduction, xxv–xxvi. Chapel Hill: University of North Carolina Press, 1950.
25. Lemay, 698–703.
26. *Ibid.*, 561.
27. Aldridge, 204.
28. Lopez, C. A. *My Life with Benjamin Franklin*, 105–11. New Haven, CT: Yale University Press, 2000.

3. Benjamin Franklin at the Dawn of the Space Age

1. *Writings*, ix, 123
2. Norgaard, Erik, *The Book of Balloons*, 17. New York: Crown, 1971.
3. *Writings*, ix, 79–81.
4. *Ibid.*, 79–81.
5. Magoun, F. A., and Hodgins, E., *A History of Aircraft*, 29–30. New York: Whittlesey House, 1931.
6. *The Romance of Ballooning*, 17. New York: Viking Press, 1971.
7. Norgaard, 20.
8. Lopez, Claude-Anne, *Mon Cher Papa: Franklin and the Ladies of Paris*, 218, 220. New Haven: Yale University Press, 1966.
9. Norgaard, 22–23.
10. *Writings*, 119–21.
11. Lopez, 219.
12. Jeffries, John, "John Jeffries Diary — Edited by Joy Jeffries." *Magazine of American History*, 13: 66–68 (1885).
13. Magoun and Hodgins, 41.

14. *Ibid.*, 69.
15. *Ibid.*, 71.
16. Jeffries, John, "A Narrative of the Two Aerial Voyages of Dr. Jeffries and Mons, Blanchard." 47, 48. London, 1786. Photocopy in Stetson University Library, Deland, Florida.
17. *Writings*, 479–80.
18. Jeffries, *A Narrative*, 75, 78, 79, 80, 81, 82, 83.
19. *Ibid.*, 80.
20. *Ibid.*, 75, 76.
21. *Ibid.*
22. *Ibid.*, 82, 84.
23. Norgaard, 34, 40.
24. Lopez, 222.
25. Writings, 155.
26. Magoun and Hodgins, 51–52.
27. Lopez, 223.
28. *Writings*, 156.
29. Jobe, 67.
30. Magoun and Hodgins, 65, footnote 3.
31. *Ibid.*, 82–83.
32. *Encyclopedia Britannica*, Vol. 3, 47. Chicago: Encyclopedia Britannica, 1973.

4. THAT FAMOUS KITE

1. Priestley, Joseph, *History and Present State of Electricity*, 4th ed. London, 1775.
2. *Writings*, vol. 3, 99–100.
3. Priestley, 172–73.
4. Cohen, 1; Bernard, *Benjamin Franklin's Science*, 102, 106–108. Cambridge: Harvard University Press, 1990. Will be referred to as *Science*.
5. Van Doren, 163.
6. Cohen, 1; Bernard, *Benjamin Franklin's Experiments*, 272. Cambridge: Harvard University Press, 1941. Will be referred to as *Experiments*.
7. *Ibid.*, 164–435.
8. *Science*, 71.
9. *Writings*, vol. 5, 94.
10. *Experiments*, 103–104.
11. *Science*, 84–85.
12. Brands, 101–102.

13. Herschbach, Dudley, R., "Scientific Amusements." *Harvard Magazine* (November–December 1995): 41.
14. *Experiments*, 200.
15. *Ibid.*, 221–22.
16. *Ibid.*, 334.
17. *Ibid.*, 129–30.
18. *Ibid.*, 356.
19. *Ibid.*, 356–58.
20. Ford, 370.
21. *Experiments*, 63.
22. Schonland, B. F. J., *The Flight of Thunderbolts*, 31. Oxford: Clarenden Press, 1950.
23. *Science*, 105.
24. Schonland, 106.
25. *Experiments*, 138.
26. Uman, Martin A., University of Florida, Gainesville, personal communication.
27. Krider, E. P. "Atmospheric Electricity and the Heritage of Benjamin Franklin," in *Benjamin Franklin Des Lumieres à Nos Jours*, ed. J. Hughes and Daniel Royot, 10. Lyon: University Jean-Moulin, 1995.
28. Schonland, 33.
29. *Science*, 145.
30. Herschbach, 43.
31. Schonland, 8–10.
32. *Ibid.*, 10–12.
33. *Experiments*, 346–47.
34. *Ibid.*, 67, 335–36, 346–47.
35. *Science*, 89–90.
36. Herschbach, 44.
37. Schonland, 22.
38. *Experiments*, 271.
39. Uman, Martin A., *All About Lightning*, 49–50. Dover, 1986.
40. Krider, 112.
41. Uman, 93.
42. Krider, 98, 103.
43. *Experiments*, 219.
44. Herschbach, 41.
45. Uman, chapters 3, 4.
46. *Ibid.*, 55, 65.
47. Schonland, 59, 60.
48. Sobel, Dava, "Jove's Thunderbolts." *Harvard Magazine* (July–August 1979): 40–49.
49. Sharp, Deborah, "Sudden Light-

ning Strikes." *USA Today*, Aug. 9, 1994, pp. 1, 2.

50. Heath, Fred, Gainesville, FL, personal communication.

51. Sobel, 45.

52. Uman, 47–49.

53. Sharp, 1, 2.

54. National Lightning Safety Institute, Louisville, CO.

55. Lightning Protection Institute, Arlington Heights, IL.

56. Matana, D., and DiPilla, S., "Lightning Causes Electrifying Losses." *National Underwriter* (April 29, 1996).

57. Industrial Risk Insurers, Hartford, CT.

58. Krider, 110.

59. Schonland, 106–15.

60. Aldini, Giovanni. "Dissertation on the Origin and Development of the Theory of Animal Electricity," in *A Translation of Luigi Galvani's "Effect of Electricity on Muscular Motion,"* ed. Robert M. Green, 1. Elizabeth Licht, Cambridge, MA, 1953.

61. Sanford, Charles L., ed. "Benjamin Franklin and the American Character," 24–25. Boston: D. C. Heath, 1955.

5. THAT FAMOUS STOVE

1. *Papers of Benjamin Franklin*, vol. 2, p. 420. New Haven: Yale University Press, 1960. Hereafter called *Papers*.

2. Fisher, Sydney George, *The True Benjamin Franklin*, 170. Philadelphia: Lippincott, 1899.

3. Papers, vol. 2, 421–46.

4. Edgerton, Samuel Y., Jr., "Heating Stoves in Eighteenth-Century Philadelphia," *Bulletin of the Association for Preservation Technology* (1971) 3: 55–104.

5. Edgerton, Samuel Y., Jr., "Supplement: The Franklin Stove." In *Benjamin Franklin Science*, ed. I. Bernard Cohen, 199–211. Cambridge: Harvard University Press, 1990.

6. To Hugh Roberts, August 9, 1765. *Papers*, vol. 12, 1236.

7. Hugh Roberts to Benjamin Frank-

lin, November 27, 1765. *Papers*, vol. 12, 386–88.

8. Hart, Sidney, *New Perspectives on Charles Wilson Peale*, ed. Lillian B. Miller and David C. Ward, chapter 13, p. 247. Pittsburgh: University of Pittsburgh Press, 1991.

9. "On Ventilation." In *The Works of Benjamin Franklin*, ed. Jared Sparks, vol. 6, 311. Chicago: Townsend Mac Coun., 1882. Hereafter called *Works*.

10. To James Bowdoin, December 2, 1758. *The Writings of Benjamin Franklin*, ed. Albert Henry Smyth, vol. 3, 465. London: McMillan, 1907. Hereafter called *Writings*.

11. To Mary Stevenson, September 20, 1761. *Works*, vol. 6, 237–38.

12. See note 3, 434.

13. To John Ingenhousz, August 28, 1785. *Works*, vol. 6, 530–31.

14. To James Bowdoin, December 2, 1758. *Writings*, vol. 3, 463–64.

15. John Adams. *Works*, vol. 3, 75–76. Boston, 1850–1856.

16. "On Ventilation." *Works*, vol. 6, 309.

17. *Ibid.*, 310.

18. See note 14, 465–66.

19. To Cadwallader Colden, October 11, 1750. *Papers*, vol. 4, 68, 1961.

20. See note 13, 505–42.

21. Shakespeare, *King Henry IV*, Part 1, Act 3, Scene 1.

22. Lord Kames, February 18, 1768. *Papers*, vol. 15, 50–51, 1972.

23. See note 13, 510.

24. *Ibid.*, 524.

25. *Ibid.*, 505–6.

26. *Ibid.*, p. 514.

27. *Ibid.*, p. 516.

28. *Benjamin Franklin's Writings*, 18. J. A. Leo Lemay, ed., The Library of America, 1987.

29. See note 13, 529–30.

30. *Works*, vol. 10, 178–79.

31. To Sir Alexander Dick, June 21, 1762. *Papers*, vol. 10, 15–16, 1966.

32. Description of a new stove for burning pitcoal and consuming all its smoke. *Works*, vol. 6, 543–61.

33. *Writings*, vol. 1, 130–31.
34. See note 8, 247.
35. See note 5, 211.
36. "Autobiography of Benjamin Franklin." In *Benjamin Franklin's Writings*.
37. See note 32, 559–60.
38. Writings, vol. 3, 187–88; also 388–89.
39. "On Fire. London. 1762." *Works*, vol. 6, 239.
40. The "Resolute Acclaim" by Vermont Castings, Bethel, VT.
41. Ross, Bob, and Carol Ross. *Modern Classic Woodburning Stoves*, 71–80. Woodstock, NY: Overlook Press, 1978.
42. Vivian, John. *Wood Heat*, 173–74. Emmaus, PA: Rodale Press, 1976.
43. See note 4, 102.
44. Internet URL http://hearth.com/what/epa.html.
45. Vermont Castings.
46. *Works*, vol. 6, 532.
47. *Writings*, vol. 3, 468.
48. *Ibid.*, 469.
49. Shelton, Jay, *The Woodburner's Encyclopedia*, 7. Waitsfield, VT: Vermont Crossroads Press, 1976.
50. See note 41, 87.
51. Barnard, Charles N., *Modern Maturity Magazine*, Washington, D.C.
52. See note 41, 262.
53. See note 50.
54. Duggan, Kerry, *The Wood Stove. A store in Gainesville, FL.
55. See note 48, 7.
56. *Works*, vol. 6, 382–83.

6. BENJAMIN FRANKLIN AND THE FRENCH REVOLUTION

1. Durant, Will, and Durant, Ariel. *Rousseau and Revolution*, 937–40, 897–94. New York: Simon and Schuster, 1967.
2. Hale, Edward E., and Hale, Jr., Edward E. *Franklin in France*, vol. 2, 257. Boston: Roberts Bros., 1888.
3. Aldridge, Alfred Owen, *Franklin and His French Contemporaries*, 16. New York: New York University Press, 1957.
4. Lopez, Claude-Anne, *Mon Cher Papa: Franklin and the Ladies of Paris*, 14. New Haven: Yale University Press, 1966.
5. Aldridge, 61.
6. Adams, Charles Francis, *The Works of John Adams*, vol. 1, 660–63. Boston: Little Brown, 1856.
7. Fay, Bernard, *Franklin, the Apostle of Modern Times*, 223. Boston: Little Brown, 1929.
8. *The World Book Encyclopedia*, vol. 12, 855. Chicago: Field Enterprises, 1954.
9. Hale, vol. 1, 171.
10. Van Doren, 655.
11. Shaw, Peter, *The Character of John Adams*, 114. Chapel Hill: University of North Carolina Press, 1976.
12. *Ibid.*, 116.
13. Jouve, Daniel; Jouve, Alice; and Grossman, Alvin, *Paris: Birthplace of the U.S.A.*, 27. Paris: Grund, 1995.
14. Brands, 245–47.
15. *Writings*, vol. 10, 72.
16. Hale, vol. 2, 395.
17. Durant, 946.
18. Jouve, 70.
19. Reynolds, C. P., "Benjamin Franklin: Poor Richard in Paris." *Gourmet* (April 1990): 137.
20. *Durant*, vol. 10, 899.
21. Van Doren, 656.
22. Durant, Will, and Durant, Ariel. *The Age of Napoleon*, 66, 312. New York: Simon and Schuster, 1975.
23. Lopez, 148–49, 171, 189, 210.
24. Woodward, W. E., *Lafayette*. New York: Farrar and Rinehart, 1938.
25. *Writings*, vol. 7, 595
26. Woodward, 428.
27. Jouve, 19–24.
28. Aldridge, Alfred Owen, *Man of Reason: The Life of Thomas Paine*.
29. Jouve, 74–76.
30. *Ibid.*, 85.
31. Brissot de Warville, J. P., *New Travels in the United States of America, 1788*, ed. Durand Echeverria, 182. Cambridge: Belknap Press of Harvard University, 1964.
32. Brissot, 85.
33. Aldridge, Franklin, 45–46.

34. Jouve, 84–86.
35. Lopez, 210.
36. Watson, K. D., *Chemical Heritage* 13 (1) (1995–1996): 2–4.
37. Van Doren, 31.
38. *Ibid.*, 707–708.
39. *Ibid.*, 710.
40. Reynolds, 138.
41. *Ibid.*, 138.
42. Van Doren, 721.
43. Schoenbrun, David, *Triumph in Paris*, 382–84. New York: Harper and Row, 1976.
44. Alsop, Susan Mary, Yankees at the Court, 249–50. New York: Doubleday, 1982.
45. Dull, Jonathon R., "Franklin the Diplomat: The French Mission." Trans. American Philosophical Society, Philadelphia. Part 1, p. 72, 1982.
46. Fay, 415.
47. Van Doren, 781.
48. Jouve, 48.
49. *Ibid.*, 91.
50. Lafayette's words, spoken on June 17, 1825. Inscription on bronze plaque in Boston Common.

7. BENJAMIN FRANKLIN, MONEY MAKER

1. Newman, Eric P., "Benjamin Franklin's Numismatic Accomplishments." Proceedings 1987 of the International Congress of Numismatics, 631–38.
2. Newman, Eric P., "The Early Paper Money of America," 3d ed., Iola, WI: Krause, 1990.
3. Newman, Eric P., "Nature Printing on Colonial and Continental Currency." *The Numismatist* (Feb. 1964): 154.
4. See note 1, 635.
5. *Ibid.*, 634–35
6. See note 2, 27.
7. *Ibid.*, 11.
8. *Ibid.*, 13, 14.
9. *Ibid.*, 14, 15.
10. Hoober, Richard E., "Franklin, The Money Printer." *Numismatic Scrapbook Magazine* (Feb. 1966): 258.

11. *Ibid.*, 265.
12. See note 2, 14, 15.
13. *Papers*, vol. 1, 139–57.
14. *Writings*, vol. 1, 306–307.
15. Hoober, 267.
16. *Ibid.*, 269.
17. See note 2, 15.
18. Van Doren, *Benjamin Franklin*, 618.
19. *Papers*, vol. 29, 354–56.
20. *Writings*, viii, 151–52.
21. Newman, Eric P., "Benjamin Franklin and the Chain Design." *The Numismatist* (Nov. 1983): 2271–81.
22. Newman, Eric P., "Sources of Emblems and Mottoes for Continental Currency and the Fugio Cent." *The Numismatist* (Dec. 1966): 1597.
23. See note 2, 29.
23. Newman, Eric P., "Franklin Making Money More Plentiful." Proceedings of the American Philosophical Society 113 (5) (Oct. 1971): 348.
25. Newman, Eric P., "Franklin and the Bank of North America." The Numismatist (Dec. 1956): 1368–70.
26. See note 2, 26.
27. Scott, Kenneth, Counterfeiting in America, 13. New York: Oxford University Press, 1957.
28. Glaser, Lynn, Counterfeiting in America, 13-14. New York: C. N. Potter, 1968.
29. *Ibid.*, 9.
30. Scott, 46–49.
31. Glaser, 13–14.
32. *Ibid.*, 263.
33. Scott, 11.
34. *Ibid.*, 8.
35. *Ibid.*, 254.
36. See note 2, 27.
37. Scott, 259.
38. *Ibid.*, 262.
39. Glaser, 48.
40. Writings, vol. 10, 106–16.
41. See note 2, 17.
42. Glaser, 9.
43. *New York Times*, July 14, 2002. Sec. 3, p. 4, col. 1. "Paper or Plastic?"
44. Nova Television #2314, "Secrets of Making Money." Online transcripts at www.pbs.org/wgbh/nova, 1996, 2–4.

45. U.S. Treasury press release, June 20, 2002. Washington, D.C., "Plans for redesigned notes."

46. Nova, 5.

47. Wertheim, Cecilia, U.S. Bureau of Engraving and Printing. Washington, D.C., personal communication, 1999; Haxby, James, and Bellin, Barbara Ann, *United States Obsolete Bank Notes, 1782–1866*, vol. 4. Iola, WI: Kraus, 1998.

48. Nova, 6.

49. *Ibid.*, 8.

50. *Ibid.*, 12–13.

51. *Ibid.*, 11–12.

52. U.S. Treasury press release, May 13, 2003. Washington, D.C., "The new color of money." See www.moneyfactory.com/newmoney

53. See note 43.

54. Nova, 10–11.

8. DETERGENTS, EMULSIONS, AND FOAMS

1. Becher, P., *Dictionary of Colloid and Surface Science*, 63. New York: Marcel Dekker, 1990.

2. *Philosophical Transactions of the Royal Society of London*, vol. 64, Pt. 1, 1774, pp. 447–48.

3. Bartlett, J., Familiar Quotations, 16th ed. Ed. J. Kaplan, 104. Boston: Little Brown, 1992.

4. See note 2, 448–49.

5. *Ibid.*, 452

6. Cohen, I. Bernard, *Science and the Founding Fathers*, 149. New York: W. W. Norton, 1995.

7. *Papers*, vol. 10, 158–59.

8. See note 2, 447.

9. *Ibid.*, 449.

10. See note 2, 451.

11. Van Doren, 419.

12. Block, 291–92.

13. *Bede's Ecclesiastical History of the English People*, vol. 3, chap. 15. Oxford: Clarendon Press, 1969.

14. Giles, C. H., "Franklin's Spoonful of Oil." Part 1. *Chemistry and Industry*, (Nov. 8, 1969): 1620.

15. Lemay, 889.

16. See note 2, 457.

17. *Ibid.*, 458.

18. U.S. Hydrographic Office, Bureau of Navigation, "The Use of Oil to Lessen the Dangerous Effect of Heavy Seas," no. 82. U.S. Government Printing Office, 1886. 27 pp.

19. Giles, C. H. and Forrester, S. D., "Wave Damping: The Scottish Contribution." Part 2. *Chemistry and Industry* (Jan. 17, 1970): 80–83.

20. See note 2, 450.

21. Tanford, C., *Ben Franklin Stilled the Waves*, 83. Durham, NC: Duke University Press, 1989.

22. See note 14, 1622.

23. See note 21, 115–16.

24. See note 19, 80–83.

25. See note 21, 105–21.

26. Rayleigh, Lord, "Foam." *Proceedings of the Royal Institution*, vol. 13, 85–97 (1890).

27. Giles, C. H., and Forrester, S. D., "The Origins of the Surface Film Balance." Part 3. *Chemistry and Industry* (Jan. 9, 1971): 43.

28. *Ibid.*, 43–50.

29. *Ibid.*, 52.

30. Hardy, W. B., "Films." *Collected Scientific Papers*, 741. Cambridge University Press, no. 47, 1936.

31. *Ibid.*, 741–42.

32. Langmuir, I., "The Shapes of Group Molecules Forming the Surfaces of Molecules." *Proceedings of the National Academy of Science*, vol. 3, 251–57 (1917).

33. See note 21, 164–65.

34. Langmuir, I., and Schaefer, V. J., "Rates of Evaporation of Water through Compressed Monolayers on Water." *Journal of the Franklin Institute* 235 (1943): 119–62.

35. La Mer, V. K. and Hardy, T. W., "Evaporation of Water: Its Retardation by Monolayers." *Science* 148 (1965): 36.

36. Lemay, 1409.

37. See note 14, 1617.

38. See note 21, 118.

39. Davies, J. T., and Rideal, E. K.,

"Interfacial Phenomena," 2d ed., 21. New York: Academic Press, 1963.

40. Florida Coordinating Council on Mosquito Control, "Florida Mosquito Control," University of Florida (1998).

41. Meyers, Drew, "Surfactant Science and Technology," p. 65–67. New York: VCH Publishers, 1988.

42. See note 14, 1622.

43. See note 19, 87.

44. Adam, N. K., *The Physics and Chemistry of Surfaces*, 105. London: Oxford University Press, 1941.

45. Shah, Dinesh, University of Florida, Gainesville, FL. Personal communication.

46. See note 43, 213.

47. Meurn, R. J., *Survival Guide for the Mariner*, 101. Centreville, MD: Cornell Maritime Press, 1993.

48. "Safety of Life at Sea." Intergovernmental Maritime Consultative Organization. London. 1974.

49. R. L. Markle, Chief of Lifesaving and Fire Safety Standards Division, U.S. Dept. of Transportation , Washington, D.C. Personal communication.

50. See note 14, 1619.

9. The Hypnotist

1. Wyckoff, J., *Franz Anton Mesmer: Between God and Devil*. Englewood Cliffs, N.J.: Prentice-Hall, 1975. 148 pp.

2. Buranelli, V., *The Wizard from Vienna: Franz Anton Mesmer*, 36. New York: Coward, McCann & Geoghegan, 1975. 265 pp.

3. Walmsley, D. M., *Anton Mesmer*, 48. London: Robert Hale, 1967.

4. See note 2, 27–44.

5. *Ibid.*, 39.

6. *Ibid.*, 60–61.

7. *Ibid.*, 67.

8. *Ibid.*, 99–100.

9. Lopez, C. A., "Franklin and Mesmer: An Encounter." *Yale Journal of Biology and Medicine* 66 (1993)ı 325–31

10. See note 2, 94–96.

11. Poirier, J. P., "Benjamin Franklin's Social and Scientific Activities in Paris. 1776–1785," 5. Academy of Medicine, Paris. Dec. 30, 1995.

12. See note 9, 12.

13. See note 2, 110–11.

14. See note 11, 5.

15. See note 2, 137–42.

16. *Ibid.*, 148–54.

17. *Ibid.*, 154–56.

18. See note 3, 129–33.

19. See note 9, 328.

20. See note 11, 7.

21. *Ibid.*, 6.

22. *Writings*, vol. 9, 268.

23. *Ibid.*, 320–21.

24. See note 2, 166.

25. See note 2, 330.

26. Hoyle, Martin, *Mozart and His Operas*, 109. Omnibus Press, 1996.

27. See note 11, 7.

28. See note 2, 189–91.

29. *Ibid.*, 200–204.

30. Darnton, R., *Mesmerism at the End of the Enlightenment in France*, 141–42, 146. Cambridge: Harvard University Press, 1968. 218 pp.

31. See note 3, 177.

32. See note 2, 219–26.

33. See note 30, 142.

34. *Ibid.*, 146.

35. See note 2, 205–11.

36. See note 3,185–86.

37. See note 2, 217.

38. *Writings*, vol. 9, 181–83.

10. America's First Senior Citizen

1. Lemay, 1471–95.

2. Van Doren, *Benjamin Franklin*.

3. Van Doren, *Benjamin Franklin's Autobiographical Writings*, 680. New York: Viking Press, 1945.

4. Van Doren, 551–52.

5. Rush, Benjamin, "Excerpts from the papers of Dr. Benjamin Rush." Pennsylvania Magazine of History and Biography (1905): 29.

6. Lopez, *Mon Cher Papa*.

7. Lemay, 1350.

8. *Ibid.*, 1185–1304.
9. *Ibid.*, 302–303.
10. *Papers*, vol. 6, 481–82.
11. Van Doren, Carl, *The Letters of Benjamin Franklin and Jane Mecom*, 57–58. The American Philosophical Society. Princeton, NJ: Princeton University Press, 1950.
12. *Papers*, vol. 7, 69-71.
13. *Ibid.*, vol. 7, 95.
14. *Writings*, vol. 9, 359.
15. *Ibid.*, 488.
16. *Ibid.*, 621.
17. *Ibid.*, 588–89.
18. *Ibid.*, 576, 540.
19. Van Doren, 737.
20. Rush, Benjamin, *Letters of Benjamin Rush*, 870, ed. L. H. Butterfield. The American Philosophical Society. Princeton, N.J.: Princeton University Press.
21. *Writings*, vol. 9, 512.
22. Aldridge, 393.
23. Van Doren, 750–51.
24. Lopez, C. A., *Franklin Gazette* 10(3) (2000): 6.
25. *Writings*, vol. 9, 685.
26. *Ibid.*, 579.
27. *Ibid.*

28. *Ibid.*, 694.
29. *Ibid.*, 591.
30. *Ibid.*, 489.
31. Lopez, *Franklin Gazette* 10(3) (2000): 6.
32. *Writings*, vol. 9, 582–83.
33. *Ibid.*, 682–83.
34. Ford, P. L., *The Many Sided Franklin*, 84. New York: Century Co.
35. *Ibid.*, 59.
36. Lopez, *My Life with Benjamin Franklin*, 17–24.
37. Aldridge, 368.
38. *Writings*, vol. 9, 622.
39. *Ibid.*, 657–58.
40. *Ibid.*, vol. 3, 339.
41. *Ibid.*, vol. 9, 676.
42. Lemay, 1307.
43. *Ibid.*, 1308.
44. *Writings*, vol. 9, 491.
45. Lemay, 1017.
46. *Writings*, vol. 10, 41.
47. Jefferson, vol. 1, 161–62.
48. *Writings*, vol. 10, 84–85.
49. *Ibid.*, 91.
50. Rush, *Letters*, 564.
51. Van Doren, 779–81.
52. *Writings*, vol. 9, 589.

Index